THE NEW WORLD ORDER

Manifest Destiny

RICHARD MCKENZIE NEAL

AuthorHouse™
1663 Liberty Drive
Bloomington, IN 47403
www.authorhouse.com
Phone: 1-800-839-8640

Published by AuthorHouse 7/9/2013

ISBN: 978-1-4817-7362-1 (sc)
ISBN: 978-1-4817-7361-4 (hc)
ISBN: 978-1-4817-7360-7 (e)

Library of Congress Control Number: 2013911753

Preamble

Almost 50 years ago (1965), legendary ABC commentator Paul Harvey tried to warn "us" of the perils awaiting America if we continued down the path of enlightenment and a culture of personal gratification. In looking back at his words today, it's as though he had a crystal ball...because everything he lamented about has come full circle. His words and the reality of our country today have come together like a hand and a glove.

Foreword

I don't mind that I belong to another time and place. I will probably never fully accept the sterile cold world that surrounds me and allows no comfort. As I learn, I accept the fact that yesterday has become more precious than today or tomorrow could ever be. As my time draws nearer, I am becoming more silent and watchful...the recorder of time, and aware that I have become the albatross of these days...the dinosaur that awaits its extinction.

A few years after I was born, my Dad met a stranger who was new to our small town. From the beginning, Dad was fascinated with this enchanting newcomer and soon invited him to live with our family. The stranger was quickly accepted and was around from then on.

As I grew up, I never questioned his place in my family. In my young mind, he had a special niche. My parents were complementary instructors: Mom taught me good from evil, and Dad taught me to obey. But the stranger...he was our storyteller. He would keep us spellbound for hours on end with adventures, mysteries and comedies.

If I wanted to know anything about politics, history or science, he always knew the answers about the past, understood the present, and even seemed able to predict the future! He took my family to the first major league ball game. He made me laugh, and he made me cry. The stranger never stopped talking, but Dad didn't seem to mind.

Sometimes, Mom would get up quietly while the rest of us were shushing each other to listen to what he had to say, and she would go to the kitchen for peace and quiet. I wonder now if she ever prayed for the stranger to leave.

Dad ruled our household with certain moral convictions, but the stranger never felt obligated to honor them. Profanity, for example, was not allowed in our home…not from us, our friends or any visitors. Our long time visitor, however, got away with four-letter words that burned my ears and made my dad squirm and my mother blush. My Dad didn't permit the liberal use of alcohol, but the stranger encouraged us to try it on a regular basis. He made cigarettes look cool, cigars manly, and pipes distinguished. He talked freely (much too freely!) about sex. His comments were sometimes blatant, sometimes suggestive, and generally embarrassing.

I now know that my early concepts about relationships were influenced strongly by the stranger. Time after time, he opposed the values of my parents, yet he was seldom rebuked...and "never" asked to leave.

More than fifty years have passed since the stranger moved in with our family. He has blended right in and is not nearly as fascinating as he was at first. Still, if you could walk into my parents' den today, you would still find him sitting over in his corner, waiting for someone to listen to him talk and watch him draw his pictures.

His name...?
We just call him "TV."

He has a wife now...we call her "Computer."
Their first child was "Cell Phone."
The second child was "I Pod."

Their family has continued to grow and amaze...while guiding the masses down the same destructive path that has, over time...caused many other great cultures to implode due to their self-indulging populace. We have now reached that proverbial "point of no return."

Most of you will understand my metaphor because by now, we've come to accept the always-evolving nature of our world...and that with each new generation we lose more and more of America...Americana.

> "Life has got a habit of not standing hitched. You got to ride it like you find it. You got to change with it. If a day goes by that don't change some of your old notions for new ones, that is just about like trying to milk a dead cow."
>
> ~ Woody Guthrie ~
> 1912 – 1967

Table of Contents

Chapter 1

Our Forefathers and Founders did not intend to invest this much power in one person.

I fear for our country but never thought it would be because of our president.

We no longer have the checks and balances that our founding fathers gave us. What muscle does the congress have? They do not control any part of the military, FBI, Border Patrol, ICE, and the list goes on. All of those police and military force type agencies fall under the executive branch. The only real power congress has is the purse, and with a president who is willing to force the issue by shutting things down, congress will yield. Forget the courts. Who can enforce their rulings? The executive branch does. The last four years have painted us into a corner that can only be solved by changing presidents.

America is a nation divided. We can't seem to agree on anything. America is divided on everything from abortion to politics, from homosexuality to the Iraqi invasion. The divorce rate has skyrocketed in America because our homes are divided. America's churches have never done so little to save our nation, wasting precious time fighting amongst each other like little immature babies. A house divided is a house that is at war with itself. Marriages are destroyed from within, not without. Churches are destroyed from within, not without.

Our government and way of life are being destroyed from within, not from external forces. America is the land of lawsuits, by the tens-of-thousands every year. If you want to see what a haughty and sinfully proud nation looks like, then look no further than the United States of America. America's pastors and preachers are asleep at the wheel.

We are still One Nation, but divided and ignoring each other. Obama's rejection of the notion that there's a Red America and a Blue America has been an Obama staple ever since his keynote speech, at the 2004 Democratic National convention, elevated him to the national spotlight. Everyone still expects him to trot out his tired "hope and change" distortions despite the fact that even his supporters now realize it has always been just an elegant fiction.

A fiction, I should stipulate, but not necessarily a lie. The evidence would suggest that Obama's 2008 campaign genuinely believed that George W. Bush was the source of the nation's political polarization. He had it exactly backwards. Bush was, just as Obama would become... the symbol of one half of our polarized nation. Both men are symptoms, not causes.

There are, however, real differences between the two Americas. One tends to be churchgoing, the other secular. One is more likely to have pets than children. One values free enterprise and entrepreneurialism. The other tends to see capitalism as a vehicle for the double homicide of labor and the environment. One sees guns as an instrument of violence. The other sees guns as an instrument for resisting violence.

Here's the problem with Obama's "professed unity" mantra: The fact that these people conceive the world in fundamentally different ways is a lot less crazy than the idea that some Washington wunderkind, no matter how elegant the crease in his trousers...is going to somehow bridge the extensive gap between them. People who cluster around absolutes aren't much interested in meeting in the middle.

In surveys conducted at 339 United States colleges and universities, more than one-fourth of students and administrators did not list freedom of speech as an essential right protected by the First Amendment to the Constitution, the Washington Times reported Friday. And more than three-fourths did not name freedom of assembly and association or the right "to petition the government for a redress of grievances." This is sad. Do you know your First Amendment Rights...all five of them? No, you probably don't.

America is a house divided in politics. This is the deliberate intent of the controlling powers behind the scenes. Do you really believe that America's government has been Democrat and Republican for the past 229 years by chance? This is by design. America serves a two-party system. More specifically, the coin is the same no matter which way it lands after the toss...heads or tails, we lose! The recent "staged election" between President George W. Bush and Senator John Kerry provided us with a "choice" between a One-World democrat or a One-World republican. Both candidates are occult members of the order of Skull and Bones. Both are members of the anti-American Council on Foreign Relations.

No matter who wins or loses such a staged election (2004), the New World Order wins. Read about the theft of the 2000 presidential election. By the way, you are contributing to America's desolation every time you vote for these occult members! If you voted for George W. Bush, then the innocent blood of the Iraqi people and their children are on your hands. Unfortunately, their blood is on my hands too because I am an American. It is called "corporate responsibility," we are responsible for the actions of our leaders. Most people could care less. The stench from the Bush administration reaches far into Hell. And the Democrats are no less evil.

As long as the government can successfully keep us Americans fighting amongst ourselves, they are free to do their dastardly deeds with little or no resistance. Adults who are products of the American public school system are unwitting imbeciles in most cases when it comes to thinking for themselves (sheep). It's sickening to hear some of the lame excuses I hear from people who have no clue as to the truth about what is going on in the world today. Much misinformation is propagated through the mainstream news media.

Moral cowards who are afraid of being accountable to the truth prefer to adhere to the illusions provided to them through the news media. The truth is out there folks, but you have to look for it.

America's churches are divided. It's the Christians within our churches who gossip, backstab, mistreat, defraud and hurt other people that are helping to destroy America. Instead of fighting against the evils of our day, we are fighting amongst ourselves. Sadly, many of America's churches are no better than the secular workplace or a liquor tavern. I don't think we should have unrealistic expectations when we go into a church because people are going to be people; however, the immature and sometimes senseless behavior of Pastors, Christian workers and church members across America is anything but Christ-like. Unfortunately, money seems to be king in most churches, and not the Lord. America's churches are "a house divided!"

The devil is crafty and knows how to toss a monkey wrench into the production line. The best way to prevent people from thinking is to give them misdirection...lead them down the wrong path. Do you think that this Michael Jackson trial is such a high-profile case by coincidence? It is directing most people's minds away from the criminal activities in Washington. Do you think Monica Lewinski really had Bill Clinton? Hundreds of acquaintances of the Clintons have died premature, strange and untimely deaths (including Vincent Foster).

Monica would have been dead overnight if they wanted her gone. No, the sexual encounter set a mindset (a major distraction) for the American people for the rest of Clinton's presidency. The Oklahoma City Bombing is still a big mystery. Well Mr. Clinton, what about those two un-detonated explosive devices which were found in the Murrah building? Where did they go? Why were they white washed with a bogus story of an exploding rental van? The devil is a master of propaganda.

One of the sins that God hates in the Bible is "sowing discord." God hates it when anyone causes a house to divide. Gossip divides houses! Sin separates and divides families. Sin divides churches. Sin divides nations. Sin divides marriages. Words are truly more powerful than weapons of war, for words are the perpetrators that have caused many wars. Nothing divides a house like gossip!

A house divided cannot stand forever. A house of cards will eventually collapse. As America's dollar continues to devalue, as our total national debt soars ever higher, as we plunge further into the immoral abyss of sin, and as the thugs and criminals in Washington continue to build a police state...the destruction of America is imminent! America is "a nation divided!"

> "Only a virtuous people are capable of freedom. As nations become corrupt and vicious, they have more need of masters."
>
> ~ Benjamin Franklin ~

Chapter 2

There are some very serious issues at stake in this year's election…so many that some people may not be able to see the forest for the trees. Individual issues are the trees, but the forest is the future of America, as we have known it.

The America that flourished for more than two centuries, is being quietly but steadily dismantled by the Obama administration, during the process of dealing with particular issues.

For example: The merits or demerits of President Obama's recent executive order, suspending legal liability for young people who are here illegally, presumably as a result of being brought here as children by their parents, can be debated pro and con. But such a debate overlooks the much more fundamental undermining of the whole American system of constitutional government.

The separation of powers into legislative, executive and judicial branches of government is at the heart of the

Constitution of the United States...and the Constitution is at the heart of freedom for Americans.

No president of the United States is authorized to repeal parts of legislation passed by Congress. He may veto the whole legislation, but then Congress can override his veto if they have enough votes. Nevertheless, every president takes an oath to faithfully execute the laws that have been passed and sustained...not just the ones he happens to agree with.

If laws passed by the elected representatives of the people can be simply over-ruled unilaterally by whoever is in the White House, then we are no longer a free people, choosing what laws we want to live under.

When a president can ignore the plain language of duly passed laws, and substitute his own executive orders, then we no longer have "a government of laws and not of men" but a president ruling by decree, like the dictator in some banana republic.

When we confine our debates to the merits or demerits of particular executive orders, we are tacitly accepting arbitrary rule. The Constitution of the United States cannot protect us unless we protect the Constitution. But, if we allow ourselves to get bogged down in the details of particular policies imposed by executive orders, and vote solely on that basis, then we have failed to protect the Constitution...and ourselves.

Whatever the merits or demerits of the No Child Left Behind Act, it is the law until Congress either repeals it or amends it. But for Obama to unilaterally waive whatever provisions he doesn't like in that law undermines the fundamental nature of American government.

Obama has likewise unilaterally repealed the legal requirement that welfare recipients must work, by simply redefining "work" to include other things like going to classes on weight control. If we think the bipartisan welfare reform legislation from the Clinton administration should be repealed or amended, that is something for the legislative branch of government to consider.

There have been many wise warnings that freedom is seldom lost all at once. It is usually eroded away, bit by bit, until it is all gone. You may not notice the gradual erosion while it is going on, but you may eventually be shocked to discover one day that it is all gone, that we have been reduced from citizens to subjects, and the Constitution has become just a meaningless bunch of paper.

Obamacare imposes huge costs on some institutions, while the President's arbitrary waivers exempt other institutions from having to pay those same costs. That is hardly the "equal protection of the laws," promised by the 14th Amendment.

John Stuart Mill explained the dangers in that kind of government long ago: "A government with all this mass of favors to give or to withhold, however free in name, wields a power of bribery scarcely surpassed by an avowed autocracy, rendering it master of the elections in almost any circumstances but those of rare and extraordinary public excitement."

Since Obama was reelected, he knows that he no longer has to worry about what the voters think about anything he does. Never having to face them again, he can take his arbitrary rule by decree as far as he wants. He may be challenged in the courts but if he gets just one more Supreme Court appointment, he can pick someone who will rubber stamp anything he does and give him a 5 to 4 majority.

Obama appears to be a tormented man and is filled with resentment, anger, and disdain for anyone of an opinion or view other than his. He acts in the most hateful, spiteful, malevolent, vindictive ways in order to manipulate and maintain power and control over others. Perhaps, because as a child, he grew up harboring an abiding bitterness toward the United States that was instilled in him by his family and mentors. It seems to have never left him.

It is not the color of his skin that is a problem for anyone in America. Rather it is the blackness that fills his soul and the hollowness in his heart where there should be abiding pride and love for this country.

Obama is a man without value...or values.

> "We must be especially aware of that small group of selfish men who would clip the wings of the American eagle in order to feather their own nest."
>
> ~ Franklin D. Roosevelt ~

Chapter 3

I think one of the leading mistakes the Western world has made in the 21st century is assuming that democracy always produces good things. It does not.

Quite a few of history's most unsavory characters rose to power through democratic means. Adolf Hitler, Robert Mugabe, Hugo Chavez, Mahmoud Ahmadinejad, and Vladimir Putin readily come to mind.

In Europe, especially in Germany, hoisting a swastika-emblazoned Nazi flag is a crime. For decades after World War II, people have hunted down and sought punishment for Nazi murderers who were responsible for the deaths of more than 20 million people.

Why are the horrors of Nazism so well known and widely condemned but not those of socialism and communism? What goes untaught...and possibly even covered up... is that socialist and communist ideas have produced the greatest evil in mankind's history. Socialists, communists and their fellow travelers, such as the Wall

Street occupiers supported by our president, care about the little guy in his struggle for a fair shake! "They're trying to promote social justice." Let's look at some of the history of socialism and communism.

The unspeakable horrors of Nazism, a form of socialism, didn't happen overnight.

What's not appreciated is that Nazism is a form of socialism. In fact, the term Nazi stands for the National Socialist German Workers' Party. The unspeakable acts of Adolf Hitler's Nazis pale in comparison with the horrors committed by the communists in the former Union of Soviet Socialist Republics and the People's Republic of China. Between 1917 and 1987, Vladimir Lenin, Josef Stalin and their successors murdered and were otherwise responsible for the deaths of 62 million of their own people. Between 1949 and 1987, China's communists, led by Mao Zedong and his successors, murdered and were otherwise responsible for the deaths of 76 million Chinese. The most authoritative tally of history's most murderous regimes is documented on University of Hawaii Professor Rudolph J. Rummel's website, at http://www.hawaii.edu/powerkills, and in his book "Death by Government."

How much hunting down and punishment has there been for these communist murderers? To the contrary, it's acceptable both in Europe and in the United States to hoist and march under the former USSR's red flag emblazoned with a hammer and sickle. Mao Zedong has been long admired by academics and leftists across our country, as they often marched around singing the praises of Mao and waving his little red book, "Quotations From Chairman Mao Tse-tung." President Barack Obama's communications director, Anita Dunn, in her June 2009 commencement address to St. Andrews Episcopal High School at Washington National Cathedral, said Mao was one of her heroes.

Whether it's the academic community, the media elite, stalwarts of the Democratic Party or organizations such as the NAACP, the National Council of La Raza, Green for All, the Sierra Club and the Children's Defense Fund, there is a great tolerance for the ideas of socialism...a system that has caused more deaths and human misery than all other systems combined.

Today's leftists, socialists and progressives would bristle at the suggestion that their agenda differs little from those of Nazi, Soviet and Maoist mass murderers. One does not have to be in favor of death camps or wars of conquest to be a tyrant. The only requirement is that one has to believe in the primacy of the state over individual rights.

The unspeakable horrors of Nazism didn't happen overnight. They were simply the end result of a long evolution of ideas leading to consolidation of power in central government in the quest for "social justice." It was decent, but misguided earlier generations of Germans... who would have cringed at the thought of genocide... who created the Trojan horse for Hitler's ascendancy. Today's Americans are similarly accepting the massive consolidation of power in Washington in the name of social justice.

If you don't believe it, just ask yourself: Tiny steps at a time...which way are we headed, toward greater liberty or toward more government control over our lives? Perhaps we think that we are better human beings than the German people who created the conditions that brought Hitler to power. I say, don't count on it.

The fact is that very little is ever heard from the media, our politicians, academia nor our mainstream religions about the millions and millions of human beings murdered in the name of the Marxist/Leninist philosophy. In those systems the method of dealing with those opposed to big totalitarian government is to kill them.

I'm just calling out the double standard here: Tolerating Communism, where the red flag with the hammer and sickle is allowed to be displayed without any argument, while any flag or banner with the Swastika on it, especially in Germany, is forbidden. Anyone giving the Roman or fascist salute, with an open hand held high, can be arrested and thrown in jail where as if anyone gives the clenched fist, the communist salute, it is no big deal. I also believe the Communist Party has representatives in the German Parliament and/or Bundestag. I have to wonder if any of them have read any of Alexander Solzhenitsyn's books, remember or even know about the Katyn Forest massacre or the 1930s communist-imposed famine in the Ukraine where up to 6 million people starved to death or the wonders of the Siberian gulags.

Furthermore, we Americans have been brainwashed by the media and other aforementioned institutions to regard such murders as Che Guevara, who was responsible for the executions of countless Cubans by kangaroo courts after Castro's take over, as folk heroes, modern day Robin Hoods. People even go around with Guevara's face printed on T-shirts whereas you will never see Adolf Hitler or Benito Mussolini on a T-Shirt.

Americans, especially our young people who are the future of our country, should be taught and made aware of the horrors inflicted on the people of Russia, the former republics of the Soviet Union, mainland China, Vietnam and Cambodia. Millions were murdered because they held opinions contrary to beliefs of the communist, dictatorial government. They should be made aware that tyranny in the form of communism will often come in silently, like fog, on little cat's feet to the point that one's religious and political beliefs are no longer accepted or tolerated and they will be branded with derogatory labels and ostracized and/or even sent to reeducation facilities to attain political correctness.

Don't ever doubt that over the decades...and beyond, while we were going about our lives making a living, creating families, supporting our communities and just generally being good Americans...that forces were at work undermining our freedoms. We never really noticed for various reasons; we were busy with life, it was done incrementally (incrementalism) and behind the scenes, it was done under the guise of good intentions and necessity...but the main reason we didn't see it coming was that we trusted our government. Then of course, there's the denial factor...the atrocities that have been perpetrated around the world by dictators and/or narcissistic individuals in positions of power and control... could never happen in America. Wake-up America...it's currently staring you in the face!

The famed Russian news site "Pravda," which ironically was formed as the official Communist publication of the former Soviet Union, recently released a scathing opinion column entitled, "Obama's Soviet Mistake." The author (Xavier Lerma) unabashedly labels the United States' president a "Communist" who was, without question, promoting the Communist Manifesto...but without labeling it as such.

The author goes on to note how Obama's "cult of personality" has mesmerized the ignorant in America, who will follow the hope and change icon in much the same way as "fools" still praise Lenin and Stalin in Russia.

"Obama's fools and Stalin's fools share the same drink of illusion."

The biggest mistake would be the excessive interference into the economic life of the country and the absolute faith in the all-mightiness of the state.

The unreasonable expansion of the budget deficit and growing accumulation of national debt, are as destructive as an adventurous stock market game.

During the time of the former Soviet Union, the role of the state in the economy was made absolute, which eventually lead to the total non-competitiveness of the economy. That lesson cost us very dearly. I am sure no one would want history to repeat itself.

After referring to liberalism as a "psychosis," the writer blasts "O'bomber" over Fast and Furious before continuing with his Communist theme:

The author questions if Americans have ever read history and went on to conclude that American schools have been "conquered by Communists long ago," paving the way for a revisionist of history that would eventually lead to the election of a Communist president in the United States.

President Vladimir Putin could never have imagined anyone so arrogant and/or so willing to destroy his own people as Obama appears to be, much less seeing millions vote for someone like Obama, the writer quipped. But America's president wasn't the only one to feel the author's ire. He also noted the pervasive influence of the ACLU and the eroding of America's Christianity... something that was, of course, also a key tenet of the Soviet Union.

Christianity in the United States is under attack as it was during the early period of the Soviet Union when religious symbols were against the law, the writer noted astutely.

In addressing the situation of America's states that have filed petitions to secede from the union, the journalist likened these Americans to hostages of the Communists in power...and who will eventually need to rise up in the face of "tyranny." He concluded with a powerful comparison of the suffering endured for nearly a century under the oppression and brutality of the USSR to... "his spin" on verbiage from Don McLean's famed song, "American Pie":

> Russia lost its civil war with the Reds and millions suffered torture and death for almost 75 years under the tyranny of the

> United Soviet Socialist Republic. Russians survived with a new and stronger faith in God and an ever-growing Christian Church. The question is how long will the once "Land of the Free" remain the United Socialist States of America? Their suffering has only begun. Bye, Bye Miss American Pie!

Those who recall the days of the former Soviet Union, or who have friends and/or family members who fled a life of degradation, will see much truth in the writer's words. Even envisioning the now-famous "Hope and Change" campaign posters, that elevated Obama to a cult of personality, strikes fear and anxiety in the hearts of those who lived through eerily similar propaganda behind the iron curtain. It is ironic that this opinion column, so scathing of Communism and so keenly perceptive of how history is repeating itself in President Obama, comes to us from the publication that was formed to be the official Communist mouthpiece of the former Soviet Union itself.

Perhaps that is what lends it all the more weight.

Now, should one be mindful of the fact that the author of this opinion column also considers Vladimir Putin to be somewhat of a "conservative?" Yes, however, more disturbing still is that the writer finds Putin conservative in comparison to Obama. Opinions on Putin vary greatly among those living in Russia in much the same way as Americans differ in their opinions regarding Obama. But what's more important here is that the writer's personal views on Putin do not necessarily negate that there is merit to his observations on President Obama. Russians, who have witnessed the trappings of the former Soviet Union either during its height or in its aftermath, tend to speak from a place of personal experience...something that warrants careful consideration.

Based on my Google search of the author, he does appear to be a Russian columnist for Pravda.

> "When Injustice becomes Law, Resistance becomes Duty."
>
> ~ Thomas Jefferson ~

Chapter 4

Well before my Dad brought "TV" to live with our family, there were (once again) forces at work to control other facets of American's lives. I accept that change and progress are inevitable in the course of mankind's evolution...but it seems that individuals seeking power and/or financial advantages, more often than not, manipulate those changes.

Looking at the fallen civilizations of Easter Island, Sumer and Rome, we can try to understand the conditions that led to the downfall of those societies. We know the definition of "progress" but we don't understand...and/or don't want to acknowledge its long-term implications for civilizations...past and present. We would prefer to believe that the twentieth century's runaway growth in human population, consumption, and technology, which has now placed an unsustainable burden on all natural systems, was an anomaly.

"The assumption that this pattern of 'change' that has existed throughout the history of mankind...consisting of irreversible changes in one direction only, and that the direction is always towards improvement of the human experience...is a self-serving fallacy."

Easter Island and Sumer both flourished, but collapsed as a result of resource depletion, both were able to visually see their land being eroded but were unwilling to reform. On Easter Island, logging...in order to erect statues and build boats destroyed their ecosystem and led to wars over the last planks of wood on the island. In Sumer, a large irrigation system, as well as over-grazing, land clearing and lime burning led to desertification and soil salinization.

The fates of the Roman and Mayan civilizations are comparable; both peaked with centralized empires but ended with power being diffused to their periphery as the center collapsed when leadership refused reformations. Both were built on "Pyramid Schemes" that inevitably succumb to diminishing returns and the ever-rising cost of operating an empire.

So where are we going? Technological advancements in bioengineering, Nan-technology, cybernetics, amongst others, have the potential to be progress traps, and the global scale of modern society means that a societal collapse could impact all of mankind. History tells us that needed reforms are usually blocked by vested interests that reject multi-lateral organizations, support laissez-faire economics and transfers of power to corporations. The subject never seems to come up, but these economic principles are the leading causes of the social and environmental degradation that led to the collapse of previous civilizations. Our present behavior is typical of failed societies at the "zenith of their greed and arrogance."

We have been living in a "Fool's Paradise."

The Obama administration is unwilling to agree to substantial cuts in federal spending. Profligacy continues unabated and on a level that is unsustainable. I don't know about you, but I no longer believe that this president has the best interests of the nation at heart. His unrestrained spending is, I suspect, nothing more than an intentional attempt to run the American economy off its tracks so that he can implement his own political vision.

To understand the nature of his vision, ask yourself this question: To whom will millions of American citizens, who will be homeless and hungry, look to for aid when the dollar collapses and the economy is devastated? The answer is to a sovereign in whom there is virtually absolute power. This sovereign will be all that stands between most people and death, since political and civil chaos will be rampant and will issue in a war of all against all.

This Orwellian prospect has caused me to reflect upon what the most appropriate motto for our new, emergent nation should be. Forget about the Latin words, E Pluribus Unum ("Out of Many, One"), in which motto the nation was cradled. Restoring that relic of nostalgia won't work, because multiculturalism has destroyed whatever national and cultural solidarity we once had. Also, delete the phrase in "In God We Trust." The idea of a supreme being is, heaven help us, "religious," and that means it is imposing and divisive and serves only to lessen citizens' devotion to the state.

The new state to which Obama is helping to give birth, needs another motto. I suggest that it be: "We Squandered All." These words suit a nation that has thrown away its resources with both hands and continues to do so.

Consider a few of the natural resources we have wasted or destroyed. Buffalo in the millions once roamed wild on the vast prairies of this country and were relied upon by indigenous peoples for food and clothing. They were slaughtered wantonly to the point of extinction. What pleasure it must have been to hunt and to kill them, leaving their carcasses to rot in the untamed wilderness. Rich timberlands with which the country was endowed have all but vanished. They have been, and are still being, decimated in order that a handful of greedy developers can become filthy rich. Huge corporate interests have fouled clear spring water, and the world's majestic oceans and waterways have been rendered toxic sewers. Why? - Because the same monetary interests need a place to dump their wastes.

Americans have also squandered a treasure trove of tradition, or sat passively by while elites have waged war against it. Thanksgiving has become "Turkey Day." The Christmas tree has become the "holiday tree." The greeting "Merry Christmas" has been replaced by "Happy Holidays" in department stores and shopping malls throughout the country. The singing of Christmas carols is disallowed in public schools and viewed as favoring one faith over others. Any public prayer or invocation of God, no matter how nonsectarian, is questionable, if not verboten. Obama has even emphatically announced that America is not a Christian nation. Still open, of course, is the question whether America' culture is de facto

Christian, but please say nothing about that to Obama or to the cadre of secularists who have surrounded him.

This country by the year 2050 is projected to have over 400 million people. A large percentage of them will have come from the Third World. America's public square will replicate a Tower of Babel, teeming with impoverished masses of people, speaking their own native tongues and conducting their lives according to the habits, traditions, and mores of their respective homelands. Democracy cannot exist with these divisions and differences. To put it mildly, we have set ablaze the Anglo-Christian heritage of our country. Mark these words: Eventually the democratic principles that flourished from that heritage will also be incinerated.

Don't forget to look closely at the church, which once stood on all fours at the heart of American life. When one observes television evangelists, he or she hears that God wants us all to be wealthy and to make it to the top of the food chain. It's as if Bruce Fairchild Barton's description of Jesus as "the founder of modern business" has now made it into the mainstream of current "prosperity theology." Barton's book, The Man Nobody Knows, published in 1925, was once regarded as a bad joke among responsible clergy, but the breakdown of the Protestant church, its morality, and its preaching appears to have changed that.

"We Squandered All"...yes, in the government, the classroom, the culture, and the church. We have razed every standard of decency and moderation in American life. I never thought that I would agree with the Reverend Jeremiah Wright on anything, but when he preached

"God damn America," perhaps he was, however obliquely, pointing to a truth. We might want to adopt a new national motto along the lines of what I've suggested. If "We Squander All" proves too much of a challenge because of its brutal honesty, maybe the Black, Hispanic, and Asian caucuses in Congress can agree upon another motto, or maybe Obama, "the Chosen One," can accomplish this feat by the stroke of his pen.

As history is inclined to foretell, we've traveled a predictable course filled with many of the same minefields that brought Easter Island, Sumer, Rome and the Mayan civilizations to their knees. Human nature has always been mankind's worst enemy.

> Human nature refers to the distinguishing characteristics, including ways of thinking, feeling and acting that humans tend to have naturally, independently of the influence of culture. The questions of what these characteristics are, what causes them, and how fixed human nature is, are amongst the oldest and most important questions in western philosophy. These questions have particularly important implications in ethics, politics, and theology. This is partly because human nature can be regarded as both a source of norms of conduct or ways of life, as well as presenting obstacles or constraints on living a good life.

There are various theories used in the fields of advertising and politics that I find very fascinating. They include tracing the development of American's society, the fields of advertising and politics, and exploring the intriguing connections between the three.

Sigmund Freud's nephew, Edward Bernays, is credited with creating the field and the term "public relations." Bernays took Freud's understanding that human beings are essentially irrational beings that act mainly out of self-interest, and applied it to advertising. Until then, advertising was primarily based on facts; this pillowcase will last longer, or that gasoline gets better mileage. What Bernays did is move advertising away from facts while embracing the customer's abstract "irrational feelings" about the intangibles a product may provide. Example: This pillowcase will show what a conscientious homemaker you are. He was the first to shift consumption to desires as opposed to needs.

His first triumph was during the late 20s, convincing women to smoke. He surveyed psychoanalysts to determine why women wouldn't smoke. The reason, they said, was that women see cigarettes as phallic symbols that represent men's power, and feel it would be improper for a woman to smoke. Bernays hired a bunch of women to pose as suffragettes in a parade, and had them pull out cigarettes in front of a group of reporters, calling them "torches of freedom." He succeeded in making women's smoking an issue of women's rights, and women never went back.

Another coup came with the advent of instant cake mix in the 40s. Women weren't buying it. Psychoanalysts were interviewed, and they concluded that women felt that they weren't doing enough when they made an instant cake, and they were ashamed to give it to their husbands. The answer...requires the inclusion of an egg in the mix. That way, the baker feels like he or she is contributing in some way...and symbolically, women are presenting an egg to their husband. Sales took off.

These insights were also applied to politics, detailing the two views of human nature...that people are irrational, and have to be kept comfortable and controlled by the ruling elite, or that they can be trusted to make rational decisions if given the correct information. One example given of Bernays' work came in the 50s when a ruler came to power in Guatemala and promised to get rid of all the United States' companies in the country, because they controlled their large banana business. What Bernays simply did was convince the American public, through various implications, but entirely without basis in fact, that Guatemala was a communist front. From there it wasn't difficult to gather support for a political overthrow. The anti-United States leader was thrown out and Americans could feel good that they had helped defeat communism, though in reality the change was entirely about American business. It is hard not to think about the Bush administration's constant linking of Iraq with "terrorists" (the "communists" of the new millennium) in this context.

By the 60s, people were beginning to become angry at being considered just consumers, and began to rebel against what they considered consumerist brainwashing. In the 70s, parties such as the Esalen institute and EST groups were helping people to break down their social conditionings...that advertising was considered to be a part of, and find their true selves. Advertisers did extensive focus groups (Bernays, by the way, also invented the focus group) and discovered that a great many of the people who became involved in the counterculture movements of the 60s weren't so much looking for political change... as they were excited by the idea of personal expression. So what's the answer? Convince people that the products they buy express who they really are inside.

Previously, industry was set up to only be economical to produce millions of the exact same item. But new manufacturing processes made it possible to produce different versions of the same thing. This combined with the message that your adornments were a great way to express yourself. It changed the way advertising is delivered to this day. People were convinced that not only is it not selfish to think of yourself, it is, in fact, your highest calling. As these new groups were studied, the idea of breaking people down into purchasing personas and demographics was born, which was described with the new term: "Lifestyle." With these new insights, marketers could predict which products certain people would buy.

From here we can delve more into politics, arguing that as people's ultimate goal became social expression, society as we used to know it broke down, as there were only individuals now, no society. And these individuals were interested primarily in themselves. Politically, they wanted to pay taxes only for things that would benefit them.

Reagan is presented as taking advantage of this by planting the image of the welfare recipient driving around in the Cadillac, doing nothing but receiving all the reward, and using it to cut social programs. This social idea was also the basis of Reagan's basic message of "getting the government off of people's backs" and letting the public make their own decisions. At this time the field of public relations went from being perceived as seedy and manipulative, to becoming glamorous and exciting. And "conservative" came to mean thinking primarily about oneself and requiring self-reliance, "liberal" to mean having fellow-feelings and contributing to others. This perspective adds new insight to the unfortunate, but seemingly true, perception that the altruistic children of the 60s turned into the selfish narcissistic yuppies of the 80s through today.

Clinton is presented as the first president who held near-constant focus groups and polls with swing voters, and to shape his policies around them. This is when the V-chip for TV sets and other government initiatives that were centered on the small issues that matter to voters came into vogue. Clinton's idea was to use anything to get elected, and make larger changes once in power, as opposed to doing what one believes-in from the start.

It seems that these politics are still in place, if you're only talking to the swing voters and setting policy around them in order to be more assured of winning, you are paying the most attention to the smallest amount of people, and even then, the ones who just can't make up their minds. Furthermore, voters don't know how to run the country. They want the government to worry about that, and will blame the government for not taking care of issues in a timely manner, which isn't happening, because the government is too busy chasing votes.

This leaves us with a great deal to think about, and gives one an interesting perspective from which to process the advertising and political messages we are being bombarded with today…and everyday.

One should never doubt the power of indoctrinating the public with repetitive advertising/promotional messages. These, more often than not, innocuous sounding promos, marketing ploys, political campaigns and even general public communication…the full gambit, is coming at us from all directions…24 hours a day. These innocent sounding ads almost always have subliminal connotations embedded in the verbiage. But there is a common thread… the government-controlled media.

Our government has a long history of seeking to control its populace through mind-control. Project MK Ultra was the code name of a United States government covert research operation experimenting in the behavioral engineering of humans (mind control) through the CIA's Scientific Intelligence Division. The program began in the early 1950s and was officially sanctioned in 1953. The program engaged in many illegal activities; in particular it used unwitting United States and Canadian citizens as its test subjects, which led to controversy regarding its legitimacy. MK Ultra involved the use of many methodologies to manipulate people's individual mental states and alter brain functions, including the surreptitious administration of drugs (especially LSD) and other chemicals, hypnosis, sensory deprivation, isolation, verbal and sexual abuse, as well as various forms of torture.

The scope of Project MK Ultra was broad, with research undertaken at 80 institutions, including 44 colleges and universities, as well as hospitals, prisons and pharmaceutical companies. The CIA operated through these institutions using front organizations, although some top officials at these institutions were aware of the CIA's involvement.

After the Church Committee of the United States Congress was commissioned to investigate CIA activities within the United States, project MK Ultra was exposed to public attention in 1975. Investigative efforts were hampered by the fact that CIA Director Richard Helms ordered all MK Ultra files destroyed in 1973. The Church Committee and Rockefeller Commission investigations were forced to rely on the sworn testimony of direct participants and on the relatively small number of documents that survived Helms' destruction order.

It's good to know that our government is always hard at work, working on more subtle ways to manipulate the system while expanding their control over..."things."

> "The government consists of a gang of men exactly like you and me. They have, taking one with another, no special talent for the business of government; they have only a talent for getting and holding office."
>
> ~ H. L. Mencken ~

Chapter 5

Unfortunately it's becoming increasingly apparent that our government has morphed into a self-serving, "God-like" entity that knows what's best for its subjects...and its own continued growth and control. Of course this didn't happen overnight...

The Select Committee to Investigate Tax-Exempt Foundations and Comparable Organizations was an investigative committee of the United States House of Representatives between 1952 and 1954. The committee was created by "House Resolution 561" during the 82nd Congress and was charged with investigating the use of funds by tax-exempt organizations (non-profit organizations) to see if they were being used to support communism. When the committee was originally created it was known as the Cox Committee (Edward E. Cox), but later an alternate chairman was named (B. [Brazilla] Carroll Reece) and it became known as the Reece Committee.

In April 1952, the Cox Committee Investigation, led by Edward E. Cox, of the House of Representatives, began an investigation of the "educational and philanthropic foundations and other comparable organizations which are exempt from federal taxes to determine whether they were using their resources for the purposes for which they were established, and especially to determine which such foundations and organizations might be using their resources for un-American activities and subversive activities or for purposes not in the interest or tradition of the United States."

In the fall of 1952 all foundations with assets of $10 million or more received a questionnaire covering virtually every aspect of their operations...and the foundations cooperated willingly. In the committee's final report, submitted to Congress in January 1953, it endorsed the loyalty of the foundations. "So far as we can ascertain, there is little basis for the belief expressed in some quarters that foundation funds are being diverted from their intended use," the report stated.

Unhappy with the Cox Committee's conclusions, Representative Reece pushed for a continuation of its work. In April 1954, the House authorized the Reece Committee. Unlike its predecessor, that limited its attention to generalities, this Committee mounted a comprehensive inquiry into both the motives for establishing foundations and their influence on public life. Norman Dodd, a former banker and bank manager and businessman, headed the investigative inquiry.

The final report was submitted by Mr. Dodd, and because of its provocative nature, the committee became subject to attack. He began by listing criticisms of the Cox Committee, and then moved on to content.

In the Dodd report to the Reece Committee on Foundations, he gave a definition of the word "subversive," saying that the term referred to "any action having as its purpose the alteration of either the principle or the form of the United States Government by other than constitutional means." He then proceeded to show that the Ford Foundation, Rockefeller Foundation and Carnegie Endowment were using funds excessively on projects at Columbia, Harvard, Chicago University and the University of California, in order to enable "oligarchical" (to rule or command by a few) collectivism. He stated, "The purported deterioration in scholarship and in the techniques of teaching has apparently been caused primarily by a premature effort to reduce our meager knowledge of social phenomena to the level of an applied science." He went on to reveal that his research staff had discovered that in 1933 - 1936, a change took place that was so drastic as to constitute a "revolution." They also indicated conclusively that the responsibility for the economic welfare of the American people had been transferred heavily to the Executive Branch of the Federal Government; that a corresponding change in education had taken place from an impetus outside of the local community, and that this revolution" had occurred without violence and with the full consent of an overwhelming majority of the electorate. He stated that this revolution "could not have occurred peacefully, or with the consent of the majority, unless education in the United States had been prepared in advance to endorse it."

He stated that the grants given by the Foundations had been used for:

- Directing education in the United States toward an international viewpoint and discrediting the traditions to which, it had formerly been dedicated.
- Training individuals and servicing agencies to render advice to the Executive branch of the Federal Government.
- Decreasing the dependency of education upon the resources of the local community and freeing it from many of the natural safeguards inherent in this American tradition.
- Changing both school and college curricula to the point where they sometimes denied the principles underlying the American way of life.
- Financing experiments designed to determine the most effective means by which education could be pressed into service of a political nature.
- He cited a book called The Turning of the Tides, which documented the literature from various tax-exempt foundations and organizations like UNESCO showing that they wished to install World Government and collectivism along the lines of Plato's Republic.

He then listed various policy organizations that had been supported by the Foundations, noting in particular the

American Historical Association. He said the following about the association:

- "The American Historical Association was established in 1889 to promote historical studies. It is interesting to note that after giving careful consideration, in 1926, to the social sciences, a report was published under its auspices in 1934 which concluded that the day of the individual in the United States had come to an end and that the future would be characterized, inevitably, by some form of 'collectivism' and an increase in the authority of the State."

The text he was referring to, the American Historical Association's Report on the Commission on Social Studies, supports these claims. Excerpts follow:

- "The Commission is under special obligation to its sponsor, the American Historical Association. Above all, it recognizes its indebtedness to the Trustees of the Carnegie Corporation, whose financial aid made possible the whole five-year investigation of social science instruction in the schools, eventuating in the following Conclusions and Recommendations."

- "The Commission could not limit itself to a survey of textbooks, curricula, methods of instruction, and schemes of examination, but was impelled to consider the condition and prospects of the American people as a part of Western civilization now merging into a world order."

- "The Commission was also driven to this broader conception of its task by the obvious fact that American civilization, in common with Western civilization, is passing through one of the great critical ages of history, is modifying its traditional faith in economic individualism, and is embarking upon vast experiments in social planning and control which call for large-scale cooperation on the part of the people."

- "The Commission recognizes the further fact of the inter-relationship of the life of America with the life of the world. In all departments of culture-intellectual, aesthetic, and ethical...the civilization of the United States has always been a part of European, or Western, civilization. To ignore the historical traditions and usages that have contributed, and still contribute, to this unity is to betray a smug and provincial disregard of basic elements in American life and to invite national impoverishment, intolerance, and disaster. Moreover, the swift development of technology, industry, transportation, and communication in modern times is obviously merging Western civilization into a new world civilization and imposing on American citizens the obligation of knowing more, rather than less, of the complex social and economic relationships which bind them to the rest of mankind."

- "There are certain clearly defined trends in contemporary technology, economy, and society of the utmost importance in creating new conditions, fashioning novel traditions, reorienting American life, and thus conditioning any future program of social science instruction."

- "Under the molding influence of socialized processes of living, drives of technology and science, pressures of changing thought and policy, and disrupting impacts of economic disaster, there is a notable waning of the once widespread popular faith in economic individualism; and leaders in public affairs, supported by a growing mass of the population, are demanding the introduction into economy of ever-wider measures of planning and control."

- "Cumulative evidence supports the conclusion that in the United States as in other countries, the age of laissez faire in economy and government is closing and a new age of collectivism is emerging."

- "As to the specific form which this 'collectivism,' this integration and interdependence, is taking and will take in the future, the evidence at hand is by no means clear or unequivocal. It may involve the limiting or supplanting of private property by public property or it may entail the preservation of private property, extended and distributed among the masses. Most likely, it will issue from a process of experimentation and will represent a composite of historic doctrines and social conceptions yet to appear. Almost certainly it will involve a larger measure of compulsory as well as voluntary co-operation of citizens in the conduct of the complex national economy, a corresponding enlargement of the functions of government, and an increasing state intervention in fundamental branches of economy previously left to individual discretion and initiative-a state intervention that in some instances may be direct and mandatory and in others indirect and facilitative. In any event the Commission is convinced by its interpretation of available empirical data that the actually integrating economy of the present day is the forerunner of a consciously integrated society, in which individual economic actions and individual property, rights will be altered and abridged."

- "While stressing the necessity of recognizing the emergence of a closely integrated society in America and the desirability of curbing individualism in economy, the Commission deems highly desirable the conscious and purposeful employment of every practicable means to ward off the dangers of goose-step regimentation in ideas, culture, and invention, of sacrificing individuality, of neglecting precious elements in the traditional heritage of America and the world, and of fostering a narrow intolerant nationalism or an aggressive predatory imperialism."

- "The Commission deems possible and desirable an enlightened attitude on the part of the masses of the American people toward international relations, involving informed appreciation of the cultural bonds long subsisting among the nations of Western civilization and now developing rapidly among all the nations of the world, and special knowledge of the increasing economic interdependence of politically separate areas and peoples, and of the emerging economic integration of the globe."

- "The Commission, under the frame of reference here presented, deems desirable the vitalizing of the findings of scientific inquiry by the best social thought of the present and of the past, and the incorporation into the materials of social science instruction in the schools of the best plans and ideals for the future of society and of the individual."

- "The implications for education are clear and imperative; the efficient functioning of the emerging economy and the full utilization of its potentialities require profound changes in the attitudes and outlook of the American people, especially the rising generation. A complete and frank recognition that the old order is passing, that the new order is emerging."

- "Organized public education in the United States, much more than ever before, is now compelled, if it is to fulfill its social obligations, to adjust its objectives, its curriculum, its methods of instruction, and its administrative procedures to the requirements of the emerging integrated order."

- "If the school is to justify its maintenance and assume its responsibilities, it must recognize the new order and proceed to equip the rising generation to cooperate effectively in the increasingly interdependent society and to live rationally and well within its limitations and possibilities."

- "The program of social science instruction should not be organized as a separate and isolated division of the curriculum but rather should be closely integrated with other activities and subjects so that the entire curriculum of the school may constitute a unified attack upon the complicated problem of life in contemporary society."

In summary:

Our study of these entities and their relationship to each other seems to warrant the inference that they constitute a highly efficient, functioning whole. Its product is apparently an educational curriculum designed to indoctrinate the American student from matriculation to the consummation of his education. It contrasts sharply with the freedom of the individual as the cornerstone of our social structure. For this freedom, it seems to substitute the group, the will of the majority, and a centralized power to enforce this...presumably in the interest of all. Its development and production seems to have been largely the work of those organizations engaged in research, such as the Social Science Research Council and the National Research Council.

The result of the development and operation of the network in which Foundations have played such a significant role seems to have provided this country with what is tantamount to a national system of education under the tight control of organizations and persons unknown to the American public. Its operations and ideas are so complex as to be beyond public understanding or control. It also seems to have resulted in an educational product that can be traced to research of a predominantly empirical character in the inexact or social sciences.

It has been difficult for me to dismiss the suspicion that, latent in the minds of many of the social scientists was the belief that given sufficient authority and enough funding, human behavior can be controlled and that this control can be exercised without risk to either ethical principles or spiritual values and that therefore, the solution to all social problems should be entrusted to them.

In the light of this suspicion and the evidence it supports, it's difficult to avoid the conclusion that if social scientists of the persuasion I have been discussing have been accepted by Foundations, Government and education as though their claims were true, this flies in the face of the fact that their validity has been disputed by men well trained in these same disciplines.

In spite of this dispute within his own ranks, the social scientist is gradually becoming dignified by the title "Social Engineer." This title implies that the objective viewpoint of the pure scientist is about to become obsolete in favor of an increased focus on techniques of control. It also suggests that our traditional concept of freedom as the function of natural and constitutional law has been abandoned by the social engineer and brings to mind our native fear of controls...however well intended.

The end of the report, following the Transcript of Dodd's address, contains the following message.

The effect of the Dodd Report was electric:

Moves were launched within a matter of hours to block an effective probe. On Capitol Hill, the Committee found itself confronted with obstacles at every turn. The Nation itself was deluged with stories that openly or by inference suggested that the investigation was futile, if not worse. The national board of Americans for Democratic Action formally urged the House to disband the Committee, stating it was conducting a "frontal attack on learning itself."

Many citizens, on the other hand, believe that such a committee should be made a permanent Standing Committee of the House..."to gather and weigh the facts."

> "I have never let my schooling interfere with
> my education."
>
> ~ Mark Twain ~

Chapter 6

One should never doubt that collectivism and communism are one and the same; and that the House's investigation in the 50s only served to force the movement underground for the next 60 or 70 years.

Many, many years ago, I read an interesting book about the rise of the Communists to power in China. In the last chapter, the author tried to explain why and how this had happened. Among the factors he cited were the country's educators. That struck me as odd, and not very plausible, at the time. But the passing years have made that seem less and less odd, and more and more credible. Today, I see our own educators playing a similar role in creating a mindset that undermines America's society. Schools were once thought of as places where a society's knowledge and experience were passed on to the younger generation.

But, about a hundred years ago, Professor John Dewey of Columbia University came up with a very different conception of education...one that has spread through

American schools of education, and even influenced education in countries around the world. John Dewey saw the role of the teacher, not as a transmitter of a society's culture to the young, but as an agent of change... someone strategically placed, with an opportunity to condition students to want a different kind of society.

A century later, we are seeing schools across America indoctrinating students to believe in all sorts of politically correct notions. The history that is taught in too many of our schools is a history that emphasizes everything that has gone bad, or can be made to look bad, in America...and that gives little, if any, attention to the great achievements of this country.

Even the official communist newspapers, back in the days of the Soviet Union, didn't attempt to degrade the United States quite as low as Howard Zinn's book, "A People's History of the United States."

That book has sold millions of copies, poisoning the minds of millions of students in schools and colleges against their own country. This book is one of many things that has enabled teachers to think of themselves as "agents of change," without having the slightest accountability for whether that change turns out to be for the better or for the worse...or, indeed, utterly catastrophic.

This misuse of schools to undermine one's own society is not something confined to the United States or even to our own time. It is common in Western countries for educators, the media and the intelligentsia in general, to single out Western civilization for special condemnation for sins that have been common to the human race, in all parts of the world, for thousands of years.

Meanwhile, all sorts of fictitious virtues are attributed to non-Western societies, and their worst crimes are often passed over in silence, or at least shrugged off by saying some such thing as, "Who are we to judge?"

Even in the face of mortal dangers, political correctness forbids us to use words like "terrorist" when the approved euphemism is "militant." Milder terms such as "illegal alien" likewise cannot pass the political correctness test, so it must be replaced by another euphemism, "undocumented worker." Some think that we must tiptoe around in our own country, lest the sight of an American flag or a Christmas tree in some institutions might offend some foreigners living or visiting here.

In France between the two world wars, the teachers' union decided that schools should replace patriotism with internationalism and pacifism. Books that told the story of the heroic defense of French soldiers against the German invaders at Verdun in 1916, despite suffering massive casualties, were replaced by books that spoke impartially about the suffering of all soldiers...both French and German, at Verdun.

Germany invaded France again in 1940, and this time the world was shocked when the French surrendered after just six weeks of fighting...especially since military experts expected France to win. But two decades of undermining France's patriotism and morale had done its work.

American schools today are similarly undermining American society as one unworthy of defending, either domestically or internationally. If there were nuclear attacks on American cities, how long would it take for us to surrender, even if we had nuclear superiority, but were not as willing to die as our enemies were?

> "Those who do not remember their past are condemned to repeat it."
>
> ~ George Santayana ~

Chapter 7

In an earlier book I expressed my concerns regarding the erosion of rural America. As our populace continues its migration to the urban melting pots, we're losing our Americana heritage...our individualism, our uniqueness and our traditional Christian values. Subliminal forces are at work moving us along, like mindless sheep descending into that rabbit hole of collectivism.

A shrinking world has room for one less dialect:

In a remote fishing town on the tip of Scotland's Black Isle, the last native speaker of the Cromarty dialect has passed away, taking with him a little fragment of the English linguistic mosaic.

Academics said Wednesday that Bobby Hogg, who was 92 when he died last week, was the last person fluent in the dialect once common to the seaside town of Cromarty, 175 miles north of Edinburgh.

"I think that's a terrible thing," said Robert Millar, a linguist at the University of Aberdeen in northern Scotland. "The more diversity in terms of nature we have, the healthier we are. It's the same with language."

The demise of an obscure dialect spoken by a few hundred people may not register for most English speakers...but it's another part of a relentless trend toward standardization that has driven many regional dialects and local languages into oblivion.

Linguists often debate how to define and differentiate the many dialects, but most agree that urbanization, compulsory education and mass media have conspired to iron out many of the kinks that make rural speech unique.

Cromarty, which counts just over 700 people, is at the very end of a sparsely populated peninsula of forest and farmland. The Beauly Firth, a wide body of cold water where salmon run and dolphins play, separates it from Inverness, the closest city.

The Cromarty dialect included a helping of archaic "thees" and "thous" as well as a wealth of seafaring vocabulary, including three sets of words for "second fishing line." The aspirate "h" was often added or subtracted, so that "house" would be pronounced "oos" and "apple" would be pronounced "haypel." The "wh" sound was often dropped entirely.

Urban dialects may be strong, but they don't replace what's being lost. Urban dialects tend to be more similar to one another than their rural counterparts, with an emphasis on differences in pronunciation over differences in vocabulary. And even rival cities like Glasgow and Edinburgh "sound more like each other than they used to."

Author Mark Abley, who has written about the dynamism of the English language, agrees. "I don't believe there's a straightforward balancing act in which urban dialects grow as rural ones shrink. Cities are always melting pots, and isolation for any group is very hard to maintain."

As the worlds' melting pots grow ever bigger, half the Earth's population now lives in cities...lesser-known dialects are evaporating.

Worldwide, languages are disappearing regularly, with half of the globe's 6,000-plus languages expected to be extinct by the end of the century, according to UNESCO. The British Isles saw two languages go extinct within living memory, UNESCO says. The last native speaker of Alderney French, a Norman dialect spoken in the Channel Islands, died around 1960, and the last speaker of traditional Manx, the language once spoken on the Isle of Man, died in 1974.

Donna Heddle, the director of the Center for Nordic Studies at Scotland's University of the Highlands and Islands, said the loss of each language or regional dialect leaves the world poorer than it was before.

"It's one less little sparkle in the firmament, one little star might go out and you might never notice it, but it's not there anymore."

We could very well apply the above analogy to our personal freedoms...one at a time, a little here...a little there; we could wake up some morning and realize...it's not there anymore.

Collectivism/socialism, whatever you choose to call it, is like a black hole that's slowly, but persistently swallowing up more and more of life's personal intangibles.

Chapter 8

Encyclopedia Britannica:

Collectivism can be defined as any of several types of social organizations in which the individual is seen as being subordinate to a social collectivity such as a state, a nation, a race, or a social class. Collectivism may be contrasted with individualism, in which the rights and interests of the individual are emphasized.

The earliest modern, influential expression of collectivist ideas in the West is in Jean-Jacques Rousseau's Du contract social, of 1762, in which it is argued that the individual finds his true being and freedom only in submission to the "general will" of the community. In the early 19th century the German philosopher G.W.F. Hegel argued that the individual realizes his true being and freedom only in unqualified submission to the laws and institutions of the nation-state, which to Hegel was the highest embodiment of social morality. Karl Marx later provided the most succinct statement of the collectivist view of the primacy of social interaction in the preface to his Contribution to the Critique of Political Economy: "It is not men's consciousness," he wrote, "which determines their being, but their social being which determines their consciousness."

Collectivism has found varying degrees of expression in the 20th century in such movements as socialism, communism, and fascism. The least collectivist of these is social democracy, which seeks to reduce the inequities of unrestrained capitalism by government regulation, redistribution of income, and varying degrees of planning and public ownership. In communist systems collectivism is carried to its furthest extreme, with a minimum of private ownership and a maximum of planned economy.

Collectivism is the opposite of individualism. The belief or socio-economic policy which states that the interests of the collective outweigh the interests of the individual and that the individual exists solely to serve the collective. Under collectivism the individual is subordinate to the collective. Utilitarianism, Communism, and to some extent all statist philosophies practice collectivism.

The path we're currently on is irreversible. We have been (for over a hundred years), and continue to be...swept along with the current that is driven not only by natural forces, but also more decisively...by governmental forces. Our government, in conjunction with "the powers that be"... worldwide, have been guiding us and the world toward their ultimate goal..."The New World Order." Collectivism just sounds more palatable...less ominous or threatening than New World Order, Socialism or Communism.

But for Americans to buy into such an un-American concept, America had to be changed to a more secular populace...less white conservative, less Americana heritage, marginalize Christianity and its values while creating major changes in our demographics. Those demographics changes have come about by our government continually, albeit incrementally...increasing the immigration quota. We've now...pretty much, reached the point where the door has just been propped open. All the above to produce cultural divide...and we all know that a house divided against itself cannot stand.

The United States today is a nation that is much less white, much less married and less traditional than it once was. These are growing trends and reflected in the various large and growing constituency groups with values supportive of Obama's worldview...activist government and moral relativism.

What was once the exception to the rule in America...not being white, not being married, not having traditional views on family, sex and abortion...is now becoming the rule. And these constituencies are becoming sufficiently large enough to elect a president.

National Journal released a poll right before the debate showing Obama and Romney dead even nationwide...47 percent each, among likely voters. The poll shows Obama's white support at just 38 percent. Obama was elected in 2008 with 43 percent of the white vote. It appears now that he could be re-elected with even less.

In recent Gallup's polling, Obama's approval among white voters stood at 39 percent. He got 38 percent approval among those who attend church weekly compared to 55 percent among those who attend church seldom or never. And his approval among married voters is 40 percent compared to 57 percent among those not married.

According to data compiled by the Tax Foundation, the large majority of those now filing tax returns in the United States are single. In 1960, 65 percent of all tax filers were married and 35 percent single. In 2010, it was reversed...61 percent of filers were single and 39 percent married. When Obama pushes for taxing the rich, he's not just pitting those with the highest incomes against everyone else. He's pitting married against singles. Eight of 10 tax filers in the top 20 percent of earners are married. The majority of filers at the middle income and below are single.

It's really a cultural divide, one you can be sure that Obama is very aware of, that is keeping his bubble inflated.

The fact that Obama's support is still this strong despite his terrible record sends a clear warning to those looking for a new birth of American freedom.

Romney and Paul Ryan should consider taking these constituencies on directly...blacks, Hispanics and singles...and explain why America's future hinges on shutting down the government plantation.

> "Beware of him who promises something for nothing."
>
> ~ Bernard Baruch ~

Chapter 9

The nation's problems are not all about money. As big a problem as our debts and deficits are, they are emblematic of deeper and actually more significant moral and cultural issues.

We've often heard of those who Tom Brokaw dubbed "the greatest generation," those who sacrificed through a world war to vanquish fascism and imperialism and leave a stronger America for their children. We can go back further to speak of the generation that took the risks to establish this country in the late 18th century or of the generation that fought the Civil War. In each case, said generation sacrificed in order to leave a better and more prosperous country of opportunity for their children.

But, what are we doing today? What will be the legacy of our generation(s)? Our debt and deficit crisis is largely caused by giving ourselves health care and retirement benefits without paying for them. But, we "deserve" them. We are "entitled." We paid for them. The problem is that none of that is true. I have paid Medicare taxes since its inception (1965), and in spite of that...I have only paid about one-third of the cost of the benefits I will likely receive. The rest, fully two-thirds of every doctor visit or medical procedure, will be borrowed. That means upcoming generations will have to figure out how to pay for it.

No one receiving Medicare now or about to receive it has paid anywhere near the full cost. The same is true of Social Security (1935), although those numbers are not as lopsided. And, we all want to care for the indigent, but we do not pay enough taxes to cover those Medicaid expenses either.

So, as a society, we have decided that we want a bunch of stuff right now so that our standard of living will be higher. And, we don't want to pay for it. Instead, we demand that people in the future pay for it through less opportunity and lower expectations and a lower living standard. Instead of sacrificing to leave the next generation a brighter future, we are rewarding ourselves more than is our due while leaving the next generation(s) in a state of serfdom. It is selfish...and it is just wrong.

The financial markets are also a part of the problem right now. Traders, rather than investors dominate the markets today. Those traders have a very short-term outlook. They are interested in the next week or maybe, at most, the next quarter. So, they want any accommodation that preserves their outlook for a few months and the heck with the long-term future. Short-term markets will hate what we might have to do to fix our current problems. But, we must become less concerned about the next three weeks in order to build a brighter future for the next three decades.

In the final analysis, that's really what this debt-limit fight is about. The president and his allies want to give you something for nothing. That's the source of their political strength. You get healthcare and retirement and education all for free because you are "entitled" to it and somebody else will pay for it. The problem is that those other "somebodies," like the "rich" and the "corporations," don't have even 10 percent of the money necessary to pay for it. So, the people paying will be our children. And, they will pay dearly.

I understand that the world moves on, and things change. But, some principles are enduring. Whatever happened to the idea that you are entitled to nothing that you didn't earn or demonstrate that you're deserving of? What about the idea that, no matter how grand or how modest my station in life is, I want my kids to have it better?

Our debt and this president's perpetual trillion-dollar deficits are not just bad economic policy…they are morally reprehensible. If we don't take a stand today, we condemn our children to the consequences of a future collapse.

It's unfortunate, but I think we deceive ourselves to permit the assumption that values and behavior are not the real drivers behind our economic problems. The fact is that the current fiscal crisis of our entitlement programs "is… the direct result of our values and behaviors."

The fiscal soundness of Social Security, Medicare and Medicaid is rooted in the assumption that those who work can fund the needs of our elderly through payroll taxes. In the case of Social Security, we're talking about retirement income. In the case of Medicare, it is health costs of the aged and for Medicaid, it is long-term care of low-income elderly. When these programs were founded, using payroll taxes to fund care for our elderly seemed like a viable idea.

The bottom has fallen out, however, because of changes in our behavior. There are fewer and fewer workers per retiree as a result of longer life spans and a shrinking workforce. In 1950, there were 16 working Americans for every retiree. Today, there are fewer than three. By 2030, it's projected there will be fewer than two.

It doesn't take a supercomputer to realize that if we don't reduce the retirement and health care resources available to our elderly, the burden on each working American to provide those resources increases substantially. Yet the discussion about this crisis is 100 percent focused on how to cut the spending and zero attention is spent on restoration of values that could rebuild families, produce more children and stop destroying the unborn.

According to a new report just out from the Centers for Disease Control and Prevention, the overall fertility rate of American women...defined by the number of births per 1,000 women ages 15 to 44...is the lowest ever recorded since the government started gathering this information. After years of hovering slightly above 2.1, it has now dropped below 1.9. According to demographers, a fertility rate of 2.1...in which each adult woman produces 2.1 children on average over her lifetime...is necessary to keep the overall population steady. Which means the overall United States' population is shrinking.

We generally look to Europe to see low fertility rates and shrinking populations. However, according to the Economist magazine, the United States, at 1.9, now has a fertility rate lower than France, whose fertility rate stands at 2.0.

A change in prevailing values could reverse this trend. But the opposite is happening. According to a new Gallup poll, for the first time the majority of Americans feel that government should not promote any particular set of values. In 1993, the first year that Gallup did this annual survey, 53 percent said that government should promote "traditional values" and 42 percent said that no particular set of values should be promoted. Now, in this latest survey, it is the opposite, 52 percent say no particular set of values should be promoted and 44 percent say government should promote traditional values.

With no rebirth of traditional values that could lead to more babies, caring for our elderly will become an increasingly onerous burden. Where can this soulless materialism lead?

In a September New York Times articles, Steven Rattner...a New York investment banker and former counselor to the Treasury secretary in the Obama administration... provided a shockingly candid answer.

The editorial began by saying, "We need death panels."

Rattner then qualified this by saying, "Well, maybe not exactly."

He concluded: "We may shrink from stomach-wrenching choices, but they are inescapable."

I would suggest that with this administration's stance on partial-birth abortions, we already have death panels.

To sin by silence, when we should protest, makes cowards out of men.

> "It is natural for man to indulge in the illusions of hope. We are apt to shut our eyes against a painful truth...and listen to the song of that 'Siren' (Greek Mythology: One of a group of sea nymphs who by their sweet singing lured mariners to destruction on the rocks surrounding their island), till she transforms us into beasts. Is this the part of wise men, engaged in a great and arduous struggle for liberty? Are we disposed to be the number of those who, having eyes, see not, and having ears, hear not, the things which so nearly concern their temporal salvation? For my part, whatever anguish of spirit it may cost, I am willing to know the whole truth; to know the worst, and to provide for it."
>
> ~ Patrick Henry ~

Chapter 10

As the growth of this shortfall, between the producers and the non-producers, continues to ratchet-up...the strain (of entitlements) on the system has reached a breaking point. We have a government that's unwilling to cut welfare benefits from its co-dependency constituency for fear of losing their seats. So what's the answer...? The solution is always the same, force the producers to pony-up more..."redistribution" has been around for a long time, it's just more blatant in our progressive world today.

- Redistribution of wealth is the transfer of income, wealth or property from some individuals to others caused by a social mechanism such as taxation, monetary policies, welfare, nationalization, charity, and divorce or tort law. The desirability and effects of redistribution are actively debated on ethical and economic grounds.

Conservative, libertarian and neo-liberal arguments against property redistribution consider the term a euphemism for theft or forced labor, and argue that redistribution of legitimately obtained property cannot ever be just. Public choice theory states that redistribution tends to benefit those with political clout to set spending priorities more than those in need, who lack real influence on government.

In the United States, some of the founding fathers and several subsequent leaders expressed opposition to redistribution of wealth.

- Samuel Adams stated: “The utopian schemes of leveling (redistribution of wealth), and a community of goods, are as visionary and impracticable as those that vest all property in the Crown. These ideas are arbitrary, despotic, and, in our government, unconstitutional.”

- James Madison, author of the Constitution, wrote, “I cannot undertake to lay my finger on that article of the Constitution which granted a right to Congress of expending, on objects of benevolence, the money of their constituents.”

United States President Grover Cleveland vetoed an expenditure that would have provided $10,000 of federal aid to drought-stricken Texas farmers. When explaining to Congress why such an appropriation of taxpayer money was inappropriate, he stated:

- I can find no warrant for such an appropriation in the Constitution; and I do not believe that the power and duty of the General Government ought to be extended to the relief of individual suffering, which is in no manner properly related to the

> public service or benefit. A prevalent tendency to disregard the limited mission of this power and duty should, I think, be steadily resisted, to the end that the lesson should be constantly enforced that, though the people support the Government, the Government should not support the people. The friendliness and charity of our fellow countrymen can always be relied on to relieve their fellow citizens in misfortune. This has been repeatedly and quite lately demonstrated. Federal aid in such cases encourages the expectation of paternal care on the part of the Government and weakens the sturdiness of our national character, while it prevents the indulgence among our people of that kindly sentiment and conduct which strengthens the bonds of a common brotherhood.

Recently when the Republican National Committee released an audio clip featuring a young Barack Obama declaring, 14 years ago…"I actually believe in redistribution," the mainstream media just rolled their eyes. They dismissed Obama's affirmation as old news, Joe the Plumber from 2008 all over again. And the Washington Post and New York Times chimed with we're all "redistributionists" now, so what's the fuss?

"To tax is to redistribute. To govern is to redistribute," lectured the Post. And aren't Romney and the Republicans the greatest redistributionists of them all, only in reverse Robin Hood-style, shunting money from the poor to the rich?

All these arguments confirm President Obama's success at shifting the national debate leftward. This is part of the long game he is playing, the gradual introduction of topics that the public would once have rejected as extreme, even preposterous, which, with repetition, become familiar, legitimate, and, eventually, compelling items on the liberal agenda.

He's comfortable with it, and wants Americans to get comfortable with it.

In truth, however, a policy explicitly designed to equalize incomes would mark a radical turn in our politics, the likes of which has not been seen since George McGovern's ill-fated "Demogrant" proposal. Though the progressive income tax and the welfare state have been around for decades, full-bore redistribution is something else again.

Progressive taxation was usually justified, in Franklin Roosevelt's words, as an instrument "to obtain just contribution from those best able to bear it and to avoid placing onerous burdens upon the mass of our people." Not redistribution but equality of sacrifice was the main goal. Walter J. Blum and Harry Kalven Jr.'s enduring study, "The Uneasy Case for Progressive Taxation," argued that it was precisely this "non-re-distributive" argument that allowed the progressive income tax to become respectable in America.

Many government programs have re-distributive effects, of course, but that's different from building an altar to and worshiping the fatted calf of redistribution. Even the welfare state was typically justified as a combination of social insurance programs to provide for lean times, and charitable programs for those who simply couldn't provide for themselves even in good times. The transfers from wealthier to poorer citizens that occurred were incidental, strictly speaking, to those charitable or prudential purposes.

To be sure, the Progressives who brought us the federal income tax and the liberals who brought us the welfare state were open to re-distributionist goals. The public, however, was always less enthusiastic. Even today, most Americans believe that the money they earn belongs to them, and that taxes, therefore, are a necessary evil, to be kept as low as the costs of government will allow.

By contrast, pure re-distributionists assume that your income is not your own, but society's. Under that theory, as Mark F. Plattner argued in a classic article in the Public Interest, "in assessing the rate of tax on an individual the government is deciding not how much of his own income it will require him to pay, but how much of the society's income it will allow him to keep."

Or in President Obama's words: "You didn't build that! If you've been successful, you didn't get there on your own."

But the public recoiled from "You didn't build that!" and so the president won't press the point further, at least right now. The modest redistribution he contemplates is just "to make sure that everybody's got a shot," he averred on the audio clip. Before a full embrace of the re-distributive state, liberals have to tend to the slow work of planting its premises in the public mind. What Obama called in the first debate the "new economic citizenship" is the next baby step in that direction.

As he likes to explain, or rather warn: "You're not on your own, we're in this together."

Obama's reoccurring theme is to demonize the wealthy (the 1 "per centers") as he panders to the middle-class and those who are already well into the early stages of socialism.

"Though a democracy, we are becoming a country of ominous social extremes between the super rich and the increasingly many who are deprived. In America today the top 1 percent of the richest families own around 35 percent of the nation's entire wealth, while the bottom 90 percent own around 25 percent. It should be a source of even greater concern that the majority of all currently serving Congressmen and Senators, and similarly most of the top officials in the executive branch, fall in the category of the very rich, the so-called top 1 percent."

For those with more income, is it due to greater work effort, higher labor productivity, innovation, entrepreneurship, better technology and more efficient management or was it acquired by favoritism, nepotism, collusion, bribery, fraud, insider trading, special privilege and/or other forms of corruption? If the explanation lies in higher productivity and better management, then the income inequality warrants encouragement. If the inequality is due to nepotism and corruption, it should be combated and reversed.

It's all starting to look and sound more and more like socialism, where the middle class disappears...leaving the elite to manage (control) an ever-growing populace of have-nots.

Growing up in rural Arkansas I was told that "anyone" could grow up to be president, but I have only come to accept that premise during the current administration.

Chapter 11

Because big time economics has never been a forte of mine, I've been hesitant about trying to understand/ explain the dynamics of this "fiscal cliff" dilemma that seems to be holding America hostage. Even though it's a very troubling situation, it is being used as political leverage, by both parties...to control the bigger issue, America's direction...socialism or capitalism.

Politicians and the media have been gripped by predictions of what they have characterized as ghastly consequences if Congress and the president do not come together to save us from the fiscal cliff. Put in perspective, however, the cliff is little more than a pothole that may slow our dash toward economic decline.

Whatever compromise may be negotiated, it will not alter the reality that we are motoring recklessly down the wrong road. The fiscal cliff is but a helpful symptom of the disease that we suffer. To disguise the pain with an anesthetic will only delay treatment, enabling the malady to persist.

Most Americans are of the opinion that our nation's debt is too large and that something ought to be done about it. What is less understood is the immensity of the financial abyss with which we are dealing. The national debt currently stands at about $16 trillion, more than double the amount we owed in 2000. But the critical dilemma is that we are continuing to amass debt at the rate of over $1 trillion annually.

In contrast, the consequences of the fiscal cliff, those that Congress and the media represent as so calamitous, are hardly noteworthy. Such timid spending reductions may slow our race toward bankruptcy but will hardly reverse it.

President Obama proposes cutting spending by some $400 billion coupled with raising taxes on the rich, thereby seizing loads of new tax revenue. The net result, it is hoped, will trim the deficit to "only" $640 billion per year.

However, history has shown that higher taxes on the wealthy do not result in the projected revenue increases because the top 3 percent (Obama's tax target and bracket) are smart enough to avoid a portion of the new taxes by taking advantage of tax loopholes that Congress itself has devised and promoted.

Moreover, even Obama's economic sages admit that higher taxes are likely to slow economic growth thus rendering the revenue projections optimistic.

Much like the "advanced" nations of Greece, Spain, France, Italy and Portugal, our problem is not a lack of revenue... but too much spending. Only spending cuts will return us to the road to prosperity, not in 2013, but eventually. As with any road trip, when we make a wrong turn we must pay the cost of backtracking. Slowing our speed yet continuing in the wrong direction is not a solution. And as for taxing the rich, if government seized all the wealth of the Forbes 400 richest Americans, it would not be enough to cover even two years of government deficits. And such a tyrannical act would be like confiscating the plow from the farmer.

Although our predicament was years in the making, and entirely predictable, it is only recently that we have perfected the spendthrift habit. The lion's share of our nation's credit card debt was rung up in just the past 10 years, advanced by Democrats and Republicans alike.

And so, as for the menacing fiscal cliff, it is but a ripe pimple on Uncle Sam's nose. But as for dealing with the consequences of our shortsighted spending habits, there is greater anguish yet to come, and whatever pain we avoid for now, the more pain we, but even more so, our children...will suffer in the future.

To paraphrase Samuel Johnson, nothing focuses the mind like a crisis. And, perhaps that is why the political class continually manufactures fiscal crises. The manufactured crises can be used to focus the collective political mind and help solve the underlying fiscal problem.

The fiscal cliff, the tax increases and indiscriminate budget cuts that, without action, could become official policy on January 1, 2013...is most appropriately viewed as the latest installment in this long list of manufactured fiscal crises.

The underlying fiscal problem is that the federal government continues to spend too much money today, while promising to spend even more money that it simply does not have tomorrow...and has created a tax system that is costly, complex and anti-competitive.

Over the past 50 years, the federal government has spent $113 for every $100 in tax revenues. Over time, these cumulative budget deficits have created our current $16 trillion federal debt, which is now the size of our entire economy.

A $16 trillion debt, on a per capita basis, implies that every man, woman and child in the United States now owes over $52,000. And, the $16 trillion is only the debt that we acknowledge.

The actual federal debt is much higher. Most of the Social Security, Medicare, and other federal benefits promised to retiring Americans are not funded. There is no savings account somewhere in Washington, D.C. that the Treasury will access to pay for the future benefits. Tomorrow's benefits can only be financed by taxing the income of tomorrow's workers.

The un-funded (and unaccounted) debt of the United States government is estimated to exceed $100 trillion. And, this debt is in addition to the $16 trillion debt from our past spending binges that we are only now acknowledging. For those keeping track, unless entitlement changes are made, every man, woman and child will owe $373,000. A family of four would owe $1.5 million.

The federal tax system is just as problematic. The federal tax system is complex and filled with special interest carve outs that rewards political influence over market acumen. It is also costly for taxpayers to comply with the tax code. A recent study estimated that for every $100 in taxes paid to the federal government, taxpayers must spend an additional $30 to comply with the tax system. In other words, taxpayers spend $130 to give the government $100. Additionally, the United States levies a corporate income tax rate that is higher and more burdensome than all of our major trading partners.

The combination of these trends has put the United States on an unsustainable fiscal path. Fiscal cliffs, debt ceilings, and other crises de jour will continue... and worsen, until the long-term fiscal soundness of the federal budget is restored.

The reforms that will put the United States on a sustainable fiscal path include: spending restraint that constrains the size and growth of the federal budget to an affordable level; entitlement reform that limits the uncontrolled growth in these programs; and, a pro-growth tax reform that raises the necessary revenue for the government while minimizing the tax distortions and costs on the economy.

Unfortunately, the fiscal cliff does not appear to be causing the collective political minds to focus enough. President Obama has stated that he will not allow the fiscal cliff to be resolved unless the tax rates for the top income earners are allowed to rise. As if the additional $82 billion a year in tax revenues, raising the top tax rate, will materially change the country's fiscal crisis.

However, longer-term imbalances are even a larger problem. The fiscal cliff created an opportunity to fix this longer-term imbalance. But is only an opportunity if the politicians don't let this crisis go to waste.

But more importantly, if you're naive enough to believe that these tax increases on the wealthy will not affect us (the middle class) down the road, then you don't understand the government's trickle-down shell game.

To frame our government's state of affairs today, we need only to look at the debt levels of countless everyday Americans who persist in living beyond their financial means. We all know...or know of, individuals and/or couples who have amassed many, many hundreds of thousands of dollars of long-term credit debt (often high interest rates)...and to make matters worse, they have also accumulated thousands of dollars of credit card debt...on multiple cards. They're drowning in debt but continue sliding those cards...while paying the minimum or just the interest each month. We know there is no logic in their method and that their house of cards will collapse at some point in time.

We have all heard the old adage regarding what we call someone who continues to repeat the same failures over and over again while expecting a different outcome. Yes, a fool...

As a dog returns to its vomit, so a fool returns to his follies.

Footnote:

In America's earliest days, there were barn-raising parties in which neighbors helped each other build up their farms. Today, in some churches, there are debt liquidation revivals in which parishioners are chipping in to help free each other from growing credit card debts that are driving American families to bankruptcy and desperation.

However, the reality of today's world is that we're seeing the emergence of a powerful debt-and-credit industrial complex that is the driving force behind the phenomenon we're seeing today, the ever-increasing numbers of Americans being strangled by debt.

While Americans continue "maxing out" their credit cards, there is a deeper story. Power is shifting into fewer and fewer hands everyday, with frightening consequences. The mall has replaced the factory as America's dominant economic engine, big banks and credit card companies are manipulating Congress while driving us into, what a former major bank economist calls modern serfdom. Americans and our government owe trillions in consumer debt and the national debt, a large amount of it to big banks and billions to Communist China.

A top government official compared the United States to Rome before its fall and warns that our bubble could burst. A former prosecutor stated that many of these loans are worse than mafia loan-sharking practices. An ex-credit card executive explains how advertising campaigns are deliberately deceptive and misleading. A real estate expert stated that tens of billions of dollars (from rip-off loans charging exorbitant, predatory interest rates) are being transferred from the pockets of the poor into the vaults of big banks (as foreclosures increase) that use front groups and subsidiaries to camouflage their association. The "until payday" loans, the college loans ($20,000 plus) and home-improvement scams are all part of this bigger picture.

I have recently come to realize how deeply all this affects me, and to understand how many ways policies and practices are tied to a growing national debt burden and how it all impacts my personal finances.

This is a problem involving millions of people and billions of dollars yet it is downplayed and rarely discussed in all of its disastrous dimensions. It's about a growing inequality that some experts fear will lead to a 21st century of serfdom (serfdom mentioned again). It's about the transfer of wealth from working people into the vaults and accounts of a relatively small number of financial institutions and real estate interests. The lenders are profiting by charging usurious rates and doing so legally, in part, because they have mastered the art and science of marketing products and then manipulating the media, politicians, and by extension...political institutions.

Credit card abuses are usually examined in terms of individuals and consumer scams like identity theft, but has evolved into a much deeper look at what's been called "financialization." This is an institutional problem involving a growing debt-and-credit complex that threatens the very fabric of our nation, not just in terms of a possible financial crash in the future, but how it is impinging upon our lives and livelihoods today.

What's been called the democratization of credit has led to the democratization of dependency. It has created an unsustainable society, trapping millions in a financial hole they can't escape from and often...do not even understand.

Over the past 25 years, America has moved from a society based on production to a nation driven by consumption, from a country that once shared its resources with the world to one deeply in debt to foreign banks and countries to the tune of trillions of dollars. As the growing number of bankruptcies and foreclosures testifies, our national debt is mirrored by a skyrocketing consumer debt, with an increasing number of individuals and families unable to cope.

It is shocking to me that intelligent people, educated people, have not taken the time to think about this. We cannot sustain, over an extended period of time, these high levels of debt. What will happen is that whenever it comes to an end, and there will be an end to the amount of credit…in other words, when it gets so leveraged, it will create an economic crisis so deep that it will threaten us as a nation. This is a real threat and no one seems to be concerned about it.

Most of those ensnared in the debt trap were seduced by the false promise of "free money." But we should all know…by this point in our life, that there is "no free money!" My personal opinion has always been that we, as individuals, have the "free will" to make our own "common sense" choices and decision. No matter how the salesperson spins his snake oil sales pitch, we always have the last word…no one makes us sign those contracts.

The distinction between genius and stupidity is that the former has its limits.

Chapter 12

From my limited perspective, I feel that this self-perpetuating, always growing, slippery slope of lack-of-responsibility, poverty and welfare programs...has actually been by design. I would also suggest that our government has had a hand in the process; and that it has been promoted at a subliminal level and facilitated incrementally (there's that word again, incrementally) over a long period of time. At the risk of sounding like a conspiracy, it seems to me that the government's goal has been to develop a constituency of dependable voters that could be counted on to support an always-growing government.

I've frequently heard statements by leftist academics, think tank researchers and policymakers that suggest: "People were not just struggling because of their personal deficiencies; there were structural factors at play. People weren't poor because they made bad decisions; they were poor because our society creates poverty."

Who made these statements and where they were made is not important, but its corrosive effects on the minds of black people, particularly black youths, can be devastating.

There's nothing intellectually challenging or unusual about poverty. For most of mankind's existence, his most optimistic scenario was to be able to eke out enough to subsist for another day.

Poverty has been mankind's standard fare and has remained so for most of mankind's subsistence. What is unusual and challenging to explain is affluence...namely, how a tiny percentage of people, mostly in the West, for only a tiny part of mankind's existence, managed to escape the fate that befell their fellow men.

To say "our society creates poverty" is breathtakingly ignorant.

In 1776, the United States was among the world's poorest nations. In less than two centuries, we became the world's richest nation by a long shot. Americans who today are deemed poor by Census Bureau definitions have more material goods than middle-class people as recently as 60 years ago.

Doctor Robert Rector and Rachel Sheffield give us insights in "Understanding Poverty in the United States: Surprising Facts About America's Poor" (September 13, 2011). Eighty percent of poor households have air conditioning. Nearly three-fourths have a car or truck, and 31 percent have two or more. Two-thirds have cable or satellite TV. Half have one or more computers. Forty-two percent own their homes. The average poor American has more living space than the typical non-poor person in Sweden, France or the United Kingdom.

Ninety-six percent of poor parents stated that their children were never hungry during the year because they couldn't afford food. How do these facts square with the statement that "our society creates poverty?" To the contrary, our society has done the best with poverty.

Maybe the professor who made the statements about poverty...who, by the way, is black...was thinking that it's black people who have been made poor by society.

One cannot avoid the fact that average black income today is many multiples of what it was at emancipation, in 1900, in 1940 and in 1960, even though average black income is only 65 percent of white income.

There is no comparison between the black standard of living today and that in earlier periods. Again, the statement that "our society creates poverty" is just plain nonsense.

What about the assertion that "people weren't poor because they made bad decisions?"

The poverty rate among blacks is 36 percent. Most black poverty is found in female-headed households, but the poverty rate among black married couples has been in single digits since 1994 and stands today at 7 percent.

Today's black illegitimacy rate is 72 percent, but in the 1940s, it hovered around 14 percent. Less than 50 percent of black students graduate from high school, and most of those who do graduate have a level of academic proficiency far below that of their white counterparts. Black men make up almost 40 percent of the prison population.

With all that said, I now have a few questions: Is having babies without the benefit of marriage a bad decision, and is doing so likely to affect income? Are dropping out of school and participating in criminal activity bad decisions, and are they likely to have an effect on income?

Finally, do people have free will and the capacity to make decisions, or is their behavior a result of instincts over which they have no control?

The message taught to so many of today's black youths isn't what was taught back in the 1930s, 1940s and 1950s, when the civil rights struggle was getting into gear.

As a teenager growing up in Arkansas, one of my best friends (James "Snowball" Jones) was Black. On Friday and Saturday nights when my white friends and I were out doing what teenagers did, James was bussing tables and washing dishes at a local restaurant.

James was a hard working Christian...and he often told me that his parents motivated him to be "a credit to his/their race."

Almost 50 years later, when I returned to Arkansas in search of my friend, I learned that he had died in a car crash. I located his sister and brother and was informed that he had remained a hard working Christian, but died in his mid-20s...a passenger in a car driven by his brother.

While I leave little doubt about where I stand in regard to our current administration, I understand the dynamics behind "his" election. He's a mirror image of a large portion of our "it's not my fault, entitlement mentality, celebrity worshiping...clueless population."

The real danger to America is not Obama, but a citizenry of fools willing to entrust their country to a man like Obama. America can survive Obama, but it is less likely to survive the multitude of fools, such as those who made him their President.

Chapter 13

Political Correctness: Organized Orwellian intolerance and stupidity, disguised as compassionate liberalism. It's the leading element in stifling free speech today but is presented (by our progressive leadership) as a social buffer to encourage and/or promote communal civility.

The irony:

When Obama and others on the Left are not busy admonishing the rest of us to be "civil" in our discussions of political issues, they are busy letting loose insults, accusations and smears against those who dare to disagree with them.

If you want to know what community organizers do, this is it...rub people's emotions raw to hype their resentments. And this was Obama in his old community organizer role, a role that should have warned those who thought that he was someone who would bring us together, when he was all too well practiced in the art of polarizing us apart.

Political correctness is most well known as an institutional excuse for the harassment and exclusion of people with differing political views.

The West will either reject the logic of Political Correctness or suffer a catastrophic failure of vision, will, power and influence...while destroying our civil society, as we know it. This may sound drastic, and of course it is, but why is it being embraced here in America? The ideas in the doctrines of Political Correctness and related notions like Multiculturalism are so destructive that, much like magma...they cannot indefinitely be safely contained before spilling over and causing tremendous damage, chaos and destruction of our society.

The reason it must be eliminated is because Political Correctness is a Trojan horse for Marxism, which always destroys everything it touches. Political Correctness is a curse which must be denounced before it mangles its host society, especially since it is the very opposite of Free Speech. More importantly, individual responsibility is eliminated by Political Correctness standards, which make personal morality irrelevant.

Political Correctness (PC) is shorthand for an ideology, which implies ethical or moral superiority for various positions that challenge traditional morality.

PC has become, in practice, a set of standards by which communication is purified from unacceptable content. But PC has also deeply affected public policy and law, and ultimately ideas about morality, itself. For example, against the longstanding notion of the right of free expression, even thinking many forbidden thoughts would break PC norms. And for this reason, PC has evolved from being rules for "sensitivity" training into a set of social mores that cannot be breached.

Politically correct definition of "Political Correctness":

- Relating to, or supporting broad social, political, and educational change, especially to redress historical injustices in matters such as race, class, gender, and sexual orientation.

Racism:

- The belief that race accounts for differences in human character or ability and that a particular race is superior to others. Discrimination or prejudice based on race.

Racist:

- A label given to a person, or group of people who hate/dislike those who belong to a different race. This typically applies to hatred based on skin-color. A racist could also be someone who thinks that people of other ethnicities are inherently inferior to his race.

Racists can occur within any ethnicity, and no one ethnicity as a whole is racist. In fact, to say that all members of a given ethnicity are racist, or that all racists are of a given ethnicity, that is, well...racist. Talk about being no better than those you complain about.

If you're a white man, this is what you are. It doesn't even matter if your wife is black and you have an adopted child from India, or how many black friends you have, somehow you're going to end up being a racist according to how the media portrays the white man as "racist whities."

All of this is interesting because the white man is the one that is stereotyped as being racist, which is hypocrisy at its best. It's racist to assume that the white race is automatically racist.

If racial insults don't offend you, then you're apparently racist, but it would offend an actual racist. When you hear a certain word too much (I'm sure we've all heard "cracka" hundreds of times thanks to standup comedy) then you become desensitized to it.

That and the other words white people get called sound stupid and/or non-offending. "Cracker" came from cracking whips. Indiana Jones cracked whips too, and he was a badass. "Honkey" sounds like some kind of gigantic sandwich, and "white boy" makes you seem like the lone white kid in break dance movies that stands out amongst the other races of kids. Most people only really think of rednecks when they think of "white trash," so it doesn't offend them if they're not rednecks.

Political Correctness and racist allegations work together like a "glove and hand" to shout down opposing views, and or to control those within an ethnicity who might disagree with the blanket ideology embraced by the group. I would also suggest that the white race (as a whole) doesn't receive equal protection under the "hand and glove" equalizer system. It just seems that only whites are accused of racism...of course the white race doesn't have community advocates like Jackson and Sharpton.

This mantle of racist bestowed upon America's white population has grown and prospered because slavery is widely misunderstood, and as such has been a tool for hustlers and demagogues. Slavery has been part of the human condition throughout recorded history and everywhere on the globe. Romans enslaved other Europeans; Greeks enslaved other Greeks; Asians enslaved Asians; Africans enslaved Africans; and in the New World, Aztecs enslaved Aztecs and other native groups. Even the word slave is derived from the fact that Slavic people were among the early European slaves.

Though racism has been used to justify slavery, the origins of slavery had little to do with racism. In recent history, the major slave traders and slave owners have been Arabs, who enslaved Europeans, black Africans and Asians. A unique aspect of slavery in the Western world was the moral outrage against it, which began to emerge in the 18th century and led to massive efforts to eliminate it. It was Britain's military might and the sight of the Union Jack on the high seas that ultimately put an end to the slave trade.

Unfortunately, the facts about slavery are not the lessons taught in our schools and colleges. The gross misrepresentation and suggestion in textbooks and lectures is that slavery was a uniquely American practice done by racist white people to black people. Despite abundant historical evidence, youngsters are taught nothing about how the founding fathers quarreled, debated and agonized over the slave issue.

But there are just certain topics or arguments that one should not wade into in the presence of children or those with little understanding...or willingness to hear anything (factual or not) that might contradict their long held opinions on divisive subjects...like slavery and racism. In those cases anything that might go against what they "want to believe" is going to be met with adamant denial. They might even imply that by your explanation you're trying to give the subject matter moral sanction or justification.

As rules by the Government are one-size-fits-all, any governmental determination of an individual's abilities must be based on a bureaucratic assessment of the lowest possible denominator. The government, for example, has determined that black people (somehow) have fewer abilities than white people, and so...must be given certain preferences. Anyone acquainted with both black and white people knows this assessment is not only absurd, but also outrageous. And yet it is the law.

Your beliefs don't make you a better person...your behavior does.

Chapter 14

Racial attitudes "have not improved" in the four years since the United States elected its first black president, an Associated Press poll found, as a slight "majority" of Americans now express prejudice toward blacks whether they recognize those feelings or not.

Racial prejudice has increased slightly since 2008 whether those feelings were measured using questions that explicitly asked respondents about racist attitudes, or through an experimental test that measured implicit views toward race without asking questions about that topic directly.

In all, 51 percent of Americans now express explicit anti-black attitudes, compared with 48 percent in a similar 2008 survey. When measured by an implicit racial attitudes test, the number of Americans with anti-black sentiments jumped to 56 percent, up from 49 percent during the last presidential election. In both tests, the share of Americans expressing pro-black attitudes fell.

Most Americans expressed anti-Latino sentiments, too. In an AP survey done in 2011, 52 percent of non-Latino whites expressed anti-Latino attitudes. That figure rose to 57 percent in the implicit test. The survey on Latinos had no past data for comparison.

Experts on race said they were not surprised by the findings. We have this false idea that there is uniformity in progress and that things change in one big step. That is not the way history has worked. When we've seen progress, we've also seen backlash.

Although Republicans were more likely than Democrats to express racial prejudice in the questions measuring explicit racism (79 percent among Republicans compared with 32 percent among Democrats), the implicit test found little difference between the two parties. That test showed a majority of both Democrats and Republicans held anti-black feelings (55 percent of Democrats and 64 percent of Republicans), as did about half of political independents (49 percent).

Just saying...it's always about white racism...we're the only racists. The article went on to suggest that Obama's presidency has been hindered by his skin color...when in fact, his skin color is the only reason he was in the running in the last election.

In an earlier book I wrote about the possibility of civil unrest regardless of which party comes out on top in the up-coming election. But there's another unsettling line of thought to consider...

We know that America is becoming less and less white and that in the near future, Caucasians will cease to be the majority. As the percentage of whites in the United States dwindles, the likelihood of race wars is a hot topic out there in cyberspace.

I recently read an article written about a "local professor," with a doctorate in bio-behavioral sciences that agrees with the possible race wars scenario. He replied to one of the interviewer's leading questions by saying: "I merely report on my observations of human nature, historical events and the collapsing of America's traditional values (I would add that we're becoming more and more tribal, and less and less united). He then quickly dismisses the idea that he's a neo-Nazi. He calls himself a "white advocate" and that he simply reports cause and effect.

If you haven't heard of American Third Position, here's part of its mission statement:

- "Government policy in the United States discriminates against white Americans...white Americans need their own political party to fight this discrimination."

It also publishes a webzine, Occidental Observer. Its mission statement promises to present "themes of white identity, white interests, and the culture of the West."

During the sometimes-jarring interview, the professor stated his local case: "The white working class can't compete in Southern California."

If Third Position is indeed a hate group, it isn't alone. According to Southern Poverty Law Center (SPLC), a watchdog for hate groups, the number of militia groups, a harbinger of extreme organizations...has increased nine fold in the past three years.

The professor rejects the name-calling, saying he's against discrimination on either side. Interestingly, SPLC and the professor agree about the reasons for the spike in extreme groups. Both attribute the increase to the recession and the fact that there's a black president in the White House.

Their webzine echoes his comments, acknowledging that his ideology is sure to be dismissed as extremism of the worst sort in today's intellectual climate...perhaps even as a sign of psychiatric disorder. "A great many other identifiable groups in the multicultural West have a strong sense of identity and interest, but overt expressions of white identity...are rarely found among the peoples who founded these societies."

He went on to say that Democrats have forsaken their white working class core and that, by default the Republican Party has become the party for white people. While there are many in both parties - white and people of color...who would heatedly deny the statement; the professor went on to forecast doom for the GOP, saying the party can't win in the long run. He blames what he calls the cost of multiculturalism and the loss of white values.

Statements like that prompted his employer to distance itself from him while at the same time defending his academic tenure, a reaction similar to that of the SPLC and the Anti-Defamation League. Both organizations condemn his views while defending his right to free speech.

When asked why he didn't just keep his mouth shut, play it safe, stop feeding the fire, he admits that his world is a "difficult environment." "I have a sense of duty for my people and the culture I grew up in. As someone whose job is protected by tenure, I have a special obligation."

His biggest concern isn't illegal immigration, although he says that's a problem. One of his biggest concerns is legal immigration. To stem the tide, he advocates deporting those who immigrated illegally and implementing immigration policies that would restore the nation to racial percentages that existed in 1950. Feasible plan... or not, he says the country has no choice if it hopes to maintain law and order.

"Ethnicity remains a huge source of conflict throughout the world, he pointed out...Blacks, Jews, and Mexicans have historical prejudices.

Then there's the IQ issue: There is a school of thought that IQs vary by race. Here's his rundown of IQ averages: Jews, 110; Asians, 104; whites, 100; Latinos, low 90s; blacks, 85.

He admits he's not an expert on IQs, but referred to studies he had read in saying..."I take them pretty seriously."

<u>Just in:</u> October 12, 2012, Florida Passes Plan For Racially Based Academic Goals.

The Florida state Board of Education passed a controversial plan to set reading and math goals based upon race.

On Tuesday, the board passed a revised strategic plan that says by 2018, it wants 90 percent of Asian students, 88 percent of white students, 81 percent of Hispanics and

74 percent of black students to be reading at or above grade level. For math, the goals are 92 percent for Asian kids to be proficient, whites at 86 percent, Hispanics at 80 percent and blacks at 74 percent.

JFK Middle School has a black student population of about 88 percent.

The plan has infuriated many community activists in Palm Beach County and across the state. "To expect less from one demographic and more from another is just a little off-base," Juan Lopez, magnet coordinator at John F. Kennedy Middle School in Riviera Beach, told the Palm Beach Post.

"Our kids, although they come from different socioeconomic backgrounds, still have the ability to learn," Lopez said. "To dumb down the expectations for one group, that seems a little unfair."

Others in the community agreed with Lopez's assessment. But the Florida Department of Education said the goals recognize that not every group is starting from the same point and are meant to be ambitious but realistic.

As an example, the percentage of white students scoring at or above grade level (as measured by whether they scored a 3 or higher on the reading FCAT) was 69 percent in 2011-2012, according to the state. For black students, it was 38 percent, and for Hispanics, it was 53 percent.

Additionally, State Board of Education Chairwoman Kathleen Shanahan said that setting goals for different subgroups was needed to comply with terms of a waiver that Florida and 32 other states have from some provisions of the federal No Child Left Behind Act. These waivers were used to make the states independent from some federal regulations. "We have set a very high goal for all students to reach in Florida," Shanahan said.

But Palm Beach County School Board vice-chairwoman Debra Robinson isn't buying the rationale. "I'm somewhere between complete and utter disgust and anger and disappointment with humanity," Robinson told the Post. She said she has been receiving complaints from upset black and Hispanic parents since the state board took its action this week.

Robinson called the state board's actions essentially "proclaiming racism" and said she wants Palm Beach County to continue to educate every child with the same expectations, regardless of race.

I personally do not believe there is a unique IQ gene that is innately different within each of the world's various races. I've expressed my thoughts on this touchy subject before and stand by those thoughts. I believe it is, in large part, a cultural phenomenon driven by the perceived value...or lack of, an education. It starts in the home of course, but grows or wilts depending on one's surroundings and influences as they move forward in life. Their acquaintances, neighborhood, community, ambitions (or lack of) and the winds of our steadily changing American culture...and a government that's always telling you "it's not your fault!"

The "dumbing" down of our schools and the redirecting of the nation's core curriculum(s) from "critical thinking" to "what to think"...in regard to social and political issues... continues today. This conditioning (indoctrinating) of

Americans has been in progress...incrementally, for a very long time.

Education-reform advocates throughout the country recently convened to commemorate the 30th anniversary of the landmark 1983 report, "A Nation at Risk," from the National Commission on Excellence in Education. Intended as a wakeup call, the report declared, "The educational foundations of our society are presently being eroded by a rising tide of mediocrity that threatens our very future as a nation and a people."

One of its most foreboding lines warned, "If an unfriendly foreign power had attempted to impose on America the mediocre educational performance that exists today, we might well have viewed it as an act of war."

Today we remain a nation at risk. In today's global economy and with demand for international competitiveness that has pressurized and irrevocably transformed the need for a more-rigorously educated workforce, we face heightened risks.

The report's warning and call to action continue to reverberate. Today, 1 in 4 American students fail to earn a high school degree on time. We trail other nations in the percentage of students who complete college. The achievement gap between too many minority students and many of their white counterparts continues to exact demands for constitutional relief in our state and national judicial systems. Education has become an issue of national defense, economic prosperity and civil rights.

Today, 29 percent of Americans surveyed by Gallup responded that they have confidence in K-12 schools...the lowest mark since Gallup commenced asking education questions. Despite the nation spending twice as much on education than was spent 30 years ago, our international rankings on math and science remain anemic. We've seen reading scores rise only one point from 1980 – 2008 among 17-year-olds about to graduate from high school.

But now is not the time for more educational research, reports or commissions. We have enough commonsense ideas, backed by decades of research, to significantly improve American schools.

The problem ingredient isn't educational at all...it's a political thing! Too often, state and local leaders have tried to enact reforms of the kind recommended by "A Nation at Risk," only to be stymied by organized special interests and political agendas.

After 30 years, the wake-up-call is still unanswered. How many more anniversaries will we "commemorate" before we realize the enemy is not an "unfriendly foreign power"...but "internal entities, posing as Americans?" We are slowly losing this war as the "powers that be" relentlessly pursue their goal of transforming America into just another non-descript component of a secular new world order.

> "There are more instances of the abridgment of the freedom of the people by gradual and silent encroachments of those in power than by violent and sudden usurpation."
>
> ~ James Madison ~

Chapter 15

Today's national educational course of action (curriculum) is too often biased toward, and/or sublimely intended... to steer students toward a particular social ideology. Those philosophies then...invariably, work hand-and-hand to support and enhance the principles of political correctness.

When asked by CNN's Soledad O'Brien about the definition of critical race theory (CRT), Emory Law Professor Dorothy Brown offered the following: "Critical race theory seeks to explain judicial decisions by asking the question, what does race have to do with it? CRT simply looks at race in America," Professor Brown stated. That's a bit like saying that a religious zealot just looks at theology.

Critical race theorists do not merely look at racial questions. Like zealots, they give answers; they preach a doctrine, seek converts, and condemn nonbelievers. Indeed, CRT is the primary source of Orwellian "hate speech" proposals.

O'Brien next asked the professor whether CRT is "all about white supremacy," as Joel Pollak of Breitbart.com asserted previously. Brown replied, "No, it's nothing about white supremacy."

Yet Professor Brown should know precisely what role white supremacy plays in CRT. In her own published work on CRT, Brown wrote that CRT "seeks to highlight the ways in which the law is not neutral and objective, but designed to support White supremacy and the subordination of people of color." She then cites Emily Houh, who defined CRT thusly:

- First, critical race theory seeks to expose the entrenchment of White supremacy and the reality of the continued subordination of people of color in the United States (and throughout the world).

CRT, as Professor Brown wrote and cited, certainly does have something to do with white supremacy.

John T. Bennett writes: As a law student at Emory University, I was assigned CRT readings in several elective courses...namely; courses in hate speech and feminist legal theory. According to the Derrick Bell Reader, edited by CRT proponent Richard Delgado, CRT's "founding members" are professors Delgado, Derrick Bell, Kimberle Crenshaw, Mari Matsuda, Charles Lawrence, and Patricia Williams. The following is just a flavor of the doctrine they transmit to countless students every day. Keep in mind that these are relatively tame assertions, by CRT standards, and are all taken from assigned readings.

The late Derrick Bell, a Harvard and NYU law professor with ties to the president, wrote that CRT "goes well beyond civil rights, integration, affirmative action, and other liberal measures." What is "beyond" those measures? Specifically...Bell called for a "commitment to radical emancipation by the law." He described the unifying theme of CRT: "We use a number of different voices, but all recognize that racial subordination maintains and perpetuates the American social order." Bell proudly wrote that CRT is characterized by "an orientation around race that seeks to attack a legal system which "disempowers" people of color." What does it mean to disempower people of color? Answer: If an institution does not provide for explicit racial preferences and favoritism, it will be deemed to disempower people of color.

Kimberle Crenshaw, a UCLA law professor, provides the much-needed feminist branch of CRT, because focusing on race alone neglects the "multidimensionality of Black women's experiences." Black women are "multiply-burdened" since patriarchy is yet "another source of domination to which Black women are vulnerable." Of course, "the social experience of race creates both a primary group identity as well as a shared sense of being under collective assault." In response to the awful "collective assault" of living in America, Crenshaw has a policy recommendation at the ready: She calls for "economic or social reorganization that directly empowers and supports" her most favored group..."single Black mothers." Not just mothers, not just single mothers, but single black mothers.

For Richard Delgado, Seattle University law professor, "American society remains deeply afflicted by racism." Delgado writes, "That because they constantly hear racist messages, minority children, not surprisingly, come to question their competence, intelligence, and worth." Indeed, "racial insult and mere words, whether racial or otherwise, can cause mental, emotional, or even physical harm to their target." Delgado argues that hate speech is a severe social problem and that such speech, along with other tools of racism, keeps minorities in an inferior position. Thus, words that are "highly insulting" and/or have a "racial component" should be grounds for a lawsuit against the speaker.

Mari Matsuda, Georgetown law professor, also insists that part of the special harm of racist speech is that it works in concert with other racist tools to keep victim groups in an inferior position. Matsuda posits, the three identifying characteristics of hate speech that she proposes to regulate: The message of racial inferiority, the fact that said message is directed against a historically oppressed group, and the fact that said message is persecutory, hateful, and degrading. Just what kind of speech will be considered racist? One clue comes from Matsuda herself, who claims that "righteous indignation against diversity and reverse discrimination" is one of the "implements of racism" for upper-class whites.

The nightmarish possibilities of hate speech codes are obvious to anyone with the slightest grasp of human nature and politics, yet such codes are seriously considered as a legal reform in universities and particularly law schools.

To Georgetown law professor Charles Lawrence, there are "structures of subordination" existing in society. Inferior social standing and inequality of access to resources are deemed the products of racist structure...never the outcome of freely chosen and avoidable decisions, and never the outcome of cultural pathology. Instead, society is always to blame.

Finally, Columbia law professor Patricia Williams offers a disturbing glimpse into the logic of CRT. Williams recounts the story of a hypothetical question that she was once asked to consider, where X and Y apply for a job with firm Z, which is all white. X and Y are equally qualified. One is black; the other is white. The questions asked: Who should get the job? Williams' answer is worth repeating at length, as a window into an ideology that is not taken as seriously as it should be:

- The black person should get the job. If the modern white man, innocently or not, is the inheritor of another's due, then it must be returned.

Williams continues:

If a thief steals so that his children may live in luxury and the law returns his ill gotten gain to its rightful owner, the children cannot complain that they have been deprived of what they did not own. Blacks have earned a place in this society; they have earned a share of its enormous wealth, with physical labor and intellectual sacrifice, as wages and as royalties. Blacks deserve their inheritance as much as family wealth passed from parent to child over the generations is a "deserved" inheritance. It is as deserved as child support and alimony.

So whites should collectively be treated as the children of thieves, and blacks collectively deserve to have "returned to them" what those white thieves stole from their black forebears. This is the seething, irrational ideology at the foundation of CRT.

While in law school, Barack Obama told an audience, "Open up your hearts and your minds to the words of Professor Derrick Bell." Bell is the same man who famously said, in a recorded television interview, "I live to harass white folks," and proudly advocated what he called a "radical ideology." Even if Bell exerted no influence on Obama's thinking, which is unlikely, it should be a national scandal that critical race theory is so widely sermonized at American colleges.

Tough days for King's dream:

In August 1963, standing in front of the Lincoln Memorial in Washington, D.C., the Reverend Martin Luther King, Jr., gave an extraordinary and memorable speech about the terrible plight of African-Americans and his dream that freedom and justice for all Americans, of all races and beliefs, was soon going to become a reality.

Among many other powerful statements, he said, "I have a dream that my four little children will one day live in a nation where they will not be judged by the color of their skin but by the content of their character."

The Civil Rights Act was passed by both houses of Congress and signed into law in July of 1964 by President Lyndon B. Johnson. Racial discrimination in most realms of commerce and societal activity was outlawed.

And yet today, a massive social movement has emerged that's sole purpose appears to be to celebrate and promote division, separation and even distrust along racial and cultural lines, all in the name of national diversity. This point was proven in predictions about racial and cultural voting patterns before the recent election and in analyses afterward in broad and extensive coverage in the national news media.

This seems to be a total subversion of the ideas and dreams Dr. King so valiantly believed and taught. He envisioned an America in which the cohesive promise of our national motto would be fully realized in the lives of all citizens. The motto is, "E Pluribus Unum," which means, "From Many, One."

> "No man is more than another unless he does more than another."
>
> ~Miguel Cervantes ~

CHAPTER 16

America appears to be coming apart at the seams with more and more stress fractures developing as civility retreats. The fragmentation is producing a patchwork of tribal-like entities...all driven by their personal, self-serving agendas. The divisions run the full gambit... age, gender, culture, religion, race and just a general difference of opinions on America's direction...or lack of direction.

Given the country's internal discord, the question has been pondered, "Would Obama be willing to incite civil unrest to win re-election?" As we have all been encouraged to wear our dog-whistle decoders these days, one can hardly be blamed for wondering. Worse yet, we know the answer. He is already doing it.

His anger at the challenger is palpable...that is, carefully staged...during each of the last two presidential debates. And he has made a central theme of his campaign the warning that a Romney presidency would erase all of the "equality" victories of the 1960s and 1970s.

Consider these typical words from his October 25 rally in Las Vegas:

You can choose to turn the clock back 50 years for women and immigrants and gays. Or in this election you can stand up for the principle that America includes everybody. We're all created equal...black, white, Hispanic, Asian, Native American, gay, straight, "abled" and/or disabled...no matter who you are, no matter what you look like, no matter where you come from or who you love, in America you can make it if you try.

This, to restate, is his message down the stretch: Before the revolutionary uprisings of the 1960s, America only "included" white men. Romney is a white man who wants to return to that time. So if you are a woman, an immigrant, gay, black, Hispanic, Asian, Native American, or disabled, then you should not merely oppose Romney as a candidate who does not represent your interests; rather, you should fear him, as a man who wishes to eliminate you from the American portrait.

If Romney wins, and you are not an "abled" white male, America will no longer "include" you, according to Obama. In less than two weeks, you could be reduced to second-class citizenship...and your fortunes cast back to the bad old days of ultra-white-conservatism.

And now, after scowling at him through two debates, after his vice-president spent ninety minutes calling Paul Ryan a liar, and in the context of all this fear-mongering about the threat of a return to White Male America, Obama has branded his opponent a "bullshitter."

From Lyndon Johnson or Harry Truman, this kind of remark might have been regarded as innocuous, albeit un-presidential. From Obama, the Harvard genius with the well-creased pant leg, the best-selling author and master of political oration, it is an expression of bitter rage and supreme disdain. And in an era when representatives of Obama's base are flooding Twitter with threats to assassinate his opponent, such heated rhetoric could be dangerous.

Anyone who wonders whether perhaps Obama just does not want to be president anymore should think again. He wants to be president. What he does not want is to have to exert so much effort to retain the presidency. What he does not want is what Hugo Chávez does not want, what Vladimir Putin does not want, what Mahmoud Ahmadinejad does not want...a fair fight, an unobstructed challenger, an un-intimidated electorate.

It was so easy in the past. Swept along on a wave of adulation and enthusiasm, protected by leftist media and academia, and helped out when necessary by an Axelrod-arranged scandal or two, Obama has barely had to lift a finger to gain political office and to climb the ladder. Authoritarians do not understand why one should have to do so.

So he is angry. And this anger has become central to his campaign strategy. The fear he is seeking to inculcate among his base has an even uglier flip side. The Obama campaign is attempting to cast Romney and his supporters not as people with the wrong ideas, but as "The Enemy." In this circumstance, fear can easily give way to extreme outrage...and perhaps to violence and intimidation. This is particularly true when the target audience of this fear-inducing invective is ignorant, emotion-driven, and dominated in its thinking by entitlement greed, rather than by considerations of right and wrong.

Could Obama really be reduced to attempting to win re-election through mob protests and intimidation...through a climate of fear?

Let us examine the broad facts: According to the recent polls, most of which have been conducted by organizations sympathetic to Obama, Romney appears to be on his way to victory. Obama's policy record is insupportable on the basis of its results, and his campaign knows it. His one ace in the hole, his alleged effectiveness in the Middle East, has been exposed once and for all as a disastrous lie. And his opponent's past seems to be scandal-free, thus eliminating the one major comeback technique his inner circle has shown past skill in executing.

All appears lost for Obama according to normal campaign channels. It is time for the Hail Mary pass. But do we have any grounds for imagining that he and his team would stoop so low as to seek to incite mass incivility, on or before Election Day?

Let us examine a few more facts: Barack Obama's primary occupation before electoral politics was as a community organizer in Chicago. He was an adviser to ACORN, the election fraud racket and socialist activism organization founded by former SDS radical Wade Rathke. His mentors in Chicago included Bill Ayers and Bernardine Dohrn, the Weather Underground leaders who staged the Days of Rage in 1969; Rashid Khalidi, apologist for and promoter of anti-Israeli violence; and Jeremiah Wright, who's most famous words, are "God damn America!" In his youth, of course, Obama's primary male role model was Frank Marshall Davis, a communist and, naturally, a community organizer.

Would any of the people I just named stop short of using intimidation or civil unrest to achieve their political ends, if they believed it would be effective...or that it was their only hope?

A few more facts: On Election Day 2008, New Black Panther militants, one carrying a billy club, stood threateningly in front of a polling station in Philadelphia. They were charged with voter intimidation. Obama's Justice Department dismissed the charges.

The Obama administration funded a study redefining domestic terror threats to exclude radical Islamists, while including people who are "reverent of individual liberty" and/or "suspicious of centralized federal authority."

In short, the Obama presidency has been consistent in its lack of scruples when it comes to demonizing wealthy people, conservatives, and now Mitt Romney... not opposing them, but painting them as racist, greedy, dangerous potential terrorists...hell-bent on doing harm to women, blacks, gays, and immigrants.

But now, most remarkably, we have Obama's Benghazi gambit. The focus of the story, of course, has been on the administration's deliberate concoction and dissemination of a fairy-tale about a video protest to obscure the damaging facts concerning the murder of Ambassador Stevens and three other Americans. That story gets uglier, and more damning, by the day.

Administration officials knew, on September 11, that the attack was in no way related to the airing of the obscure YouTube video, and that in fact there was no protest in Libya on that day. In spite of this knowledge, they systematically cited the video as the primary source of the (nonexistent) protest in Benghazi and implied that the murderous attack grew spontaneously out of that protest.

The political fallout of that lie should be devastating. But we must not neglect its practical domino effect on the world beyond the Obama campaign.

By making the video the centerpiece of its various public statements over the days following the Benghazi attack...including Obama's September 25 address to the United Nations...the administration itself publicized and aggrandized it. They repeatedly branded it a "disgusting" and "intolerant" offense against Islam, thereby giving credence to the mock outrage being stoked by a television host on the Egyptian Islamist station al-Nas and Egypt's Muslim Brotherhood government. In other words, their repeated apology for the video's offense against Islam, couched as a (feeble) defense of Western values..."we protect free speech, but we hate religious intolerance" helped to justify, heighten, and prolong the Arab outrage over a video almost no one had seen.

Rather than responding to the Ansar al-Sharia attack with force in real time, labeling it accurately at once, and promising with credibility to crush any copycat incidents...a response which might have defused any further uprising from the Arab streets...Obama, Hillary Clinton, and others in the administration told a story that justified and empathized with Islamic anger, while weakly pleading for non-violent protests. In addition to inviting a bounty on the filmmaker's head; the administration's rhetoric helped to swell the protests, to increase the intensity of subsequent violence at United States diplomatic missions, potentially to endanger the lives of Coptic Christians in Egypt; and to legitimize the sharia advocacy of the Muslim Brotherhood.

In short, the administration's Benghazi cover story, by repeatedly citing and publicizing a supposedly grave insult against Islam, endangered many lives, and risked igniting a much larger outbreak of anti-Western violence in a region of the world Obama claims to admire and respect.

And it must not be forgotten that the inflammatory words with which Obama and his team carelessly stoked Muslim outrage, thereby needlessly endangering so many Arab and Western lives, were a calculated, bald-faced lie, and Obama knew it.

This lie, with all its resulting risk to human safety, was apparently judged to be worth it simply in order to shield Obama's re-election campaign from harm.

Think about that. Think about Obama's attempts to brand Romney a threat to every leftist cause of the last fifty years. Think of his supporters among the New Black Panthers, the SEIU, and the Communist Party USA. Think of his condemnation of Romney at this final, desperate hour, as a "bullshitter" from the one percent who wishes to revoke the equal rights of blacks, Hispanics, Native Americans, gays, women, and immigrants.

Benghazi teaches us that Obama is willing to risk inciting civil unrest abroad for the sake of protecting his re-election hopes. Is he willing to take the same risk at home?

One must hope that the harsh realities of life in Obama's America have dulled the enthusiasm of even his most ardent supporters, and his "new era of civility"...Chicago-style civility...will come to nothing.

But...in a recent impromptu statement to his minions, Obama chose to motivate them by framing the up-coming election with a very negative message: "In this election 'voting is the best revenge'...payback for our enemies and rewards for those who supported us." It would seem...to me (from his proclamation), that once again his divisive nature comes to the forefront when things aren't going his way. By suggesting that "they" should think revenge, rather than perhaps advocating rejuvenation...speaks to his darker side; the side that "will do whatever it takes to stay in office."

Footnote to the "undefended" Benghazi terrorist attack:

Ambassador Stevens, killed along with three other Americans, did not have a security detail of United States Marines in Benghazi. In contrast, Valerie Jarrett, senior adviser to the president, had a full Secret Service detail accompany her on vacation at Martha's Vineyard.

> "Civilization begins with order, grows with liberty and dies with chaos."
>
> ~ Will Durant ~

Chapter 17

In 2008, Barack "No Drama" Obama was the coolest presidential candidate America had ever seen...young, hip, Ivy League, mellifluous and black, with a melodic and exotic name. Rock stars vied to perform at his massive rallies, where Obama often began his hope-and-change sermons by reminding the teary-eyed audience what to do in case of mass fainting.

Money, like manna from heaven, seemed to drop spontaneously into his $1 billion campaign coffers. Ecstatic Hollywood stars were rendered near speechless at the thought of Obama's promised Big Rock Candy Mountain to come...peace, harmony, prosperity and "5 million new jobs" in renewable energy alone.

The giddy media declared Obama a "sort of god," and "the smartest man with the highest IQ" ever to assume the presidency.

And why not, when the soft-spoken, adaptable African-American candidate preached civility and visions of a post-racial America...changing his speech from a white suburban patois to Southern black evangelical cadences as needed to woo widely diverse audiences.

Obama, the most partisan member of the United States Senate, promised a new post-political nonpartisanship. Almost by fiat, he declared an end to big debts, corruption, lobbyists, wars, unpopular American foreign policies and unlawful antiterrorism protocols...almost everything that had predated the presidency of Barack Hussein Obama.

Four years of governance later, the huge crowds have mostly melted away. And those still left...are not fainting!

Instead of "no red states or blue states" healing rhetoric, Obama has sown all sorts of needless divisions in hopes of cobbling together a thin us-versus-them coalition, as independents flee. The 99 percent claim oppression by the 1 percent. Young single female professionals are supposedly at war with Republican Neanderthals. Beleaguered gays apparently must fight the bigotry of the homophobic right wing. Greens should go on the offensive against conservative polluters who are OK with dirty air and water.

Latinos must "punish our enemies" at the polls, and Attorney General Eric Holder's "my people" are to be set against "a nation of cowards." With all the advantages of incumbency and an obsequious media, why is Obama stooping this low to save his campaign?

A dismal economy, of course, explains voter discontent. So do the contradictory and illogical explanations about the recent killing of a United States ambassador and three other Americans in Libya. Mitt Romney is also proving to be a far better campaigner than were prior so-so Obama opponents like Hillary Clinton and John McCain. And don't forget Obama's first debate disaster.

A worldlier Obama no longer talks of cooling the planet or lowering the rising seas. Barely even with challenger Mitt Romney in the polls, he now alternates between the crude and the trivial in a campaign that in its shrillness on the stump evokes the last desperate days of failed incumbents like Gerald Ford, Jimmy Carter and George H.W. Bush.

The greatest problem facing Obama, however, is not just his mediocre record of governance, but the growing public perception that he is as un-cool in 2012 as he was cool in 2008. Voters no longer feel they're square for voting against Obama. Instead, it's becoming the "in thing" to shrug that enough is enough.

A common theme of classic American tales such as "The Rainmaker," "Elmer Gantry," "The Music Man" and "The Wizard of Oz" is the anger that's unleashed at Pied Piper-like messiahs who once hypnotized the masses with promises of grandeur.

The bamboozled people rarely fault their own gullibility for swooning over hope-and-change banalities, but rather, once sober, turn with fury on the itinerant messiahs who made them look so foolish.

> [In writing this I couldn't help but reflect back on the long ago tragedy of Jonestown; I was struck by the utterly unthinking way that so

> many people put themselves completely at the mercy of a glib and warped man, who led them to degradation and destruction. And I could not help thinking of the parallel with the way we put a glib and warped man in the White House. Those Jonestown believers paid the ultimate price for their continuing gullibility...]

In other words, it is not just the economy, foreign policy, poor debating skills or a so-so campaign that now plagues Obama, but the growing public perception that voters "were had" in 2008, and that now it's okay...even cool, to no longer believe in him. We can only hope...

While Obama's national job approval rating is a little less than 50 percent...among blacks, his job approval is a whopping 88 percent. I would like to ask these people, who approve of Obama's performance, "What has Obama done during the past four years that you would like to see more of in the next four years?"

I do not understand how it can possibly be that conservative writers are still addressing Obama as if he is actually trying to help the economy, but his well-intentioned policies are just failing.

Obama is the enemy. Obama is a Marxist-Communist usurper and puppet front for a cabal of Marxist-Communists who are actively trying to destroy the United States of America. Everything they have done, are doing, and will do has the single goal of collapsing and destroying the United States economy, military, constitutional government and culture. What part of "Marxist Revolution" do you not understand?

The Obama regime is not a failure. The Obama regime is not incompetent. The Obama regime has achieved more in three and a half years than anyone could have possibly foreseen. It has devalued our currency by 50 percent of the "gross domestic product" (one of the primary indicators used to gauge the health of a country's economy) and guaranteed that our economy will collapse. It has looted the treasury for more than the size of some countries' entire economy and embezzled that wealth into the hands of fellow Marxists in preparation for the final collapse of the United States. It has ground the economy of the United States to a screeching halt. It has destabilized the entire Muslim world and ensured that there will be a nuclear war centered around Israel within the decade.

The Obama regime has no interest whatsoever in "stimulus or getting folks back to work." How can you not understand this? How can we possibly win this war if we refuse to come to terms with the fact that we are in fact fighting a war?

God save the United States of America, because the people are far too stupid to do it themselves.

Black support of politicians who have done little or nothing for their ordinary constituents is by no means unusual. Blacks are chief executives of major cities, such as Philadelphia, Detroit, Washington, Memphis, Atlanta, Baltimore, New Orleans, Oakland, Newark, Cleveland and Cincinnati. In most of these cities, the chief of police, the superintendent of schools and other high executives are black. But in these cities, black people, like no other sector of our population, suffer from the highest rates of homicides, assaults, robberies and shootings. Black high school dropout rates, in these cities, are the highest in the nation. Even if a black youngster manages to graduate from high school, his reading, writing and computational proficiency is likely to be equivalent to that of a white seventh - or eighth grader. That's even with school budgets per student being among the highest in the nation.

Last year, in reference to President Obama's failed employment policies and high unemployment among blacks, Representative Emanuel Cleaver, D-Mo., who is chairman of the Congressional Black Caucus, said, "If Bill Clinton had been in the White House and had failed to address this problem; we probably would be marching on the White House."

That's a vision that seems to explain black tolerance for failed politicians...namely, if it's a black politician whose policies are ineffectual and possibly harmful to the masses of the black community, it's tolerable, but it's entirely unacceptable if the politician is white.

Black people "would not" accept excuses upon excuses and vote to re-elect decade after decade any white politician, especially a Republican politician, to office who had the failed records of our big-city mayors. What that suggests about black people is not very flattering.

> "Nothing in the world is more dangerous than sincere ignorance and conscientious stupidity."
>
> ~ Martin Luther King ~

Chapter 18

Nothing I've written so far sounds like the homogenous environment that one would expect, before introducing the populace to Collectivism...and by extension, the New World Order. But history tells us that it will transpire, whether by "consent...or force." The process has been in motion for a very long time and we're approaching the point of no return.

Long before Bill and Hillary's "it takes a village," we had Roosevelt's "New Deal," Kennedy's "New Frontier," and Johnson's "The Great Society." As the decades rolled by, this utopian concept continued to grow...fed by ambitious politicians, stroking their constituency by passing out more and more freebies to ensure they maintain their seat each election cycle. But in the last four years the various entitlement and social welfare benefit numbers have jumped off the charts. We've reached the point where "almost" 50 percent of the populace is receiving some level of government assistance. We're also nearing the tipping point where the voting numbers will favor a socialist culture and government.

I would be remiss if I didn't acknowledge the fact that Bill and Hillary's "village" notion has been a viable safety net, for the unfortunate, since the beginning of time. The difference today is that the village concept worked back when it was facilitated...and supported, by communal volunteers...not by a dictatorial government with self-serving agendas. Long-term, socialism...with the exception of our "caretakers" hurts everyone.

When push comes to shove, I believe the line will be drawn between the producers (contributors, current and past) and the non-producers (the entitlement group)... and there will not be a "consensual" agreement.

In spite of...or perhaps because of, a "slight majority" against the welfare/socialism state, the government's impetus reflects the "Manifest Destiny" model. The same doctrine/mandate used by our forefathers (at Wounded Knee) to expand across North America while confiscating the American Indians' land and subjugating their way of life. Rounding them up like buffalo and herding them onto "reservations" for their "preservation." It would seem they were already persevering pretty well before our government decided it knew what was best for the Native Americans. Of course it wasn't about what was best for the Indian nations...it was all about control.

Whether one believes it or not, that's the direction America is currently leaning.

A brief synopsis about this 19th-Century doctrine, Manifest Destiny:

- "A policy of imperialistic expansion defended as necessary or benevolence."

Rural America continues its retreat, as each and every emerging generation is motivated for various reasons, to embrace the lifestyle of the large metropolitan areas. The most recognizable logic here is that pastoral America has become caught-up in a catch 22 situation...also known as a vicious cycle; where two or more conditions require the other condition(s) to be fulfilled, but these other conditions also require the original condition to be fulfilled. In simple terms, this means neither can get fulfilled without the other being satisfied. These rural areas are losing their younger generations because there are fewer and fewer jobs available...so the quandary is that the lack of meaningful employment is driven by the absence of a skilled labor force. Hence, they can't have one without the other.

With those dynamics in play, America is moving more and more into densely populated, centralized areas of the country. One could suggest that this internal migration is in fact a survival necessity. But on the other hand, with forty-something percent of America's multicultural population dependent (at some level) on the government for their "care," wouldn't these people be easier to "manage" if we/they were more localized. You know, like the American Indians, for our own good...our preservation. Reservation, Uncle Sam's plantation, welfare, collectivism...call it what you will, but to me...it's looking and sounding, more and more...like socialism. Nevertheless, it will be promoted as a necessary benevolence...

America seems to be morphing into a government-run, assisted-living facility for slackers. Of course there are people out there who are truly in need of a "helping hand," but there are also many able-bodied individuals who are only interested in a "hand-out"...just working the system instead of a job.

I'm sure you're rolling your eyes about now and thinking, he's really reaching now...all the above is just the natural flow of man's evolutionary direction.

Just a brief refresher from Chapter 5:

- "The American Historical Association was established in 1889 to promote historical studies. It is interesting to note that after giving careful consideration, in 1926, to the social sciences, a report was published under its auspices in 1934 which concluded that the day of the individual in the United States had come to an end and that the future would be characterized, inevitably, by some form of "collectivism" and an increase in the authority of the State."

It's been years since I cared so deeply about any election, but I would venture to say that today...fewer people can watch so many loathsome campaign ads without thinking that something is dreadfully wrong with our political system.

"Evans Law," named for conservative writer M. Stanton Evans, offers a reminder of why we shouldn't put much faith in politicians: "When one of our people gets in a position where he can do us some good, he stops being one of our people." I've seen council members, in essence, switch sides almost immediately after taking office. The few politicians who stick to their guns often end up being ineffective and ignored.

The crux of the problem is that with every presidential election, the contending parties fall in line as the competitive bidding process for buying votes kicks in. Every time one group ups the ante (more freebies), one of the others will call-and-raise (more entitlements). Just like in a card game, this irresponsible, continuing cycle of "calling and raising" can prove to be financially devastating to the financier...or in this case, the taxpayers. This insanity has been the hallmark of our government from the very start; we have been in a constant state of incrementally increasing the funding that has allowed this all-consuming beast to become the albatross around America's neck today. Its growth has been a persistent escalation that interestingly enough...seems to mirror the always-growing ambitions...and egos, of the career politicians. Perhaps we can now better understand how the entitlement and dependency culture developed over many, many decades...and of course the numbers have jumped off the charts during this administration. But they (the government) don't have the money to continue this endless doling out of un-funded support to...as always, placate their constituencies. Their rational...and/or answer to the country's ever-growing deficit is always same, take it from the "the taxpayers"...you know, those of us who still pay taxes. God forbid they cut back on some of the benefits being paid to the non-tax payers, the many government supported "special interest" programs and subsidies and the foreign aid we send to over half the countries in world...and most of them don't even like us! The bottom line is that participation in this nebulous process is a requirement for retaining one's seat for another election cycle. It's a never-ending cycle that comes and goes...and before we know it, this dog and pony show will once again, be back in town...

mesmerizing and amazing as it coaxes the general public into a state of mind-numbing, lack of common sense. But the real bottom line here is that the general public and the career politicians have a co-dependency relationship that holds this self-servicing monstrosity together.

It's no wonder then that Journalist H.L. Mencken (1880 - 1956) posited that "government is a broker in pillage, and every election is a sort of advance auction in stolen goods."

It's much easier being effective as a pillager than as someone who wants to halt the auction.

My idealistic notion that Republicans might actually cut government spending died with the Reagan administration. That's not to say Reagan didn't implement cuts to take place incrementally down the road, but subsequent administrations overrode most of those cuts...defending their actions as necessary. Of course, "it's necessary" is always the rational. There's so much to cut...but all those programs have constituencies, and unions that have enough money to bury any politician seen as a threat to their members.

I don't believe Mitt Romney will fix anything either, but it's depressing to have a president, like the current one, who believes the answer to every question is..."the government."

The big statewide initiative Tuesday is Proposition 30, Governor Jerry Brown's proposed tax increase. My advice, starve the beast. California's government outspends its revenue every year, during both economic booms and busts. The best hope for restoring some fiscal responsibility is to limit the cash politicians have to spend. Brown and Company are promising Draconian cuts to schools if we don't yield to their political blackmail. It's always best to call a politician's bluff.

No matter who wins, no message will be sent; no deserved political punishment will be meted out.

I hope that if Romney wins the presidency, Americans will be reminded that wealth and the private-enterprise system are good things and should not be the objects of envy and scorn.

Then again, I don't expect much. No matter Tuesday's results, I console myself, again, with Mencken: "Every decent man is ashamed of the government he lives under."

<u>Election update:</u> America's slide continues...

Notable of course was the expected demographic separation of the voting public, but while I was intrigued by the correlation of the voting trends between tradition rural America (conservatives) and their counterparts (liberal/progressives) in the ever-expanding metropolitan areas...I wasn't surprised. Rural America is more inclined to be self-sustaining while the big city dwellers seem to be looking...more and more, to bigger and bigger government for their sustainability. Unfortunately, as we already know...rural America is slipping into irrelevance even as the urban areas continue to expand across America.

No one seems to have learned anything, and now we're stuck with another four years of economic policies based on the notion that one can take water from the deep end of the pool, and dump it in the shallow end (after spilling most of it on the sidewalk) and expect the water level to rise across the pool.

> "What has been will be again, what has been done will be done again. There is nothing new under the sun."
>
> ~ Ecclesiastes 1:9 ~

Chapter 19

Some media pundits see, in the growing proportion of non-white groups in the population, a growing opposition to the Republican Party that will sooner or later make it virtually impossible for Republicans to win presidential elections or even to control either house of Congress. But is demographics destiny?

Some Republicans question whether their party should even try to resist certain seemingly unstoppable demographic trends.

"The die is cast on this issue," said Steve Schmidt, who advised the presidential campaigns of Senator John McCain and George W. Bush and has for years urged Republicans to accept same-sex marriage. "Why should we sign a suicide pact with the National Organization for Marriage?" Schmidt asked, saying the party should instead endorse the principles of federalism and let the states decide the matter.

Conventional wisdom in the Republican establishment is that what the GOP needs to do, to win black and Hispanic votes, is to craft policies specifically targeting these groups. In other words, Republicans need to become more like Democrats. Whether in a racial context or in other contexts...the theory for Republicans to become more like Democrats has been a recurring theme of the moderate Republican establishment; going back more than half a century.

Yet the most successful Republican presidential candidate during that long period was a man who went completely counter to that conventional wisdom...namely, Ronald Reagan, who won back-to-back landslide election victories.

Meanwhile, moderate Republican presidential candidate after moderate Republican presidential candidate has gone down to defeat, even against Democratic presidential candidates who were unpopular (Harry Truman), previously unknown (Jimmy Carter and Bill Clinton) or another who had a terrible economic track record (Barack Obama). None of this seems to have caused any second thoughts in the Republican establishment. As long as that remains the case, demographics may indeed be destiny; that destiny could be Democratic administrations as far out as the eye can see. If pandering to them, with goodies earmarked for them, is the only way to get non-white voters...then Republicans are doomed, even if they choose to go that route. Why would anyone who wants racially earmarked goodies vote for Republicans, when the Democrats already have a track record of delivering such goodies?

An alternative way to make inroads into the overwhelming majority of minority votes going to the Democrats would be for the Republicans to articulate a coherent case for their principles and the benefits that those principles offer to all Americans. But the Republicans' greatest failure has been precisely their chronic failure to spell out their principles, and produce the track record...to either white or non-white voters. Very few people know, for example, that the gap between black and white incomes narrowed during the Reagan administration and widened during the Obama administration.

This was not because of Republican policies designed specifically for blacks, but because free market policies create an economy in which all people can improve their economic situation. Conversely, few policies have had such a devastating effect on the job opportunities of minority youths as minimum wage laws, which are usually pushed by Democrats and opposed by Republicans. But these facts do not "speak for themselves." Somebody has to cite the facts and take the trouble to show why unemployment among minority youths skyrocketed when minimum wage increases priced them out of jobs. The loss of income from an entry-level job is only part of the loss sustained by minority young people. Work experience at even an entry-level job is a valuable asset, as a stepping-stone to progressively higher-level jobs. Moreover, nobody gains from having a huge number of idle youths hanging out on the streets, least of all minority communities.

Labor unions push minimum wage laws to insulate their members from the competition of younger workers, and Democratic politicians are heavily dependent on union support. For the same reason, Democrats have to go along with teachers' unions that treat schools as places to guarantee their members jobs, rather than to provide the needed quality education to rise out of poverty.

What Democrats cannot say under these conditions is what Republicans are free to say, even if Republicans have seldom taken advantage of that freedom to make inroads into minority voting blocs. Inroads are all they need. If the black vote for Democrats falls to 70 percent, the Democrats are in deep trouble. But if Republicans continue to be inarticulate, then it is they who are in big trouble. But more importantly, so is the country.

From a personal perspective I understand and relate to the Republicans' hesitance to explain themselves and the benefits of their policies. They're always looking at the bigger picture (political platform), a more comprehensive... all-inclusive (rather than targeting special interest groups) package that's intended to work in the best interest of all Americans without regard to skin color, gender or national origin...the proverbial level playing field.

How can I relate to all the above? I think it's all about personal pride and conservatism...and that the two go hand-in-hand. Throughout my life I have (from time to time) struggled with people's un-founded perception of what I represent and/or who I am. As a prideful, southern conservative who worked his way up from the cotton fields of Arkansas to a California, offshore oil-platform supervisor; I've always declined to defend my character when mischaracterized. I've always known who I am, but if you can't see that...I'm not going to waste my time or yours trying to change your mind. I see that same prideful, conservatism trait as the hindrance dogging the

Republican Party. They know their program is, overall, in the best interest of America and its entire population. Conservatives (due to our character/temperament) aren't very good at responding to the progressive liberal's attack modes of shouting us down, ridicule and mockery.

The president's campaign, if you will, focused on giving targeted groups big gifts, and making big efforts on small things (because he had no real plan). Instead of focusing on America's best interest...he was focusing on Obama's best interest.

Romney said his campaign, in contrast, had been about "big issues for the whole country." He said he faced problems as a candidate because he was "getting beat up" by the Obama campaign's negative, unfounded attack ads that allowed Obama to come back.

Republican presidential nominee Mitt Romney told his top donors that Obama won re-election because of the "gifts" he had already provided to blacks, Hispanics and young voters, and because of the president's efforts to paint Romney as anti-immigrant.

Among the "gifts" Romney cited were free health care "in perpetuity," which he said was highly motivational to black and Hispanic voters as well as for voters making $25,000 to $35,000 a year.

Young voters, he said, were motivated by the administration's plan for partial forgiveness of college loan interest and being able to remain on their parents' health insurance plans. Young women had an additional incentive to vote for Obama because of free contraception coverage under the president's health care plan.

Some say that we "conservatives" should move to the Left if we want to win elections. That is not an option. I would rather see the GOP lose every election than become "light Democrats."

Some of us believe that we will have to answer to a "higher power," namely to God, as well as to our posterity; so we will not embrace abortion, amnesty, socialized medicine nor the emasculation of our military.

A liberal is someone who feels a great debt to his fellow man, which debt he proposes to pay off with your money.

> "Republics are created by the virtue, public spirit, and intelligence of the citizens. They fall, when the wise are banished from the public councils, because they dare to be honest, and the profligate are rewarded, because they flatter the people, in order to betray them."
>
> ~ Joseph Story, Commentary on the Constitution, 1833 ~

Chapter 20

More than 100 years ago, Anglican Bishop William Stubbs, describing the start of the 14th century, wrote:

> "We pass from the age of heroism to the age of chivalry, from a century ennobled by devotion and self-sacrifice to one in which the gloss of superficial refinement fails to hide the reality of heartless selfishness and moral degradation...an age of luxury and cruelty.
>
> The men are all of a meaner moral stature. The patriots work for lower objectives...the grievances of the people are the result of dishonest administration, chicanery and petty malversation."

As we enter a new year, these words remind me of our current plight. Just compare Vice President Joe Biden's scorn for serious debate with former President John F.

Kennedy, who said: "Ask not what your country can do for you, ask what you can do for your country," or "Let us not seek the Republican answer or the Democrat answer but the right answer."

He also said, "Let us accept our own responsibility for the future," to which I would like to add...and not kick our problems down the road.

The debate on entitlement reform is just the latest chapter in the epic shift of responsibility from the individual to the collective that has taken place over the past 80-plus years. The first chapter was Social Security in 1935, followed by others, including disability insurance in 1956, Medicare and Medicaid in 1965, prescription drugs in 2003 and Obamacare in 2010. The shift of responsibility to the collective is global and particularly well established in Europe. Why has this happened and what are the long-term consequences?

The shifting of responsibility normally is caused by a shock or crisis, for example, a war, depression, natural disaster or terrorist attack. The government responds to the shock, and in doing so takes on responsibility and power it did not have prior to the shock. Government power may recede when the shock is over, but normally not to its pre-shock level. The process repeats with each subsequent shock, causing increased government control over time. This phenomenon was well documented by Robert Higgs in his 1987 book, "Crisis and Leviathan."

President Franklin D. Roosevelt signed the Social Security Bill in Washington on August 14, 1935. He was joined at the signing by Chairman Doughton of the House Ways and Means Committee, Senator Wagner, D-New York...co-author of the bill, Secretary Perkins, Chairman Harrison of the Senate Finance Committee and Representative Lewis, D-Maryland...co-author of the measure.

The shifting of responsibility to the collective has at least four consequences. The first is that individuals become dependent on the government for the responsibility that has been shifted, and lose some freedom in the process. The government, now responsible, calls the shots. It tells you what you get, when, how much; whether it's indexed to inflation, whether your spouse gets anything...the list is almost endless. These are choices you once made for yourself, but now you don't.

Second, resources are also shifted because the government has to provide for its new responsibility. It gets its resources from taxing the very individuals whose responsibilities it took over. To the extent that the new taxes decrease the after-tax return on saving, investing or labor, there is less of it, which leads to slower economic growth.

The third consequence is that to the extent that the government allocates its newfound resources less efficiently than the private sector from which it took them, which is often the case...economic growth slows even more.

Finally, responsibility is rarely shifted back to the individual. This is because the collective is protective of its new power, and the individual does not have the clout to reverse it. It takes a groundswell of individuals to reverse the course, a difficult task at best.

In the case of Social Security, the shock was the Great Depression. Franklin D. Roosevelt responded to the crisis in his 1935 State of the Union address:

> "Closely related to the broad problem of livelihood is that of security against the major hazards of life. I shall send to you in a few days, definite recommendations that will cover the broad subjects of unemployment insurance and old-age insurance, of benefits for children, for mothers, for the handicapped, for maternity care, and for other aspects of dependency and illness where a beginning can now be made."

Thus, the shifting of responsibility started. When the Depression was over, Social Security didn't end. In fact, it has expanded to the point where nearly all retirees are now dependent on the collective. The government writes the rules, mind-boggling in their complexity... thereby reducing individual choice. In order to finance the benefits, the same individuals who ultimately receive benefits are required to give up resources. Given that total resources must at least equal total benefits, there is no net gain, but a redistribution of wealth from one cohort to another.

As Social Security has confronted new shocks, such as unfavorable demographics, the government has responded by decreasing benefits and raising taxes, causing an inefficient system to be more so. Given that the system faces a present un-funded liability in the trillions of dollars, scheduled taxes and benefits will not be honored. Yet, totally consistent with the fourth consequence, the collective holds on, disallowing any competition that would shift responsibility back to the individual.

These shocks and/or crises (natural or manufactured) have followed America since the two WWs and Roosevelt. Pearl Harbor and 9-11 were major events within the bigger picture of our turbulent history, but we've also experienced presidential assassinations and attempted presidential assassinations, terrorism...home and abroad, mass killings at home, and natural disasters... earthquakes and weather related events.

Each and every one of these incidents has been used by our "benevolent" government to increase its influence and control of the people, thereby...always increasing its size and power. With that said, we can see why the government...and its allies in the mainstream media are focused on the December killings in Connecticut. It's not so much about the incident, but rather the bigger goal of disarming the law-abiding citizens...leaving them/us without personal protection capabilities...or the resources to resist governmental oppression.

The president and Congress are supposedly "engaged" to save us from the fiscal cliff. It's all meaningless theater as they argue about pennies while we need to be talking about trillions of dollars. One fundamental problem is that the people deciding how to solve the problem are the same people who created the problem.

I find it difficult to believe they really care...first, because the vast majority of individuals who end up as elected officials in Washington are wealthy enough to weather any economic storm (or become wealthy enough during their tenure), but also because they have the power to exempt themselves from laws they impose on the rest of us. While it has always been true that our government has been, for the most part...executed by wealthy and powerful individuals, we now see a true ruling class developing.

We desperately need a 28th Amendment to our Constitution that requires federal lawmakers to be subject to every law they pass. Until their interests are aligned with ours, we can hardly expect them to serve our interests. But can any of us seriously say that the "Bill of Rights" could get through Congress today? It wouldn't even get out of committee.

Members of Congress and the president are corralling the American taxpayers into the jaws of the IRS like border collies herd sheep. For months they've made themselves appear to be frantically working for a solution to improve the economy when in fact...they were cunningly conditioning and wearing down their constituents into a sense of resignation about increased taxes...the highest single tax increase in our country's history.

America, wake up. It is not the so-called "1 percent" that is ripping us off; it's the president and the 535 members of Congress; a number far less than the 1 percent that the liberal progressives whine about. It is Congress as a whole that is responsible for the tsunami of debt and spending that is drowning the American taxpayer.

I would say there is a mountain of truth to the study published in the American Political Science Review: "Decision-making by voters is ill-informed," study says. Politics, December 28, 2012.

All one must do is look at the White House in Washington, D.C., and California's governor's office and the supermajority in Sacramento to see how relevant and to the point that study has been.

> "There are two ways to conquer and enslave a nation: One is by the sword...the other is by debt."
>
> ~ John Adams ~
> 1826

Chapter 21

A look back perspective from an earlier book:

> At the end of World War I, Wilson brought his famous "fourteen points," to the Paris Peace Conference with point fourteen being a proposal for a "general association of nations," which was to be the first step towards the goal of One-World Government... the "League of Nations."
>
> It was later revealed that the League was not Wilson's idea. Not a single idea in the Covenant of the League was original with the President. Colonel House was the author of the Covenant, and Wilson had merely rewritten it to conform to his own phraseology.
>
> The League of Nations was established, but it, and the plan for world government

> eventually failed because the United States Senate would not ratify the Versailles Treaty.
>
> Pat Robertson, in "The New World Order," states that Colonel House, along with other internationalists, realized that America would not join any scheme for world government "without a change in public opinion/attitude."

Today, it would be hard for anyone to deny that the majority has embraced that change of opinion/attitude. Just look around you, "that change" has been subliminally orchestrated over many decades (incrementally of course) until one day...like a train wreck, many of us realized that we no longer recognize America.

Representative Ron Paul recently made his farewell speech to a largely empty House of Representatives, aptly symbolic of a Congress that did not want to hear the message of less government he has consistently preached. He concluded that his fight to reform the American government had largely failed because a limited form of government could not work...unless the people of this country were ethical enough not to initiate force to take other people's wealth and impose their lifestyle on others.

Pandering to envy and bigotry has ruined the ideals and hopes of the founding fathers. Paul's solution: Reform the minds of the people. Rejecting the initiation of force, starting with each individual, each family, each neighborhood and organization. Do this, and reform of government will follow.

In the wake of the election, more than a handful of news stories and commentaries have suggested that any chance of a tax revolt is either dead or mortally wounded. But, as Mark Twain famously said, "The reports of my death are greatly exaggerated." I have to challenge Mark on an element of his supposition that tax revolts are still alive. The possibilities of a tax revolt are in fact still alive, but due to our changing demographics...any tax revolts would be impotent.

These reports may be based on wishful thinking on the part of the liberal commentators and bloggers, aided and abetted by a general funk among fiscal conservatives, taxpayers and free-market advocates who, understandably, were a bit down.

Which brings me to my point: The passage of Proposition 30 proves that millions of Californians will vote to raise taxes on a few thousand other Californians. Brown has told the media that Californians are ready "to tax themselves." No, they're not. They're ready to tax anyone, and anything, other than themselves.

The pro-Proposition 30 campaign shamelessly told college students that they would get a $250 check by raising taxes on the wealthy if Proposition 30 passed and, conversely, they would pay higher tuition if Proposition 30 failed. Likewise, the threat of shorter school years for K-12 students effectively frightened parents into giving Proposition 30 the benefit of the doubt.

The notion of a "tax revolt" is based on the asinine opinion that the threat of a tax revolt itself has prevented government from collecting the necessary revenue to provide essential government services. While Proposition

13 has proven remarkably successful in keeping people in their homes, it never really restrained the size and scope of government in California. Had government growth been limited to increases in population and inflation, as envisioned by the Gann Spending Limit in 1979, California would have a surplus and a massive rainy-day fund. But the Gann limit was gutted by a coalition of government and corporate interests. We are now paying the price for California's two decades of profligate spending.

Brief refresher on Proposition 13:

- Proposition 13 (officially named the People's Initiative to Limit Property Taxation) was an amendment to the Constitution of California enacted during 1978, by means of the initiative process. It was approved by California voters on June 6, 1978, and declared constitutional by the United States Supreme Court in 1992.

The most significant portion of the act is the first paragraph, which limited the tax rate for real estate:

- Section 1 (a): The maximum amount of added value tax on real property shall not exceed one percent (1%) of the full cash value of such property. The one percent (1%) tax to be collected by the counties and apportioned according to law to the districts within the counties.

- The proposition decreased property taxes by assessing property values at their 1975 value and restricted annual increases of assessed value of real property to an inflation factor, not to exceed 2 percent per year. It also prohibited reassessment of a new base year value except for (a) change in ownership or (b) completion of new construction.

- In addition to decreasing property taxes, the initiative also contained language requiring a two-thirds majority in both legislative houses for future increases of any state tax rates or amounts of revenue collected, including income tax rates. It also requires a two-thirds vote majority in local elections for local governments wishing to increase special taxes. Proposition 13 received an enormous amount of publicity, not only in California, but also throughout the United States.

Imposing a huge tax increase on a few thousand of our most productive citizens might sell well among college students and others who can't grasp basic economics, but it is another thing to take on Proposition 13, which provides enormous security for every homeowner in the state. Nothing that happened last week would suggest that Proposition 13, called the third rail of California politics, is any less popular than it has been for 33 years. Indeed, the most recent public polling suggests its popularity is increasing.

Will this stop those in political power who have an insatiable appetite for our money from at least trying to weaken Proposition13? Not hardly.

Los Angeles Mayor, Antonio Villaraigosa, spoke in platitudes until he got to Proposition 13 ("Time to invest in the future," Opinion, November 13, 2012). Here is the doozy: "We need to reform Proposition 13 and move from a tax system full of loopholes and exemptions to a system that protects homeowners, supports job creation and gives Californians the ability to generate new revenue." Translation: We…"your government" want you (those of you who actually still pay taxes) to pay even more and more toward California's out-of-control, spending deficit. Between the controlling unions and the always-growing welfare numbers, "necessity" may well dictate the altering of Proposition 13? And…after our recent election the Democrats now have that two-thirds vote majority that means they can do whatever they deem "necessary."

If Proposition 13 should go under the knife, would it resurrect a "tax revolt" movement? While I think it would stir the pot, the numbers in California would suggest (to me) that it would fail because of California's always growing populace of welfare voters (the highest in the country)…and union members (who have inflated, state sponsored retirement packages that are currently vastly under-funded) will always vote for taxing the rest of us. Yes, the state will go after Proposition 13…they are holding all the cards.

All politics is cyclical. After Lyndon Johnson crushed Barry Goldwater, the chattering class said that the Republican Party was dead. But Ronald Reagan, a Goldwater backer, proved how wrong that prediction was. More recently, in 2010, the overwhelming Republican tide had conservatives overly confident that President Obama had zero chance of reelection. The pendulum will swing again.

We have set up a system of involuntary servitude where those who work hard, save and want to enjoy the fruits of their labor are being forced to give their money to others who haven't worked hard or planned ahead, and give subsidies to benefit certain businesses that can't make it on their own. It becomes slavery when I am forced to send my money to pay for others who should be paying for themselves.

Americans have "voted themselves a lifestyle they are not willing to earn." Actually, Americans have voted for a lifestyle they would like someone else to earn for them.

As early as the mid-19th century, French philosopher and historian Alexis de Tocqueville warned that democracies would collapse once the majority realized they could elect leaders who will give them free things. He said that all democracies die on the rocks of loose fiscal policies.

He also warned that the world's great civilizations only lasted about two centuries. Well, we're working on our third century and America's electorate has developed an insatiable appetite for government's free goodies, welfare and other handouts.

"The lessons of history...show conclusively that continued dependence upon relief induces a spiritual and moral disintegration that's fundamentally destructive to the national fiber. To dole out relief in this way is to administer a narcotic, a subtle destroyer of the human spirit."

Some would argue that America has already crossed the Rubicon; that the "gimme" generation has reached critical mass; that from this point on a majority of Americans will always vote for a President based on what he will give them, not on how wisely he will lead the nation.

And the majority will vote this way because they are ensnared in the "entitlement trap." And unfortunately, this situation did not come to pass by accident.

What else could explain the re-election of a leader who failed miserably to accomplish anything he promised in his first campaign; yet repeatedly and clearly guaranteed that, if re-elected, he would double-down on his failures?

Wait a minute. I stand corrected. He did come through on one promise: Obamacare. And it may help bankrupt America, which is not what he promised, but almost surely intended.

The Congressional Budget Office has been telling America for years that Obamacare is not budget neutral as Nancy Pelosi and Obama kept saying when they forced the legislation through Congress, so it should not be a surprise to anyone. It is hugely expensive, and when added to Social Security, Medicare, Medicaid, welfare and disability programs, and the myriad of other so-called social justice programs, it is the program that will push the cost of the federal government so deep into the red that the result may produce the worst depression this country has ever experienced.

It is more than irresponsible government at work here; it is insanity. The only logical conclusion to what is happening is that the Obama administration and the progressives in our country want to see a major financial crash while they are in control of the government. They must believe that the utter chaos and desperation that a financial crash will create will give them an opportunity to implement their socialist ideology as a baseline in our country. It gives Obama the opportunity to "transform" America from our capitalistic roots into another entitlement based socialist/communist country.

There is no other logical reason for a continuation of the uncontrolled borrowing and spending, and the huge expansion of the entitlement programs that are being pushed by the Obama administration.

Our government was set up to fund shared infrastructure costs, the military, roads and our court system, not birth control, solar panels, lifetime welfare and absurd government retirement programs.

I've recently read various articles by national columnists questioning how historians will characterize Obama's legacy given his failure to address America's stalled economy. He will of course, no matter what...always be remembered as America's first Black president. I believe he's not concerned about our capitalistic system slowly grinding to a near halt, because it's necessary for his real agenda. Those on the far Left, including the mainstream media, know exactly what's going on and are compliant... if not complicit; he's utilizing Americans to take America down. He wants his legacy to portray him as the president who single-handedly, subjugated the most powerful nation in the world. Even for a pathological narcissist, this would be big...expanding his already over-inflated ego.

> "Freedom is never more than one generation away from extinction."
>
> ~ Ronald Reagan ~

CHAPTER 22

The America many of us have known, loved and respected passed away November 6, 2012. A new America is emerging, but bearing no resemblance to the original. Alas, America went peacefully...hardly a whimper. Since history is a tale of events told by the winners, America's demise will not be mentioned in the news or history books.

Sadly, America's passing will be overlooked by the rest of the free world...embroiled as its members are in economic turmoil, disturbing demographic trends and outbreaks of violence. With America's passing, a more important concern will eventually emerge...international security. The threat will appear on two fronts...economic and military. A powerful and prosperous American economy has been, and still is, the world's best hope for security, buttressed by America's military capability that provides the majority of the resources needed for the defense of the free world. The path upon which the new America has now embarked, poses a serious threat to both fronts.

Blessed by a fortunate geography and a succession of world events in which American courage in the face of high risk enabled much of the world, both free and oppressed...to prosper; America's shining example and its role in world events is not disputed. The new America, however, is no longer capable of playing a similar role. The new America is economically unsustainable, and it no longer seeks to lead the fight against oppression or military threat.

While America's future role in world affairs may be simply speculation, a claim that the new America bears no resemblance to the original is easily supported by evidence. The evidence is all around us...hiding in plain sight:

- Exhibit 1: We must acknowledge the emergence of a new "government class"...a class so extensive, powerful and intrusive that, to many, our government is now a government of the people, by the government, for the government. The new government class is inflexible regarding business cycles, and is covered by a security blanket at taxpayer expense that defies rational fiscal policy, and its presence is felt in every aspect of our daily lives. This class poses a threat that dwarfs that of the supposed rich-versus-poor divide.

- Exhibit 2: We need only note the fatal fiscal policies promoted by our government that annually spends $1 trillion more than it takes in, and has accumulated more than $16 trillion in debt owed to others.

- Exhibit 3: Our historic morality, reason, self-reliance and our respect for the traditional family and religion...these intangibles that have always been key ingredients in the development of America and its prosperity, have been subordinated to a de-facto faith and reliance on government regulations and entitlements, designed, as we are told, to achieve a more equal economic and social equity in America's society.

The cause of America's death is undoubtedly suicide, with a self-inflicted fatal wound caused by an education system that does not support the principles upon which the country was founded, or reinforces the story of America's evolution, or articulates the benefits of our economic system, or explains our system of government at the national, state, and/or local levels. It has also failed to produce, for a large proportion of the students, thinking skills necessary for self-reliance or achievement in our society. As with any system infrastructure, failure to continually reinforce the American story leads, inevitably, to its decline, decay and destruction.

To be fair, many will dismiss all of the above as simply sour grapes and if, indeed, there is a "new America," it is, or will be, superior to the original. The "more perfect union" will be a product of the government's efforts in response to changing demographics, the global economy, and the need to redistribute society's income and wealth to mitigate the "perceived unfair" results produced by an economic system that is "perceived as rigged" against the interests of the people. History has shown, however, that efforts to legislate, or force, social or economic equality is only accomplished at the expense of liberty.

We cannot allow a myriad of government regulations be the proxy for our individual and/or collective morality in our lives. And despite demographic changes, we must not permit political correctness be the controlling force in policy decisions.

Throughout mankind's history, socialism has played out in various forms and locations around the world. That same history also tells us that socialism doesn't have a good track record in regard to sustainability. It usually surfaces as a localized phenomenon fed by too much government seeking ever more power and control over the populace. Under the cloak of altruism the politicians keep handing out more and more freebies and entitlement programs (to buy the public's favor... and votes of course) until the government bankrupts its host state or country. While socialism comes and goes, it can...and often does, mutate into communism and/or some other forms of dictatorships. But what the world has never seen or experienced is a time of structured, organized...worldwide socialism/collectivism. Well, not yet...

Suppose a cabal was working to facilitate the long conspired One World Government Dictatorship, they couldn't want any Superpowers around that might have the military and financial might to deny them when they start dictating what must happen. And because a World Government would tend to have a World Army, a World Central Bank and a World Currency...they would need to take the world's Superpower...America, out. To do that, they would have to destroy it militarily and financially...from within. And that's exactly what's currently happening.

Dictatorships, revolutions, military coups and even foreign military controlling the subjugated population of conquered countries, have been a part of world history for a very, very long time. Like socialism, these events were localized and most didn't stand the test of time. Again... like socialism, a one-world government (a one size fits all concept) has never existed in a structured, "congenial" and organized form. The United Nations is the closest thing to a world government that the world has ever known...and they rarely agree on anything because they all have their personal agendas and ultra egos.

In earlier times, during those periods of pandemonium and civil disobedience, the perpetrators were "usually" able to affectively "control" the involved population without killing millions of people. But as history tells us..."not always." Today, with the world's political awakening and the advent of real time, worldwide, information centers and the individual's Internet communication systems connecting them to the world...subjugation of a group can no longer be accomplished in the darkness of ignorance. In today's world, "control" is no longer a realistic stopgap... millions will have to be killed.

It's obvious that our world is experiencing some extreme growing pains, the likes of which our older generations would have thought unthinkable several decades ago... but today's younger generations don't appear to see the demise of America's heritage as a setback. We (the older folks) have the advantage (or disadvantage...depending on one's point of view) of the bigger-picture perspective... whereas; their snapshot perception is limited to today's ever-growing..."new norm"...progressivism. This "upheaval" isn't limited to America; our world is in the process of re-aligning everything we had come to believe in...including the naive expectations of a harmonious continuance of our American way of life. Do I think... or expect the American traditionalists will stand up for what they believe in? Yes, if push comes to shove...we could see civil unrest here in America.

Gun sales in America have skyrocketed during the last couple of years of Obama's first term. Those sales have been driven by a number of things...not the least of which is the growing knowledge of this administration's anti-guns agenda which is expected to be ramped-up in his second term when he doesn't have to worry about alienating Second Amendment rights voters. The administration has also been working with the United Nations to implement a worldwide ban on certain guns, but it's generally understood that once that door is opened, they will eventually be coming after all privately owned guns...it would just be a matter of time. It's also understood that for the One World Government to rein in its reluctant inhabitants, it must first disarm them... as Hitler did with Germany.

At a more personal level, I know (from conversation... and emails) that a growing number of everyday citizens are quietly acquiring weaponry and ammunition. In confidential conversation the driver is always the same... fear. They fear their government and they fear the real possibility of civil instability. The current administration has so divided our country with its divisiveness that we have all these different factions pointing fingers at each other. In the weeks preceding the election, the Internet was very active with Obama supporters threatening retaliation if Obama didn't win.

Recap from an earlier chapter:

- In a recent impromptu statement to his minions, Obama chose to motivate them by framing the up-coming election with a very negative message: "In this election 'voting is the best revenge'... payback for our enemies and rewards for those who supported us."

So is it any wonder that many in the general public have legitimate concerns for themselves' and their family's safety. In sharing thoughts and feelings regarding the state of affairs in America today, the most common comeback is: "I hope I never need these guns and ammunition, but I don't want to find myself needing them...and then not having them."

As frightening as all this sounds, there is an even more worrisome threat growing on the distant horizon. One can't help but realize that down the road, the continual global growth of the Muslim populace will reach a breaking point in the coming decades. We're already seeing and hearing about how the Islamic culture is making demands in the various countries that have "welcomed" them. Europe and countries around the world are feeling the pressure being exerted by Muslim emigrants for sharia laws and courts to accommodate their culture. In major cities they have settled into large enclaves where signs announcing that you're now entering a sharia law area...are blatantly posted. Even the police avoid those areas. These submissive countries are starting to look like the tribal patchwork of the Middle East. But it gets worse; given the high birth rates within the Muslim communities...they will be electing government officials in the coming years.

Political correctness aside, I'm going to go out on a limb and suggest that globally speaking, the Muslim culture clashes...in many ways, with America and its traditional values. From my perspective (again), there would seem to be a major disconnect between the one world government and the Muslim world. The push here in America is toward secularism...but the Muslims cannot separate religion from government because it's all entwined. Islam is a complete cultural doctrine with laws and religious mandates all wrapped up in the Koran...end of story.

It sounds like this one world government will be in for a turbulent tenure...given the historical nature of mankind.

> "The most dangerous man to any government is the man who is able to think things out for himself."
>
> ~ M. L. Mencken ~

Chapter 23

One of the best "sounding" Inaugural Addresses in recent times, made a good argument for "something." Obama's second one, which surely has to rank among the most "inspirational" of the past half-century, makes an argument for a pragmatic and patriotic "progressivism."

His critics have sometimes accused him of being an outsider, but Obama wove his vision from deep strands in the nation's past. He told an American story that began with the Declaration and then touched upon the railroad legislation, the Progressive Era, the New Deal, the highway legislation, the Great Society, Seneca Falls, Selma and Stonewall.

Turning to the present, Obama argued that America has to change its approach if it wants to continue its progress. Modern problems like globalization, technological change, widening inequality and wage stagnation compel us to take new "collective" measures if we're to pursue the old goals of equality and opportunity.

Obama wasn't explicit about why we have failed to meet these challenges. But his critique was implicit. There has been too much "me"...too much individualism and narcissism (he certainly has insight regarding narcissism), too much retreating into the private sphere. There hasn't been enough "us," not enough communal action for the common good.

The president then described some of the places where collective action is necessary: Address global warming, fortify the middle class, defend Medicare and Social Security, and guarantee equal pay for women and equal rights for gays and lesbians.

During his first term, Obama was inhibited by his desire to be post partisan, by the need to not offend the Republicans with whom he was negotiating. Now he is liberated. Now he has picked a team and put his liberalism on full display. He argued for it in a way that was unapologetic. Those who agree, those who disagree and those who partly agree now have to raise their game. They have to engage his core narrative and his core arguments for a collective turn.

I am not a liberal like Obama, so I was struck by what he left out in his tour through United States history. I, too, would celebrate Seneca Falls, Selma and Stonewall.

I would also mention Wall Street, State Street, Menlo Park and Silicon Valley. I would emphasize that America has prospered because we have a decentralizing genius.

When Europeans nationalized their religions, we decentralized and produced a great flowering of entrepreneurial denominations. When Europe organized state universities, our diverse communities organized private universities. When Europeans invested in national welfare states, American localities invested in human capital.

America's greatest innovations and commercial blessings were unforeseen by those at the national headquarters. They emerged, bottom up, from tinkerers and business outsiders who could never have attracted the attention of a president or some public-private investment commission.

I would have been more respectful of this decentralizing genius than Obama was, more nervous about dismissing it for the sake of collective action, more concerned that centralization will lead to stultification, as it has in every other historic instance.

I also think Obama misunderstands - no, misrepresents - this moment in time. The Progressive Era, New Deal and Great Society laws were enacted when America was still a young and growing nation. They were enacted in a nation that was vibrant, raw, under-institutionalized and needed taming.

We are no longer that nation. We are now a mature nation with an aging population. Far from being under-institutionalized, we are bogged down with a bloated political system, a tangled tax code, a Byzantine legal code and a crushing debt.

The task of reinvigorating a mature nation is fundamentally different from the task of civilizing a young and boisterous one. It does require some collective action, like investing in human capital. But, in other areas, it also involves stripping away...streamlining the special interest sinecures that have built up over the years and liberating private daring.

Reinvigorating a mature nation means using government to give people the tools to compete, but then opening up a wide range of fields so they do so raucously and creatively. It means spending more here but deregulating more there. It means facing the fact that we do have to choose between the current benefits to seniors and investments in our future, and that to pretend we don't face that choice, as Obama is doing, is effectively to sacrifice the future to the past.

Obama made his case beautifully. He came across as a prudent, non-populist progressive. But we still have one party that talks the language of government and one that talks the language of the market. We have no party that is comfortable with civil society; no party that understands the ways government...and the market can both crush and/or nurture the community, and no party with new ideas about how these things might blend together.

I know it's premature, but as I watched Obama take the oath of office for a second term, I couldn't help thinking, four years from now it could be President-elect Marco Rubio's turn.

Why do I think Rubio is likely to be our next president? Because the Florida senator has the vision, charisma, brains, and communications skills to fix the problems that will no doubt linger long after Obama has returned to Chicago.

Of course, this is not an entirely original observation. Four years out, Rubio is already at the top of what many consider to be a strong 2016 Republican bench. His background and biography (he's the son of Cuban immigrants) doesn't hurt and he's a natural communicator. He could be something special. He could be a pivotal leader, someone who redefines the GOP for the 21st century.

Here's my theory: Being elected president in the modern era requires you to be a sort of rock star. A lot of conservatives don't like this...they don't like the "cult of personality." Well, they had better get over it; it's a fact of life today.

The trend probably started with John F. Kennedy. And though it has certainly skipped a few modern presidents, if you look at Reagan, Clinton, and Obama, it's clear the messenger was special. They weren't merely traditional politicians who simply climbed the greasy pole of politics by dispensing patronage jobs.

This is not to give the impression that leadership is superficial. Winston Churchill was an inspiring and charismatic prime minister, and he didn't exactly have Hollywood looks. Leadership is about vision and character. It's also about persuasion and communication; the best leaders challenge us to do big things.

Our society is facing a leadership crisis. If America now demands charismatic presidents, the public is also yearning for someone who can inspire and persuade. Everywhere we turn, we see a failure of leadership and character.

When politicians promise things to special interests...or divide the electorate into coalitions they can do favors for, they are employing transactional leadership. When congressmen are cajoled or bribed via earmarks or committee assignments, they are doing the same. But when leaders summon us to discover our most noble calling...to sacrifice for something greater than our own personal interest, they are transformational leaders.

While too many liberals pander to voters, and too many conservatives believe stirring rhetoric is beneath them (preferring instead to get mired in the weeds or to spout tired talking points)...Rubio's rhetoric is decidedly Reaganesque. "He is one of the best orators in the GOP," says Reagan biographer Craig Shirley. "It is too early to say if he will ever rival Reagan, but he has as good a chance as anyone."

Consider this excerpt from Rubio's speech at the Republican National Convention this summer:

"That journey...that journey, from behind that bar (his father was a bartender) to behind this podium, goes to the essence of the American miracle. That we're exceptional, but not because we have more rich people here. We are special because dreams that are impossible anywhere else, they come true here.

The story of our time will be written by Americans who haven't yet even been born. Let us make sure they write that we did our part. That, in the early years of this new century, we lived in an uncertain time, but we did not allow fear to make us abandon what made us special."

Obama does not have a mandate, but he does not need one. I have read where conservative pundits are trying to assure us that Obama "has to know" that he does not have a mandate, and so he will have to govern from the middle. I don't know what they're smoking...because Obama does not care that he does not have a mandate. He does not view himself as being elected (much less re-elected) to represent individuals. He views himself as having been re-elected to complete the "fundamental transformation" of America, the basic structure of which he despises. Expect much more of the same...largely the complete disregard of the will of half the American public, his willingness to rule by executive order, and the utter inability of another divided Congress to rein him in.

America has become a nation of adolescents. The real losers in this election were adulthood, maturity, responsibility and the understanding that liberty must be accompanied by self-restraint. Obama is a spoiled child, and the behavior and language of his followers and their advertisements throughout the campaign makes it clear that many of them are, as well. Romney is a grown-up. Romney should have won. Those of us who expected him to win assumed that voters would act like grownups. If we were a nation of grownups, he would have won.

It wasn't the candidate(s), although some are already suggesting that Romney was the wrong guy and/or he should have picked Marco Rubio to get Florida or Rob Portman to get Ohio or Chris Christie to get something else. With all due respect, these assessments are incorrect. Romney ran a strategic and well-organized campaign. Yes, he could have hit harder on Benghazi; but for those who would have loved that, there are those who would have found it distasteful. No matter what tactic you could point to that Romney could have done better, it would have been spun in a way that was detrimental to his chances. Romney would have been an excellent president, and Ryan was an inspired choice. No matter whom we ran, they would have lost.

It's not about giving up on "social issues." No Republican candidate should participate in a debate or go out on the stump without thorough debate prep and a complete set of talking points that they stick to. This should start with a good grounding in biology and a reluctance to purport to know the will of God.

We do not hold the values we do because they garner votes. We hold the values we do because we believe that they are time-tested principles without which a civilized, free and prosperous society is not possible.

We defend the unborn because we understand that a society that views some lives as expendable...is capable of viewing all lives as expendable.

It's the culture, stupid! We have been trying to fight this battle every four years at the voting booth. It is long past time we admit that is not where the battle really is. We abdicated control of our culture...starting back in the 1960s. And now our largest primary social institutions...education, the mainstream media and Hollywood (entertainment) have become really nothing more than an assembly line for cranking out reliable little Leftists. Furthermore, we have allowed the government to undermine the institutions that instill good character... marriage, the family, communities, schools and our churches. So, here we are, at least two full generations later...we are reaping what we have sown. It took nearly fifty years to get here; it will take another fifty years to get back on track. But it starts with the determination to reclaim education, the media, and the entertainment business. If we fail to do that, we can kiss every election... and our freedom, goodbye from here on out.

So what did the immature choose? Sex, drugs, bad language, bad manners, vulgarity, lies, cheating, name-calling, finger pointing, blaming and irresponsible spending. This does not bode well for America. People grow up...or not, in one of two ways: They take responsibility for their life or they choose to blame circumstances. But in America, no one is forced to maintain and/or accept the circumstances they are born into. The warnings are all there, whether it is the looming economic disaster, or the inability of the government to respond to crises like Hurricane Sandy, or the growing strength and brazenness of our enemies within. It is unpleasant to think about the circumstances it will take to force Americans to grow up. It is even more unpleasant to think about Obama at the helm when those circumstances arrive.

It's possible that America just has to hit rock bottom. I truly believe that most Americans who voted for Obama have no idea what they are in for. Most simply believe him when he says that all he really wants is for the rich to pay "a little bit more." America is on a horrific bender...and has been for some time now. The warning signs of our fiscal profligacy and culture of lack of personal responsibility are everywhere. We need only look at other countries that wandered down this same dead-end corridor that we are currently on to see what's in store for America.

It's undeniable that words are important. Words can summon men to do great things or even inspire a nation.

Sincere...meaningful words (not self-serving political doubletalk) still matter: "I have a dream"...just words? "We hold these truths to be self-evident, that all men are created equal"...just words? "We have nothing to fear but fear itself"...just words? If our words no longer matter... then what's left?

Marco Rubio has the words. He has the charisma. He has the policy chops. And he has the personal narrative.

Come January 2017, hopefully America won't be inaugurating its first female president. Perhaps we'll be inaugurating our first Latino commander-in-chief.

Chapter 24

The United States reversed policy during the United Nations' meeting in New York earlier this year and said it would back launching "talks" on a treaty to regulate arms sales as long as the talks operated by consensus, a stance that would give every nation a veto. The decision, announced in a statement released by the State Department, overturns the position of former President George W. Bush's administration, which had opposed such a treaty on the grounds that national controls were better.

This was Obama's first major step in a plan to "ban all firearms in the United States." The Obama administration intends to force gun control and a complete ban on all weapons for United States citizens through the signing of international treaties with foreign nations. By signing international treaties on gun control, the Obama administration can use the State Department to bypass the normal legislative process in Congress. Once the United States Government signs these international treaties, all United States citizens will be subject to those gun laws created by foreign governments. These are laws that have been developed and promoted by organizations such as the United Nations and individuals such as George Soros and Michael Bloomberg. The laws are designed and intended to lead to the complete ban and confiscation of all firearms.

The Obama administration is attempting to use tactics and methods of gun control that will inflict major damage to our 2nd Amendment before United States citizens even understand what has happened. Obama can appear before the public and tell them that he does not intend to pursue any legislation (in the United States) that will lead to new gun control laws, but...while cloaked in secrecy, his Secretary of State, Hillary Clinton is committing the United States to international treaties and foreign gun control laws. Does that mean Obama is telling the truth?

Obama and the truth have never met.

He is the most consummate liar there is.

What it means is that there will be no publicized gun control debates in the media or votes in Congress. We will wake up one morning and find that the United States has signed a treaty that prohibits firearm and ammunition manufacturers from selling to the public. We will wake up another morning and find that the United States has signed a treaty that prohibits any transfer of firearm ownership. And then, we will wake up yet another morning and find that the United States has signed a treaty that requires United States citizens to deliver any firearm they own to the local government collection and destruction center or face imprisonment.

As sure as government health care is being forced on us by the Obama administration through whatever means necessary, so will gun control.

We are being led like lambs to the slaughter (Socialism/Dictatorship).

After two resounding wins, it is clear that liberal Barack Obama supporters strongly outnumber conservatives in the United States. He won the 2012 election with roughly seven million fewer votes than the 2008 election, and it was still more than enough. We are outnumbered.

Guess what he did on his first day back at work while you were staring sullenly at the electoral map.

He green lighted the United Nations Arms Control Treaty, which he plans to use as a springboard for a national gun registration list, followed by confiscation. Do not be surprised. All Marxists do this, and Obama has frequently stated his intentions. He is working quickly, on his first day after re-election. This treaty, even if it dies like so many other things the United Nations touches, will at least cause higher prices as it eliminates the importation of ammunition and guns. Obama has assured us that it will not threaten our Second Amendment rights. Do not believe him.

This is a man who doesn't even believe in Second Amendment rights. While teaching constitutional law at the University of Chicago, Obama told Doctor John Lott that he believed people should not be allowed to have guns. Apparently, knowing the meaning of the Second Amendment is not a requirement for constitutional law professors these days. After seeing that he has us outnumbered, it is alarming that his first priority is to ensure that we are also outgunned.

But we are not outgunned yet. If you, like millions of other Americans, noticed that the value of your stock holdings dropped precipitously the day after Obama was elected, and the following day...and the day after that too, you may be curious to know there is one sector that has been gaining big...guns and ammo. Ruger and S&W had a banner week while the rest of the market tanked. That is because millions of us all around the country rushed to our nearest gun stores on Wednesday and bought as much as we could bring home, while we still could. For the past four years the gun industry is the only sector that has seen consistent, non-subsidized growth, and it is the only sector Obama won't boast about.

Think of it as a reverse bank run. When people fear the banks aren't trustworthy, they rush to the bank to pull out their money. When people fear that the government isn't trustworthy, they rush to the gun stores to spend their money. This is a uniquely American privilege that is not possible in most other countries around the world, and may not be available here for much longer either. If you haven't participated in it, you aren't taking him seriously.

From a friend of mine in Texas: My local shop had a full parking lot overflowing onto two side streets at 11:00 AM on Wednesday after the election. They were completely sold out of 12-gauge buckshot and slugs, and running very low on 5.56×45mm NATO.

In the time it took me to browse the store, two different people walked out with AR-15s. For those who aren't familiar, AR-15s are the right hand of freedom in America. Barack Obama, like all tyrants, wants to make sure he has them and we don't. They will be the first guns he puts limits on, but not the last.

For the uneducated: Official nomenclature 5.56 NATO is a rifle cartridge developed in the United States and originally chambered in the M16 rifle. It is a standard cartridge for NATO forces as well as many non-NATO countries. It is derived from, but not identical to the 223 Remington cartridges. When the bullet impacts at high velocity and yaws into tissue, fragmentation creates a rapid transfer of energy that can result in dramatic wounding effects.

Complete control and confiscation of all civilian guns is a major goal for Obama. In 2004, while in the Illinois senate, he voted to make it illegal for people to use guns in self-defense. He has argued for a 500 percent tax on guns and ammunition sales, and voted to allow civil lawsuits against gun manufacturers, for the purpose of running them out of business. Aside from these legislative goals, there is the specter of his Supreme Court appointments, who will continue to approve any and every bill with his signature on it.

Do not chuckle about the gun store runs taking place. These people are paying attention. You can buy a box of ammo today, or you can buy it tomorrow with a 500 percent tax. Take your pick. It will get worse. His first-term experiments with executive orders will continue.

As long as he is in office your guns are not safe and your rights are not safe. The Constitution is just a piece of paper that Marxists want to burn. The Second

Amendment has no power unless the people enforce it, and our president, elected by the people, doesn't even believe in it. The Second Amendment isn't necessary until someone tries to take it, at which point it becomes absolutely paramount. If you aren't prepared for that day, there is no better time to start than today.

It has been said that during buck hunting season there are more armed men in the woods of Michigan than in all the armies of Europe. This may be true in several states, and it indicates the primary reason why no United States president has dared to enforce a true gun confiscation law. There are too many of us. Some liberals simply do not respect the ballot box, but they all respect the cartridge box. That is what the Second Amendment is for, to protect the country if the system breaks down.

The United Nations Arms Control Treaty was discussed this past July, and Obama shrewdly dropped out of all talks and kept his distance, waiting for an opportunity when he would have more flexibility. That opportunity came the morning after being re-elected. He spent his first term steering clear of gun control, knowing it would prevent him from being re-elected. Once he was free from the voters, he moved very quickly.

Americans, take a step back from your personal opinions about firearms, and look at the bigger picture regarding gun control. It is not about whether you approve or disapprove, like or dislike, fear or do not fear guns; it's about our Constitution staying intact as it was intended. This is how it begins...chipping away at the Constitution bit by bit...word by word, until we're living in a world like the countries our forefathers and other early Americans fled. Those with the power will control those who have no power. Americans, who fought for their independence and freedom, also had the foresight to protect us from those who would take our freedom away...by writing our Constitution.

Respect and honor the Constitution, and it will protect our freedom. Allow it to be changed and you and your children will pay in a much deadlier way than any gun can cause. A firearm is no more dangerous than a baseball bat unless an evil, sick or misinformed individual misuses it. It would benefit everyone to learn safe firearm handling. Understand what you fear, and the fear will disappear.

If you believe in the Constitution but do not own a gun, you have been reaping the protective benefits of an armed and free society without personally supporting its existence. It is the duty of all good men and women to own a gun and know how to use it. Gangsters, terrorists, and Marxists (I repeat myself) shouldn't be the only ones doing the shooting. The time for laziness is over. He isn't messing around anymore, so you shouldn't either. The best time to get a gun was before he came to office, but the second best time is today. There is a gunfight brewing on the horizon, and there is only one rule in gunfights. "You had better have a gun!"

Now is not the time to take up armed revolt against the government or any members of it, but it is time to remind them that you are here. Right now your duty is to pay attention and prepare. The golden rule of guns is that you don't need to use them until someone tries to take them. Better to have one and not need it than need one and not have it. Get one while you can. Then get another one, just to send a message.

How will you know when it is time to take up arms? When someone tries to take them. Tyrants always start that way. Until then, your only duty is have one ready. What a tragedy it will be on the day the jackboots come through your door, if you have nothing to greet them with. America started with a bang. Do not let it end without one.

As Edmund Burke that champion of British liberty once orated, "The people never give up their liberties but under some delusion." Americans must therefore remain informed and vigilant to preserve their traditional and constitutional liberties and prevent enactment of gun control legislation rooted in passion and emotionalism and that impacts them and not the criminals. Government efforts should be directed against criminals and felons, and should best be directed towards crime control rather than gun control.

December 29, 2012 marked the 122nd Anniversary of the murder of about 297 Native American Indians. Federal agents and members of the 7th Cavalry who had come to confiscate their firearms..."for their own safety and protection," murdered them. The slaughter began after the majority of the Sioux had peacefully turned in their firearms. When the final round had flown, of the estimated 297 dead or dying, two-third were women and children.

The bloodbath occurred, without provocation, as the Indians (men, women and children) were being relocated to the Sioux reservation at Pine Ridge. The Wounded

Knee Massacre occurred near Wounded Knee Creek on the Lakota Pine Ridge Indian Reservation in South Dakota, USA. It was the last battle of the American Indian Wars.

The preceding day, a division of the United States' 7th Cavalry Regiment had intercepted Spotted Elk's band of Miniconjou and Hunkpapa Lakota near Porcupine Butte and escorted them five miles westward to Wounded Knee Creek where they made camp. The remainder of the 7th Cavalry Regiment, led by Colonel James Forsyth, arrived later and surrounded the encampment...supported by four Hotchkiss guns.

One version of events claims that during the process of disarming the Lakota, a deaf tribesman named Black Coyote was reluctant to give up his rifle, claiming he had paid a lot for it. A scuffle over Black Coyote's rifle escalated and a shot was fired which resulted in the 7th Cavalry opening fire indiscriminately from all sides, killing men, women, and children, as well as some of their own fellow troopers. Those few Lakota warriors who still had weapons began shooting back at the attacking troopers, who quickly suppressed the Lakota fire. The surviving Lakota fled, but United States cavalrymen pursued and killed many who were unarmed.

We do not hear of Wounded Knee today. It is not mentioned in our history classes or books. What little does exist about Wounded Knee is normally the sanitized "Official Government Explanation" or the historically and factually inaccurate depictions of the events leading up to the massacre on the movie screen.

Wounded Knee was among the first federally backed gun confiscation attempts in United States history. It ended in the senseless murder of some 297 people.

Before you jump on the emotionally charged bandwagon for gun-control, take a moment to reflect on the real purpose of the Second Amendment: The right of the people to take up arms in defense of themselves, their families, and property in the face of invading armies or an oppressive government. The argument that the Second Amendment only applies to hunting and target shooting is asinine. When the United States Constitution was drafted "hunting" was an everyday chore carried out by men and women to put meat on the table each night, and "target shooting" was an unheard of concept, musket balls were a precious commodity in the wilds of early America, and were certainly not wasted on "target shooting." The Second Amendment was written by people who fled oppressive and tyrannical regimes in Europe, and refers to the right of American citizens to be armed for defense purposes should such tyranny arise in the United States.

As time goes on the average citizen in the United States continues to lose personal freedom or "liberty." Far too many times unjust bills are passed and signed into law under the guise of "for your safety" or "for protection." The Patriot Act signed into law by G.W. Bush, then expanded and continued by Obama is just one of many examples of American citizens being stripped of their rights and privacy for "safety." Now, the Right to Keep and Bear Arms is on the table, and will, most likely...be taken away (sooner or later) for "our safety."

Before any American citizen blindly accepts whatever new firearms legislation is about to be doled out, they should stop and think about something for just one-minute..."evil" does exist in our world. It always has and always will. Throughout history evil people have committed evil acts. In the Bible one of the first stories is that of Cain killing Abel. We cannot legislate "evil" into extinction. Good people will abide by the law; defective people will always find a way around it.

And another thought. Evil exists all around us, but looking back at the historical records of the past 200 years across the globe, where is "evil" and "malevolence" most often found? Yes, in the hands of those with the power...governments. The greatest human tragedies on record and the largest loss of innocent human life can be attributed to governments. Whom do governments target? "Scapegoats" and "enemies" within their own borders...but only after they have been disarmed to the point where they are no longer a threat. Ask any Native American, and they will tell you it was inferior technology and lack of arms that contributed to their demise. Ask any Armenian why it was so easy for the Turks to exterminate millions of them, and they will answer, "We were disarmed before it happened." Ask any Jew what Hitler's first step prior to the mass murders of the Holocaust was...the confiscation of firearms from the people.

Wounded Knee is the prime example of why the Second Amendment exists, and why we shouldn't be in such a hurry to surrender our Right to Bear Arms. Without the Second Amendment we have no right to defend our families and ourselves.

We were all wounded at Wounded Knee...

> "The most foolish mistake we could possibly make would be to allow the subject races to possess arms. History shows that all conquerors who have allowed their subject races to carry arms have prepared their own downfall by so doing."
>
> ~ Adolf Hitler ~

Governments that trust their citizens with guns are governments that sustain and affirm individual freedom. Governments that do not trust their citizens with firearms tend to be despotic and tyrannical. As our history of prohibition in the 1920s has shown, Americans obey just and moral laws but disobey or flout capricious and tyrannical laws.

> "The Constitution of most of our states (and of the United States) assert that all power is inherent in the people; that they may exercise it by themselves; that it is their right and duty to be at all times armed."
>
> ~ Thomas Jefferson ~

Chapter 25

CBS, 12/14/2012: Twenty children are among 27 people who were killed Friday morning after a gunman opened fire at Sandy Hook Elementary School in Newtown, Connecticut.

The rampage, coming less than two weeks before Christmas, was the nation's second-deadliest school shooting, exceeded only by the Virginia Tech massacre that claimed 33 lives in 2007.

The gunman, identified as 20-year-old Adam Lanza, was the son of Nancy Lanza; she was later found dead at her Newtown home. The vehicle the suspect drove to the school was registered to his mother.

At least three guns were found...a Glock 9-mm and a Sig Sauer inside the school and a .223-caliber Bushmaster rifle in the back of the car. The guns used in the shooting were owned by and legally registered to...his mother.

The gunman got into an argument with people at the front office over entry issues, possibly the principal, at about 9:30 A.M. Screening cameras are used to view people before buzzing (allowing) them into the school. After being denied entry the gunman commenced shooting his way through the door.

The gunman was believed to have suffered from a personality disorder and lived with his mother in Connecticut. The New York Times reported that Lanza suffered from Asperger's syndrome, a high-functioning form of autism.

Whoa! Even I didn't think the knee jerks would come this fast…within hours.

Bloomberg: Obama Must Take 'Immediate Action' Against Guns!

New York City Mayor Michael Bloomberg, an ardent gun control advocate, moved to politicize the monstrous school shooting in Connecticut by issuing the following statement:

With all the carnage from gun violence in our country, it's still almost impossible to believe that a mass shooting in a kindergarten class could happen. It has come to that. Not even kindergarteners learning their A, B, Cs are safe. We heard after Columbine that it was too soon to talk about gun laws. We heard it after Virginia Tech. After Tucson and Aurora and Oak Creek. And now we are hearing it again. For every day we wait, 34 more people are murdered with guns. Today, many of them were five-year olds. President Obama rightly sent his heartfelt condolences to the families in Newtown. But the country needs him to send a bill to Congress to fix this problem. Calling for 'meaningful action' is not enough. We need immediate action. We have heard all the rhetoric before. (By rhetoric, he apparently means the United States' Constitution.) What we have not seen is leadership...not from the White House and not from Congress. That must end today. This is a national tragedy and it demands a national response. My deepest sympathies are with the families of all those affected, and my determination to stop this madness is stronger than ever.

At the same time that New York City Mayor Michael Bloomberg was going full bore after gun owners...on the heels of the tragic school shootings in Connecticut, Mayor Thomas Menino of Boston issued a similar statement. It was just as strident and just as political.

Boston Mayor: Time For National Policy on Guns!

As a parent and grandparent, I am overcome with both grief and outrage by the tragedy in Newtown, Connecticut. This unspeakable act of violence will forever imprint this day in our hearts and minds. My heart goes out to the families impacted by this senseless tragedy and the many others we have recently witnessed across the United States. As a Mayor who has witnessed too many lives forever altered by gun violence, it is my responsibility to fight for action. Today's tragedy reminds us that now is the time for action. Now is the time for a national policy on guns that takes the loopholes out of the laws, the automatic weapons out of our neighborhoods and the tragedies like today out of our future. (There were no automatic weapons there, but who cares about facts when liberals attack the Constitution, Freedom, and Liberty.)

Gun-ownership groups were preparing themselves on Friday for another barrage of anti-firearm moves following the horrific mass killing at the Connecticut elementary school. The National Rifle Association and most groups were keeping silent on the day that 27 people, including 20 young children, were shot dead. The NRA said it would not have any comment until the facts are thoroughly known.

But some organizations spoke out, including Gun Owners of America, which has about 300,000 members. "Gun-control supporters have the blood of little children on their hands, Larry Pratt, the group's executive director, said. Federal and state laws combined to ensure that no teacher, no administrator, no adult had a gun at the Newtown school where the children were murdered. This tragedy underscores the urgency of getting rid of gun bans in school zones, he added. The only thing accomplished by gun-free zones is to ensure that mass murderers can slay more before they are finally confronted by someone else with a gun."

Gun Owners of America called for state and federal lawmakers to immediately overturn bans on guns in schools.

Washington GOP Representative Cathy McMorris Rodgers, the incoming chairwoman of the House Republican Conference, urged caution in rushing to enact tougher gun laws. We need to find out what happened and what drove this individual to this place, we have to be careful about suggesting new gun laws. And...we must make sure that we're enforcing the laws that are currently on the books. Yes...we definitely need to do everything possible to make sure that something like this never happens again.

Yet the thought of another gun-control debate rankled other Republicans, pushing them to advocate for fewer restrictions. "What happened in Connecticut, however, is not because of...nor related in any way to actions taken by the Michigan House yesterday in approving Senate Bill 59."

Carrying concealed weapons into schools, churches and stadiums is against the law in Michigan, but it might not be for much longer.

> Lawmakers in both the House and Senate approved Senate Bill 59 to allow concealed weapons in several gun-free zones Thursday, as well as doing away with county boards currently overseeing concealed pistol licensing.
>
> "If you have pistol free zones, they are actually mass murderer empowerment zones," said Steve Dulan, attorney for the Michigan Coalition of Responsible Gun Owners, who represents sportsmen clubs throughout Michigan. "If you actually look at the history, over the past 10 years in the United States, you'll find that all but one mass shooting occurred in a so-called gun free zone."

> Under the new law schools and private establishments would be able to voluntarily remain pistol-free zones, if desired.

Former Arkansas GOP Governor Mike Huckabee told Fox News that any debate should focus on the lack of religious instruction in public schools.

"We ask why there is violence in our schools, but we have systematically removed God from our schools," the former Republican presidential candidate told Fox. "Should we be so surprised that schools would become a place of carnage? We've made it a place where we don't want to talk about eternity, life, what responsibility means, accountability…that we're not just going to have be accountable to the police if they catch us, but one day we'll stand before, you know, a holy God in judgment," Huckabee said. "If we don't believe that, then we don't fear that."

The first thought of many (gun control advocates) is that it must be all those guns out there that are the cause, as if "the guns made them do it."

Why do we never hear anything about violent military video games and movies that seem so popular among young boys? They visualize themselves with an M-16 rifle, or some other military weapon in their hands, while they're pulling the trigger. Couldn't Hollywood have some responsibility in this violent trend?

It seems there are mass shootings, school shootings or workplace shootings weekly somewhere in America, if not daily. The reasons given are many and perplexing, but I believe I know why this keeps happening.

Growing up in the 1940s, 50s and 60s these mass-shootings did not exist. There were crimes and murders and assassinations, but certainly not in the numbers we're seeing today. And it's not about the guns...guns were plentiful and un-regulated in those days. The difference today is what our culture has become...and what it revolves around.

Unlike Obama's world today (we're all in this thing together), we were on our own...sink or swim! We faced the hardships of life head on and became stronger... self-sustaining citizens; but those days are history and we know what the progressives think about history. The present is a ballooning culture of entitlement minded individuals, and a government sponsored belief that diversity and individuality deserves preferential treatment. This always-growing culture of government dependency and the enabling empowerment provided by political correctness is creating a morass of misguided human beings.

Today, everything revolves around "little people's problems." Dr. Phil, TMZ, Twitter, anti-bullying campaigns and liberalism are the order of the day. As a result, narcissists choose to go out in a sick blaze of glory and get maximum attention.

We now live in a culture where it has become acceptable, and almost encouraged that one be weird. As a result, no one can make fun of you and/or bully you, fire you, break up with you or hurt your feelings in any way. Stigmas no longer exist.

A half-day before Adam Lanza committed one of the deadliest school attacks in United States history; a

Chinese farmer took a kitchen knife and hacked at more than 20 children as they entered their rural elementary school.

Though the outcomes are different...27 dead in Connecticut, and 23 injured in China, the Friday attacks show how disturbingly frequent rampages against children and schools are. Attackers often seek out the vulnerable, hoping to amplify their outrage before they themselves often commit suicide. A news story of a mass killing can often serve as an inspiration and blueprint to other potential mass killers.

"It's these disenfranchised people who are angry at the world, who plan to take out as many people as they can, and there's some element there of notoriety," said forensic psychologist James Ogloff of Monash University in Melbourne, Australia. "It's a way of becoming infamous."

Mass killings, when an individual tries to kill as many people at one time as possible, have occurred in places as far away as Switzerland, where 14 people died in a shooting spree by an unemployed man who then killed himself in 2001, to South Korea, where a police officer killed 56 people before he blew himself up in 1982. Distinct from acts of terror that have political or collective aims, other mass killers act out of personal grievances.

Attacks against schools are a bleak subset, offering easy targets for taking down large numbers of victims. Shootings at schools have periodically occurred in Finland and Germany as well as the United States, though the American attacks have been more frequent.

China has seen more than a half-dozen school attacks in less than three years, though the death tolls have been mostly in single digits, largely because knives have been the most-used weapons. China largely prohibits private ownership of guns. "They choose to attack school students who are weak in defending themselves and are easily assaulted," according to Zhu, a researcher in psychology, at the Chinese Academy of Sciences.

Ogloff, who has studied both spree and serial killers in the United States, Canada and Australia, said that a breakdown in a relationship or a humiliating experience often acts as a triggering event for mass shooters. After Thomas Hamilton killed 16 kindergarteners and a teacher at an elementary school in Dunblane, Scotland, in 1996, reports said that he had been suspected of inappropriate behavior with boys he oversaw in a youth group and that letters he wrote talked of persecution by police and authorities for forcing him from taking part in boys clubs and for causing a business he ran to fail.

While police in Connecticut and China have so far not given motives for Friday's attacks, both began with single assaults. Twenty-year-old Adam Lanza first shot his mother in their home in the New England town of Newtown before driving to the nearby Sandy Hook Elementary School; armed with two handguns, he shot into two classrooms, killing 20 children, six adults and then apparently shooting himself.

Min Yingjun, a 36-year-old resident of Guangshan, an area of tea and rice farms in central China, burst into the home of an elderly woman and stabbed her with a kitchen knife. He then went to the Chenpeng Village

Primary School and slashed 22 students, ages 6 to 12, as they arrived for class. Seven of the students, some with severed fingers and ears, required hospitalization.

Though Min did not die, he was grabbed by police at the scene and is under arrest. These attackers are often in a state of depression, believing that society is malicious or unsafe and want others to die with them. Many mass attacks should be seen as "expanded suicide," according to Zhu.

Police described Min as possibly being "mentally ill," and a law enforcement official briefed on the Connecticut shooting told The Associated Press that Lanza was believed to suffer from a personality disorder. But overall, very few mass shooters are truly mentally ill, according to Ogloff.

Most perpetrators are young men, and their common traits...an interest in the military or violence, are so widespread as to make it impossible to identify potential killers. Spree shootings are increasing and becoming deadlier because each killing leaves a blueprint for others to follow.

Imagine you're a kid and you're 20 years old, and you're angry at the world and you're fascinated with the military and you're in a situation where you want to end your life. All the others who have gone before you...are now influencing you.

The spate of school attacks in China...six in a seven-month period in 2010, have raised concerns about copycats. News media in China, all of which are state-controlled, gave wide coverage to the Connecticut attack. But they only ran a brief report about Friday's knifings and local officials refused to provide additional information, signs that the authorities want to restrict the news to keep blame off the government...and not motivate potential copycats.

Tight controls mean that gun crimes are rare in China and make knives and sometimes explosives the weapons used in mass attacks in China. Even so, violence is on the rise as people grow frustrated with a corrupt and often indifferent officialdom and seek other means to address grievances.

In one of the worst incidents, a man described as an unemployed, middle-aged doctor killed eight children with a knife in March 2010 to vent his anger over a thwarted romantic relationship.

One's social environment is a factor behind most attacks around the world. A person who chooses extreme acts to voice his or her grievances usually believes that his or her case will not be handled fairly through normal channels or legal procedures.

Most of the attackers have been mentally disturbed men involved in personal disputes or unable to adjust to the rapid pace of social change in their cultures.

People ask, what is happening to America? Perhaps it's the reflection of what our nation has become...

> And even as they did not like to retain God in their knowledge, God gave them over to a debased mind, to do those things which are not fitting; being filled with

all unrighteousness, sexual immorality, wickedness, covetousness, maliciousness; full of envy, murder, strife, deceit, evil-mindedness; they are whisperers, backbiters, haters of God, violent, proud, boasters, inventors of evil things, disobedient to parents, undiscerning, untrustworthy, unloving, unforgiving, unmerciful.

~ Romans 1:28-31 ~

Chapter 26

Must every tragic mass shooting bring out the shrill ignorance of "gun control" advocates?

The only way man can defeat, or remove evil…is to change his heart. But because we cannot make a man change his heart, we can only use common sense to protect ourselves from it.

The key fallacy of so-called gun control laws is that such laws do not in fact control guns. They simply disarm law-abiding citizens; while people bent on violence find firearms readily available. If gun control zealots had any respect for facts, they would have discovered this long ago. There have been too many factual studies done over the years to leave any serious doubt…about gun control laws being not merely futile, but counterproductive.

Places and times with the strongest gun control laws have often been places and times with high murder rates. Washington, D.C., is a classic example, but just one among many.

The rate of gun ownership is higher in rural areas than in urban areas, but the murder rate is higher in the urban areas. The rate of gun ownership is higher among whites than blacks, but the murder rate is higher among blacks. For the country as a whole, handgun ownership doubled in the late 20th century, while the murder rate went down.

Other countries with stronger gun control laws than the United States, such as Russia, Brazil and Mexico...all have higher murder rates than the United States.

You could compare other sets of countries and get similar results. Gun ownership has been three times as high in Switzerland as in Germany, but the Swiss have had lower murder rates. Other countries with high rates of gun ownership and low murder rates include Israel, New Zealand, and Finland.

Guns are not the problem. People are the problem... including people who are determined to push gun control laws, either in ignorance of the facts or in defiance of the facts. There is innocent ignorance and there is invincible, dogmatic and self-righteous ignorance. Every tragic mass shooting seems to bring out examples of both among gun control advocates.

It is no accident that mass shootings repeatedly have occurred in designated gun-free zones, which attract lunatics looking to murder as many souls as possible before they turn their guns on themselves. Banning gun-free zones and allowing teachers to carry concealed weapons could help eliminate mass shootings at schools. Gun-free zones have become magnets for deranged killers hoping to burn their names into the history books by running up a big body count before they turn their guns on themselves.

When you ban guns, rather than making it safer for the victims, you unintentionally make it safer for the criminals, because they have less to worry about. If you had a violent criminal stalking you or your family, and was really seriously threatening you, would you feel safer putting a sign up in front of your home stating, "This home is a gun-free zone."

My guess is you wouldn't do that...and I've never run into any gun-control proponents who would do that either. The reason is pretty clear; putting a sign there saying this is a gun-free home isn't going to cause the criminals to say, "Oh, I don't want to break the law, so I'm not going to go in and attack these people." It encourages them to do it. It serves as an enticement to proceed with attack... because he knows it will be easier without the fear of encountering any real resistances. Yet every time we have one of these mass-shooting incidents, it renews the call from the media and the left for banning guns.

In the recently attack at the Aurora, Colorado movie theater, there were seven movie theaters that were showing the Batman movie when it opened at the end of July. Out of those seven movie theaters, only one was posted as banning permit-concealed handguns. The killer didn't go to the movie theater that was closest to his home. He didn't go to the movie theater that was the largest movie theater in Colorado, which was essentially the same distance from his apartment as the one he ended up going to. Instead, the one he picked was the only one of those movie theaters that banned people taking permit-concealed handguns into that theater.

The media typically spins these mass shootings as an American phenomenon but Europe has had a lot of multiple victim shootings. If you look at a per capita rate, the rate of multiple-victim public shootings in Europe and the United States, over the last 10 years, have been fairly similar to each other. A couple of years ago Finland had a couple of big shootings and about two-and-a-half years ago the United Kingdom had a big shooting where 12 people were killed.

In Norway last year, 77 were killed. Two years ago there was a shooting in Austria at a Sikh Temple. There have been several multiple-victim public shootings in France during the last few years. Over the last decade, we've seen large school shootings in Germany. Germany in terms of modern incidents has two of the four worst public-school shootings, and they have very strict gun-control laws. The one common feature of all of those shootings in Europe is that they all took place in gun-free zones, in places where guns are supposed to be banned.

Another typical media ploy is to ignore facts regarding America's mass murderers that do not support their bias against white, conservative Americans...suggesting that mass murderers are "usually white men." "Perspectives on gun control," December 23, 2012: The writer also claimed that if any of these perpetrators had been Muslim, Hispanic, Black or women...they would have been held up to more scrutiny.

What about the Muslim Army psychiatrist, Nidal Malik Hasan, who killed 13 fellow soldiers in the Fort Hood massacre? Or Islamist John Allen Muhammad, the D.C. sniper who killed 10 innocent people while terrorizing our nation's capital in 2002?

The worst school shooting in United States history with 32 dead was perpetrated by Seung-Hui Cho, a Korean national, while another Korean student, One L. Goh, shot and killed seven classmates at Oakland's Oikos University in April of this year.

So do we have to think about who is going to be obeying these "gun control laws?" It would be nice if things were that simple, that banning guns would eliminate crime. But study after study has shown that murder rates and violent crime rates go up when guns are outlawed. Why? It's a pretty simple answer...because the law-abiding citizens are the ones who turn in their guns, not the criminals.

As Senator Feinstein prepares to introduce a gun control bill in 2013, any reporter seeking to discover what medications were being taken by the alleged shooter in the Newtown massacre will find that they cannot get this information, by law.

One must assume the shooter was on some kind of psychiatric drugs since he has been described as having "anti-social" behavior problems, was slightly handicapped and suffered from Asperger's Syndrome...a form of autism. But nowhere will you find any comments about the drugs prescribed for the shooter, only that the guns were the problem.

Who do you think stands to gain by withholding this information? Yes, the drug manufacturers, of course...

certainly, not the public. The link between psychiatric drugs and senseless acts of violence has been present in nearly all recent mass-shootings and school shootings.

Psychiatric drugs have been documented, by international drug regulatory agencies, to cause suicidal and homicidal ideation, mania, psychosis, worsening depression and a host of violence inducing side effects. Numerous school shooters were under the influence of these drugs when they went on shooting rampages, including Columbine shooters Eric Harris and Dylan Kleebold (Kleebold's autopsy report was never made public), Kip Kinkel, Thurston High School in Oregon, Red Lake Minnesota school shooter, Jeff Weise, and others. Yet there has never been a federal investigation into the link between psychiatric drugs and random acts of senseless violence.

Right now, if you are on any controlled substance, you are not permitted to own firearms under the Gun Control Act of 1968. But antidepressants have not been added to that list.

Yet in almost every case of a mass shooting over the last number of years, antidepressants have somehow been involved. The medical establishment is so deeply connected to the profit motive here that we would have to fight them to get antidepressants added to that list of controlled substances. Bottom line, "no one" on psychiatric drugs should ever be allowed to own guns... period!

Despite media reports alleging that the gunman, 20-year-old Adam Lanza, the man who perpetrated the Connecticut schools' senseless massacre at an elementary school in Newton, had Asperger's, which is considered a high-functioning form of autism. Geraldine Dawson, chief science officer at the nonprofit advocacy group, Autism Speaks, and a professor of psychiatry at the University of North Carolina at Chapel Hill was quick to assert, "There really is no evidence that links autism or Asperger's to violence."

Lanza fatally shot his mother at her home before forcing his way into Sandy Hook Elementary School and killing 20 children, aged 6 and 7, as well as six adults and then himself. It is one of the worst mass shootings in United States history.

Asperger's has its own designation in the current Diagnostic and Statistical Manual of Mental Disorders (DSM-4), considered the Bible of psychiatry, which has been in use since 1994. However, as of the spring of 2013, when the new DSM-5 comes out, "autistic disorder" will be known as "autism spectrum disorder" and Asperger's will be folded within that larger category.

Certain characteristics are common across the autism spectrum, experts said.

"Two features that characterize autism spectrum disorders are difficulties in the area of social interactions and also a tendency to engage in repetitive behavior, whether this is a high-functioning person or one who's severely affected, Dawson explained. Those are the two common features."

However, in the DSM, "there is no linking of this syndrome with violence in any way," she added.

Former classmates said Lanza was painfully shy, reserved and socially awkward, according to news reports. Those characteristics can be typical of Asperger's, experts said.

People with autism spectrum disorders, including those with Asperger's, may exhibit aggressive behavior when compared with peers, but it is a completely different type of aggression than that witnessed Friday, said Eric Butter, assistant professor of pediatrics and psychology at Ohio State University.

"Research suggests that aggression among people with autism spectrum conditions can occur 20 to 30 percent more often than compared to the general population, he said. But, we are not talking about the kind of planned and intentional type of violence we have seen at Newtown."

Aggression that we see in autism can best be described as disruptive and irritable behavior and is often consistent with the communication and social difficulties that are the hallmarks of autism spectrum disorders, he added. It is a very human experience that when you cannot explain how you are feeling, that you will then act out in frustration, anger, and aggression. But, it is not consistent with the diagnosis that you would plan and execute a crime like we saw here.

"Aggression in people with Asperger's and autism tends to be more reactive, such as impulsive outbursts, being quick to anger, shoving or pushing, shouting in anger, and being slow to cool off when angry," said Butter, who is also associate director of the Child Development Center at Nationwide Children's Hospital in Westerville, Ohio.

"The types of violence seen in Connecticut and elsewhere have occurred at the hands of individuals with a range of psychological profiles, and the underlying and connected theme is that we have not done enough in our schools and mental health services systems to identify, assist, and de-stigmatize those people suffering from the illnesses of the brain," Butter said.

Added Dawson: "Whenever there are horrible tragedies like this one, people want to make sense of it and try to find answers. I think it's important that we be very clear that if this individual did have Asperger's or autism, which we don't know for sure that he did, this is not going to help us understand what happened. Because there's really no link between the two (Asperger's and structured/planned violence)."

Perhaps writing the prescription provides the link...

The liberals are always pointing fingers at the NRA's lobbyist who are paupers compared to the pharmaceutical's unlimited resources in the area of leveraging their clout in congress. Autopsies always reveal these mass killers die from gunshots...self-inflicted or otherwise, but the drugs/prescriptions are never exposed because it's private medical information.

If you don't want guns in your home or your schools...so be it, that's your choice. But don't be such a damn fool as to advertise to the whole world that you are in "a gun-free environment" where you are a helpless target for any homicidal fiend who is armed. Is it really worth a human life to be a politically correct, moral exhibitionist?

I find it interesting that the anti-gun factions are always sharing their unsolicited opinion that guns do not make us safer. Maybe it's just Obama's pompous need for ceremonial decorum...but if guns don't make us safer, why is he and his entourage always surrounded by a large force of armed bodyguards? Just asking...

Once again I must reference the old adage regarding what we call someone who continues to repeat the same failures over and over again while expecting a different outcome. Usually he's a fool...but in the case of our elected officials and their governmental regulations to protect us ("their subjects") from ourselves, they're self-serving idiots. See examples below:

- Prohibition in the United States was a national ban on the sale, manufacture, and transportation of alcohol, in place from 1920 to 1933. Effective enforcement of the alcohol ban during the Prohibition Era proved to be very difficult and led to widespread flouting of the law. The lack of a solid popular consensus for the ban resulted in the growth of vast criminal organizations, including the modern American Mafia, and various other criminal cliques. Widespread disregard of the law also generated rampant corruption among politicians and within police forces.

- Although Nixon declared the War on Drugs in 1971, the policies that his administration implemented as part of the Comprehensive Drug Abuse Prevention and Control Act of 1970 were a continuation of drug prohibition policies in the United States, which started in 1914.

- In June 2011, the Global Commission on Drug Policy released a critical report on the War on Drugs, declaring: "The global war on drugs has failed, with devastating consequences for individuals and societies around the world." The United States has the highest documented incarceration rate and total prison population in the world. At the start of 2008, more than 2.3 million people were incarcerated, more than one in every 100 adults. The current rate is about seven times the 1980 figure.

- Despite over $7 billion spent annually towards arresting and prosecuting nearly 800,000 people across the country for marijuana offenses in 2005 (FBI Uniform Crime Reports), the federally-funded Monitoring the Future Survey reports about 85 percent of high school seniors find marijuana "easy to obtain." That figure has remained virtually unchanged since 1975, never dropping below 82.7 percent in three decades of national surveys. At least 500 economists, including Nobel Laureates Milton Friedman, have noted that reducing the supply of marijuana without reducing the demand causes the price, and hence the profits of marijuana sellers, to go up, according to the laws of supply and demand. The increased profits encourage the producers to produce more drugs despite the risks, providing a theoretical explanation for why attacks on drug supply have failed to have any lasting effect. This same logic applies across the board to all the illicit drugs. The producers and dealers are just making more profit.

- The Gun-Free School Zones Act of 1990 (yes, another cure-all facilitated by our enlightened Congress) severely limited where a person may legally carry a firearm, although this was voided by United States v. Lopez as exceeding Congress' Commerce Clause authority. The act was then passed again in its current form in 1995. The act makes it generally unlawful for an armed citizen to travel on any public sidewalk, road, or highway that passes within 1,000 feet of the property line of any K-12 school in the nation. Only if one has a state permit to carry a firearm are they exempt from the 1,000 feet rule. And of course we know how well that legislation has worked out; all law-abiding citizens have respected the law.

So with that brilliant track record, Congress is now gearing up to regulate, control and at some point in time, even confiscate American's standard method of self-defense, our guns...a Second Amendment, Constitutional right. This isn't the first time, but once again...calls for the outlawing of private guns emanate from the same people that thought banning drugs would keep criminals from getting them.

A gun is an inanimate object, it has no mind of its own nor can it launch a projectile on its own or target anyone or anything. To become active it requires someone to load it, aim it and put the required pressure on the firing mechanism. Gun control advocates seem to ignore this fundamental requirement and believe that removing these inanimate objects from the hands of rational, law-abiding citizens will be the panacea for preventing gun violence.

However, this solution doesn't prevent these inanimate objects from falling into the hands of criminals and/ or mentally disturbed people who will then use them in pursuit of their objectives. Nor does it provide for enforcement of laws already on the books for the illegal use of a firearm.

A strict and severe punishment for the use of a firearm in the commission of a crime is needed. Our judicial system all too often considers the "appropriate penalty" to be "cruel and unusual punishment"...and therefore, in violation of the Constitution. Until the judiciary revises their thinking on this subject, crime will continue to flourish.

In the meantime, gun-control advocates would disarm the law-abiding populace and leave them at the mercy of the lawless.

> "A strong conviction that 'something must be done' is the parent of many bad measures."
>
> ~ Daniel Webster ~

> "A society deadened by a smothering network of laws, while finding release in moral chaos, is not likely to be either happy or stable."
>
> ~ Robert H. Bork ~

Chapter 27

Freedom vs. Security:

The progressive community wants...and expects the government to secure their safety. First, may I point out the oxymoron here? Their concern is that people are killed because guns are too accessible. Firearm homicides (intentional killings) are terrible. But these highly publicized killings account for less than 11,000 deaths per year. I am not suggesting that the pain for those families is not gut-wrenching. Many years ago, friends of mine lost their son (the same age as my oldest son) when a drug dealer with a gun murdered him. The devastation of any loss is unspeakable, no matter the cause.

While there are many senseless deaths every year, one might argue that easy access to automobiles accounts for more than 42,000 deaths per year. Shall we require our brilliant leaders in government to save us from our cars? About 195,000 people die annually because of medical error. Shall we beg benevolent politicians to save us from the evils of doctors? Twenty five thousand children under five, die daily around the world from malnutrition and illness.

I am far more afraid of those willing to give up their freedoms for a false sense of security, believing that government can save them from the dangers of this world. There are no guarantees of comfort, riches, success, health or happiness. And at some point...we will all die. No politician or legislation can stop that. Those most protected by governments are the least free and they are still subject to danger and death. You are a better caretaker of your life and property than any elected official will ever be. Take responsibility for yourself and quit whining for some politician or union leader to make you safe.

The Newtown tragedy is truly lamentable. As with other mass slayings, the media coverage will be extensive and will include the usual pleas to "do something" about it.

Regrettably, too, there will be no agreement on what "it" is that needs solving but the federal government will be seen (by many) as the source of a solution. The usual special-interest groups will demand remedies directed at their favorite targets. The president's call for "meaningful action to prevent more tragedies like this" is not unexpected, but fruitless if we depend on government action for a solution.

Those who believe that government can solve problems of this nature will be disappointed, but will pat themselves on the back for trying and be unaware that government "solutions" to these issues are more likely to be counterproductive.

To expect that federal legislators...the same group that cannot figure out how to pay the bills, can craft effective legislation dealing not only with guns, but with morality, mental health, education, family dysfunction, religion and other factors that may or may not have contributed to the Newtown event is foolhardy.

The more we turn to our government for answers to the declining morality of our society, the less morality we will have. We need to look elsewhere.

Calm heads must prevail. It is dangerous to make snap decisions about the future based on emotions from an extreme event. Specifically, I'm referring to people calling for gun control after the Sandy Hook Elementary School shooting. Here are a few examples of why gun control is an unproven knee-jerk reaction to unfortunate events and why it will not prevent similar acts in the future.

Gun control doesn't guarantee that there won't be gun violence. Mexico is proof of this.

Even if guns are illegal, they will be available to those determined to possess them, just like licit drugs (Vicodin) and illicit drugs (Cocaine) are available via the black market. Even if worldwide production of guns stopped and there was no such thing as a black market (which is impossible), it would take several generations before guns would no longer be a part of our society.

Most gun owners are responsible, law-abiding citizens. Hardened criminals and/or those with mental health issues commit a significant amount of today's gun violence. In both cases, these people should not have been permitted to have firearms in the first place. Laws in place to prevent these people from possessing firearms demonstrate that gun control is ineffective. I ask that we use logic and reason instead of resorting to a lynch-mob mentality when making decisions regarding gun ownership in America.

Needless loss of life is particularly shocking when innocent children are the victims as they were at Sandy Hook Elementary School. Evil visited the community, said Connecticut's governor, Dannel P. Malloy, but early accounts indicate the shooter had no history, or predilection, for "evil." He was not a sociopath (one who disregards normal societal mores or has no social conscience). Acquaintances and neighbors indicated that he was not one with a history of being an "evil" person. His brother said that the 20-year-old perpetrator suffered from a "personality disorder."

Guns and gun laws are always the easy target for blame, with conveniently popular political talking points, but they represent only one aspect of the issue. How about we talk seriously about the deplorable state of mental health services in our country? When one of every five Americans is on prescription medication for a psychological problem yet mental health disorders are still in the closet and stigmatized, there's a disconnect.

We have breast cancer and HIV 10K runs, pink and rainbow ribbons and wristbands, but the single most disabling disorder on the planet (according to the World Health Organization) is in hush mode. Mental illness is a brain disease, just like stroke, epilepsy and multiple sclerosis. It is not a bad or shameful behavior. There is a chemical and structural component and proper treatment is essential. Health insurance benefits for mental health are minimal compared to those for physical conditions. Indeed, mood and personality disorders are intimately intertwined with physical health disorders and greatly magnify the cost of traditional health care.

We must transform our thinking and approach to mental health disorders.

The United States' mental health system is severely broken. There is no place for families to get help for uncooperative mentally ill family members. Often the only solution for the family is to exclude the mentally ill member to protect others in the family. Most mentally ill are in denial and/or refuse help from therapy, counseling and medication. Most police officers are not trained to recognize mental illness.

Mental hospitals usually only detain the mentally ill for short periods of time and then release them onto the streets. If the person appears before a judge, he or she can often fool the judge, who then releases them.

Many medical professionals (psychologists and psychiatrists) are biased toward downgraded diagnosis, as from schizophrenic to bipolar, and are unconcerned with protecting society from mentally ill patients who may be prone to violence. They are reluctant to label mentally ill people as "violent."

Furthermore, the federal database established to verify if gun buyers should be permitted to purchase guns is another failure. Many states are negligent in reporting the mentally ill who are prone to violence to that database. My guess is that very few of the mentally ill who may commit violent acts are included in that database. I also doubt that many mentally ill people, in custody for violent acts, are in the federal database.

The focus of dealing with mentally ill people, who may be prone to violence, is on patient's rights and privacy. There is little focus on protecting society and innocent people until severe violent acts are committed and others are harmed. Society has so far been unwilling to enforce treatment (medication, therapy, and counseling) on mentally ill people who refuse to cooperate.

Of course not, the focal point and issue must always be about the guns if the mainstream-media, this administration and the United Nations are to have their way.

What Barack Obama thinks of rural America: "Bitter, gun toting, and Bible clinging xenophobes!"

While speaking to a group of his wealthier Golden State backers at a San Francisco fund-raiser, Obama took a shot at explaining the yawning cultural gap that separates a Turkeyfoot from a Marin County resident. "You go into some of these small towns in Pennsylvania, and like a lot of small towns in the Midwest, the jobs have been gone now for 25 years and nothing has replaced them," Obama said. "And they fell through the Clinton Administration, and the Bush Administration, and each successive administration has said that somehow these communities are gonna regenerate and they have not. It's not surprising then, that they become bitter, cling to their guns and religion, are hostile to people who aren't like them, and embrace anti-immigrant sentiment and/or anti-trade sentiment as a way to explain their frustrations."

Obama made a problematic judgment call in trying to explain working class culture to a much wealthier audience. He described blue collar Pennsylvanians with a series of what in the eyes of creamy Californians might be considered pure negatives: Guns, clinging to religion, antipathy and xenophobia.

Given that I'm from pastoral America, I can't help but feel that he was talking about me too. So let me enlighten Obama as to his misconceptions about us rural yokels.

We cling to guns not because we're bitter but because we still believe...strike that, we still know, that private gun ownership is a right afforded to us by our constitution. We're not anti-immigrant or xenophobic, we're against millions of people being able to stroll across our borders and partake in the benefits of being American while flouting the laws our elected leaders passed and taking on almost none of the burdens of citizenship. We may be skeptical of people who aren't like us...but then who isn't? Is Obama really suggesting that a gun-loving conservative from Middle America would be un-welcome in, say, Berkeley?

I know that my fellow rubes practice their strongly held religious beliefs as a way of edifying their moral code, creating a sense of community and passing their beliefs and standards on to future generations. That the churches in places like Pennsylvania and North Dakota seem alien to someone used to the booming diatribes of hatred and bigotry that come from the pulpits of the Reverend Wrights of the world, is hardly our fault.

And as for anti-trade, I don't doubt that many of my fellow rural Americans don't believe, as I do...and are skeptical of free trade. But I certainly don't see where Obama, who has spent a good deal of this campaign season castigating free trade agreements as having lost this country's jobs and wealth, gets off criticizing anyone for being "anti-trade."

Personally, I don't know what's worse; that Obama said those arrogant things about people like me, or that he thought he could say them to a bunch of rich liberals in California without it getting back to us in the backwoods, out-of-the-mainstream rubes.

Is anyone really surprised? I mean this is a member of Jeremiah Wright's "God Damn America" flock.

But it gets worse: The Communist Chinese government, via its state-run media front Xinhua, has called for Americans to be disarmed, arguing that the Sandy Hook school massacre demands "no delay for United States gun control."

The article calls on Obama to exploit the tragedy to push his gun control agenda, adding that his lame duck situation represents "the best position to promote it," while blaming the National Rifle Association for curtailing previous attempts to regulate firearms in the United States. Worth noting is that after previous mass shootings, efforts to impose gun control measures "disappointingly always fail." The editorial went on to suggest the "gunman's cruelty and evil should provide a strong momentum and broader public support for the restart of gun control efforts."

The editorial went on to suggest the "gunman's cruelty and evil should provide a strong momentum and broader public support for the restart of gun control efforts."

The article added that Barack Obama should begin "to prepare for a protracted civil war," with massive political fallout, if he wants to eviscerate the second amendment.

As Brandon Darby points out, "The current Chinese government, the communist People's Republic of China, was established in a revolution led by Mao Zedong, who killed an estimated 40-70 million people with starvation, executions, and re-education camps."

Indeed, it was Mao himself who said, "Political power grows out of the barrel of a gun."

This should provide a hint as to what happens when tyrants are unleashed upon a disarmed population, and why China's call to repeal the Second Amendment rings chillingly hollow.

Appearing on the nationally syndicated Alex Jones Show today, former Congressman and NRA board member Bob Barr called for members of Congress to speak out against the Chinese government, expressing his outrage that an authoritarian regime would lecture the United States about the rights of its people.

If you want to get a taste of how a state treats it's completely disarmed citizens, who refuse to submit to big government tyranny...look no further than China itself.

As reported earlier this year, a villager in northern China attempting to resist forced government relocation by remaining on his land was brutally crushed to death by a road flattening truck on the orders of a Chinese government official.

China is routinely rocked by riots staged by residents furious at the arbitrary theft of their land by the state, which under the Communist system claims that the government owns all land and that private property rights are non-existent. However, the state-owned media ensures that news of the protests does not reach a national audience.

Since the state has all the guns, the idea of government thugs arbitrarily kicking people off their own property is a routine occurrence in China. The kind of massive land grabs and forced relocations that occur almost every day in China is not a situation that has yet been visited on America primarily because Americans have the second amendment with which to protect their private property rights.

A law was recently passed in Indiana that legalizes the use of deadly force...including against a police officer, in the event of an unlawful intrusion.

The Pentagon's recent geopolitical pivot made it clear that China was the primary military threat to the United States. In addition, Chinese military and Communist Party leaders have repeatedly indicated that they are preparing for a future war with the United States. Others have threatened to launch a nuclear attack against America during any potential confrontation over Taiwan.

In this context, it's noteworthy that Japan's Admiral Yamamoto refused to invade the United States during world war two because he feared the fact that there "would be a rifle behind every blade of grass," therefore it's not surprising that the Communist Chinese regime would also want to see the American people disarmed.

Concerns that China was also interfering in the United States' media were heard after MGM was forced to delay the re-make of Red Dawn for two years after Chinese state media complained that depicting the invading villains as Chinese "would demonize their state and its citizens." The bad guys were changed to North Koreans and entire portions of the film had to be revised.

It's unprecedented to see foreigners like the Communist Chinese and others like Piers Morgan (a British journalist and television host currently working in the United States for CNN) advising Obama on ways to exploit the school shooting in order to disarm the American people.

China can keep its forced relocations, its summary execution of political dissidents, its mobile execution vans, and its draconian police state. Americans will keep their guns, no matter how many times the Communist Chinese government, and all its political allies within America...talk down the second amendment.

A writer for the Communist Party USA wrote: Re-electing Obama is absolutely essential, and warned that divisions among Democrats and a potential wave of bad economic news could combine to threaten President Obama's reelection.

Marxist John Case, who writes for various CPUSA publications, wrote a piece, "The danger of a Romney election," for the party publication People's World, which warned that "re-electing Obama is not sufficient to bring economic recovery or even relief to our people. Only a different class configuration in political power can do necessary minimum reforms to give us a chance. But re-electing Obama is absolutely essential. Now is not the time for hand washing the complexities and tactics away...or failing to triage the most critical questions from those that are less critical. We cannot win everything at once!"

In reality, the CPUSA's endorsement of Obama for a second term is not surprising. Various CPUSA officials, including Jarvis Tyner and Joelle Fishman, have openly expressed support for the United States President and "his agenda."

Since 1988, the CPUSA has not run its own candidates for president and vice-president, preferring instead to work through the Democratic Party. Its support for Obama in 2008 and again this year has been open and outspoken.

The Case article offers a rationale, mostly on economic grounds, for getting Obama re-elected to a second term. He claims that the Republicans intend to do on a national level what Scott Walker has done as governor in Wisconsin...reduce government spending and the power of organized labor. Case refers to the prospect of a national "Walker-like regime." Case laments the fact that "many private sector workers," including 25 percent of Wisconsin union members, supported Walker. In that case, as we have reported, Walker and his conservative backers soundly defeated Obama's progressive allies.

Obama's support in the CPUSA, a political entity once funded and directed by Moscow, has become an open secret, although the major media treat the subject as something not worthy of serious discussion. This silent treatment extends to the matter of Obama's mentor, a member of the CPUSA named Frank Marshall Davis. Members of the party have known of Obama's connection to Davis for many years, which may account for their support of the Democratic Party politician in 2008 and now in 2012. A congressional friend of Obama's from his Chicago days, Danny K. Davis, still associates with the CPUSA and even accepted an award from them.

Obama isn't the only Democrat getting various kinds of communist support. Workers World Party, an openly Marxist-Leninist party, endorsed Democrat Charles Barron for the United States House in the 8th Congressional District in New York City. However, in that primary election, which was held on June 26, Barron lost. The Workers World Party newspaper referred to Barron, a city council member, as "a former Black Panther who continues to connect with many sectors of the progressive movement. He has marched alongside oppressed activists and Occupy Wall Street in the fight against poverty, budget cuts, foreclosures, racial profiling like stop-and-frisk, police brutality, the prison-industrial complex, and all forms of injustice at home and abroad." It said Barron had won the endorsement of District Council 37, the city's largest public employee union, representing

125,000 members and 50,000 retirees, and the black-oriented Amsterdam News.

The CPUSA writer John Case has not been without criticism of Obama, saying that the Democratic President made a huge mistake by firing Van Jones as White House Green Jobs czar after his communist background came to light.

There is speculation that Jones was fired because the chain of command that hired him led to the Oval Office, including Obama adviser Valerie Jarrett and Obama himself (forcing his hand).

Jones remains a major figure in the progressive movement backing Obama, however, and was a featured speaker at the "Take Back the American Dream" conference recently held in Washington. Participants in the conference included Communist Party activists Jarvis Tyner and Joelle Fishman.

I'm not saying that Obama is a Communist; just that from a distance...he seems to have a lot of Communist associates and tendencies.

But there's another line of thought regarding Obama's agenda and how he rose from virtual obscurity to become one of the most powerful men on the planet.

Webster Tarpley was interviewed about his book, "The Postmodern Coup: The Making of a Manchurian Candidate" in October of 2008, just before the first election of Barack Obama for President of the United States. Tarpley made predictions about the imminent future of the geopolitical landscape should Obama be elected, based on his knowledge of the people who backed and advised Obama. As far as foreign policy strategy goes, it has been 100 percent Zbigniew Brzezinski all the way.

In retrospect, it's interesting to understand Brzezinski's vision and how much of it has been accomplished so far. The question remains as to whether the ultimate fantasies of this real-life Dr. Strangelove will be achieved by 2017.

Referring to Obama, Tarpley said, "The guy is a puppet of the worst sort of circles of Imperialism...David Rockefeller, George Soros and Zbigniew Brzezinski."

Tarpley went on to say, "Right Wingers don't know how to attack 'him,' they either want to attack him for being a Communist, which I think is not accurate...because he's a servant of finance capital...so how could he be a Communist?

Or that he's a Muslim, because his middle name is Hussein. He lived in Indonesia for a while and may have considered himself a Muslim for a while. I would note that he has known two fathers, his biological father who abandoned him...and then an Indonesian man. Both of them, it seems to me were more devoted to Johnnie Walker Black Label Scotch Whiskey than they ever were to Islam, so I don't think that the Muslim connection would make any sense.

But I would add one more thing: If you're running to be the President of the United States, you're asking to put your finger on the button; there's a thermonuclear button that launches Intercontinental Ballistic Missiles with H-bombs onboard."

Chapter 28

Distinguished journalist Bob Woodward, a darling of the political Left, called Obama a "Nixon" regarding the ongoing sequester drama. He accused him of attempting to divert culpability for the so called sequester, for which Obama must take responsibility. Even the liberal senator from Illinois, Dick Durbin, said the legislation, signed into law (2012) by the president, was Obama's idea.

But by so doing, Woodward said he has received threats from the White House in an attempt to intimidate and shut him up. Obama is guilty of practicing "Hegelism" as a way of maintaining power and popularity. G. W. Hegel, an 18th century German philosopher whose thinking was a precursor to Marxism, noted that, first, "you create a crisis, then offer solutions to the crisis you created, and finally you blame the opposition for the crisis."

It should sadden every American that we have elected a president who uses such tactics in order to maintain his popularity to an electorate that pays little attention to what is actually happening until it is too late.

I hope there are enough honest journalists left in this country to stand up for veteran journalist Bob Woodward, who spoke the truth and now is being threatened by our government. If it can happen to Woodward, it could happen to any of us.

If the White House is willing to push a Bob Woodward around on such a mundane matter as Obama's role in a budget standoff, what else will they do? A look at Wikipedia's page on Obama's communist mentor Frank Marshall Davis might give us some indication. It is apparent that Obama supporters and Internet "trolls" have sanitized the page in order to eliminate any hint that Obama's Marxist policies are being driven by the relationship he had, for almost 10 years...with a Communist Party operative who was under surveillance by the FBI.

Wikipedia's treatment of the Obama-Davis relationship demonstrates that adding any additional relevant information about a contemporary politician's socialist ties or communist background would be a waste of one's time...because it will be deleted faster than you can type it. The left has armies of minions, surfing the net, purging all information that reflects negatively on their heroes.

While Bob Woodward's spat with the White House makes for interesting reading and gets headlines, the famed Watergate reporter has barely scratched the surface of what Obama and his people will do to suppress the truth about the nature of this administration and its policies.

On one level, it seems too late, since Woodward was asleep on these matters as Obama won the presidency and re-election. But at least he could now begin to set the record straight.

The Davis-Obama relationship was a Watergate-type story that, if told by Woodward and his colleagues in the "mainstream media," could have spared America from the domestic and foreign policy catastrophes that now grip the United States.

Perhaps Woodward should not be praised for standing up to the Obama White House's alleged "threats." Rather, he should be asked what he was doing for the last several years as Obama and his allies ruthlessly suppressed the truth about his Marxist background and agenda for America and the world.

Any republican candidate for president, with Obama's background, would have been eaten alive by the mainstream media, but nothing in Obama's past concerned the left-leaning news people. It's not just that the media did no vetting of Obama during his campaign, but even over time as issues were raised and legitimate questions were asked...the Obama-media had no interest in pursuing answers. It later came to light that an agreement, to ignore the many problematic events in his less-than-patriotic background, had quietly been implemented to shield him from public scrutiny. That protective screen has remained in place (with the mainstream media) and Obama can do no wrong in their eyes. Of course the media is greatly influenced by the proverbial "powers that be."

The major newspapers were bought up almost 100 years ago by the wealthy elitist to manage and influence the general public's thoughts, and by extension...their opinions and beliefs. That subliminal indoctrination has continued to expand as the media evolved to radio, television and the Internet...until the masses are but mindless zombies. So when you hear someone speak about the "powers that be," they're talking about the super wealthy, global elite, power brokers. These entities have accumulated and/or control so much of the world's capital that they have become bored with just controlling most of the world's wealth, they're now gearing up to move forward with their long-planned new world order... so they can then not only control the world's monetary systems...but the world's population...each and every individual.

This is a very slippery slope that's currently underway... and the United States media is sponsoring it. It exposes the enormous power of a "Biased Media" to cut the heart and will out of the American public.

I can't help but be reminded of Hitler's ascent to totalitarian control of Germany. He had the same compliant, nation news media cheerleading for him... while they brainwashed the German citizenry...or as Hitler called them, "the useful idiots."

A truism worthy of note: Do not fear the enemy, for they can only take your life. Fear the media, for they can distort your grasp of reality and destroy you and your way of life in many more ways than death can ever bring about.

I've put together a short list of things that any rational person interested in the long-term continuance of our American way of life...might find very disturbing, to say the least.

Here are some of my validating reasons for my beliefs that we're being herded into a form of collectivism, and I'm not even going to mention any of Obama's policies...such as the socialist nationalization of GM and Chrysler; which with the stroke of a pen deprived private investors of billions of dollars of their legitimate property and turned it over to the state and the unions (the proletariat in Marxist parlance).

1) Obama admits attending socialist conferences and reading Marxist literature. He stated that he "chose his friends carefully...the Marxist professors, we were just resisting bourgeois society's stifling constraints."

2) Frank Marshall Davis to whom Obama refers to as "Frank" and with whom the young Obama "had a close relationship, almost like a son"...is publicly identified as a prominent member of the Communist Party USA and an acknowledged Stalinist agent.

3) Obama held receptions at the home of, and served on boards with, another mentor who has had an indelible influence on his worldview, William Ayers along with his wife, Bernardine Dohrn. The two were leaders of the terrorist group known as the Weathermen or the Weather Underground, notable for a campaign from 1969 through the middle 1970s of riots, bombings, murders, and a jailbreak. Under Ayers and Dohrn's leadership, the terrorist organization bombed the United States Capitol on March 1, 1971, The Pentagon on May 19, 1972, and the

> United States Department of State Building on January 29, 1975. Their founding document called for "the destruction of United States imperialism and the achievement of a classless world...worldwide communism." When recently asked about his terrorist activities, Ayers replied he had "no regrets" but that "we didn't do enough."

Footnote to the above paragraph: School officials at Minnesota State University Moorhead selected left-wing radical and admitted terrorist, William (Bill) Ayers...as their 2013 College of Education and Human Services "visiting scholar."

In an announcement last month, MSUM proclaimed that Ayers's campus-wide address would be called "Teaching from the Heart: Education for Enlightenment and Freedom." Ayers reportedly spent three days on the school's campus. Social justice was the big theme of his visit.

Steve Grineski, a professor at MSUM's School of Teaching and Learning, said, "Ayers's radical past didn't bother the school's administration; if they had been really concerned they would have canceled his presentation and not allowed us to do it." Grineski told Campus Reform that he and his colleagues chose to celebrate and honor Ayers because of his long history of trying to commingle social justice principles with the American education system. While Ayers received a stipend for his appearance at MSUM, the taxpayer-funded school refused to disclose how much it was.

Ayers was a co-founder of the Weather Underground, a communist revolutionary group. He was involved in Chicago's "Days of Rage" riot in 1969 and fled prosecution after an accidental Greenwich Village townhouse explosion in 1970...and killed three Weather Underground members who were preparing a bomb that prematurely detonated. In his 2001 book, Ayers admitted that he participated in bombings of the New York City Police Department headquarters, the United States Capitol Building and the Pentagon in the early 1970s.

After his days as a federal fugitive ended (because charges were dropped due to illegal FBI snooping), Ayers earned a Ph.D. and eventually became a faculty member at the University of Illinois at Chicago. Ayers also achieved notoriety as a "family friend" to a youngish politician named Barack Obama. (This must have been about the time of Ayers' epiphany; that when it comes to destroying core civilizational institutions, trying to blow them up is less effective than hollowing them out from within.) Ayers and his wife, Bernadine Dohrn still live in Chicago's Hyde Park neighborhood, where Obama formerly resided.

In 2010, Ayers was denied emeritus status after a passionate speech by the University's board chair, Christopher Kennedy...the son of assassinated Robert Kennedy. Christopher urged the board to vote against Ayers because he had dedicated his 1974 book "Prairie Fire" to a list of people...including his father's assassin, Sirhan Sirhan.

But there's more: Former Weather Underground radical Kathy Boudin, who spent 22 years in prison for an armored-car robbery that killed two cops and a Brinks guard...now holds a prestigious adjunct professorship at Columbia University's School of Social Work.

Boudin, 69, won another academic laurel this year...she was named the Sheinberg Scholar-in-Residence at NYU Law School, where she gave a lecture last month on "the politics of parole and re-entry."

Boudin bounced-back into respectability after her 2003 parole came to light...just a week before the release of Robert Redford's movie "The Company You Keep," loosely based on the $1.6 million Brinks heist.

4) At one Obama reception at the Ayers/Dohrn home, Alice Palmer...who was identified by the FBI as being on the Soviet payroll in the eighties and an enthusiastic attendee of the 27th Congress of the Communist Party of the Soviet Union, announced that she was stepping down from the office and that Obama was her chosen successor.

5) Mike Klonsky was funded to the tune of $1,968,718 by an organization headed by Obama and Ayers. His father, Robert Klonsky, was an American communist who was convicted for advocating the forcible overthrow of the United States government. Mike founded a precursor of the Weatherman terrorist group, formed the American Communist Party (Marxist/Leninist), was feted in China by Maoists, and spoke in front of Hugo Chavez for the need to bring the Marxist revolution into the classroom.

6) Obama admits that one of his close friends was Rashid Khalidi, who was the President of Columbia University's Communist Party and a former spokesperson for the PLO. They had frequent dinners together and the Obamas even babysat Khalidi's children. Obama led organizations funded the Arab American Action League an organization calling for the demolition of Israel and chaired by Khalidi's wife. Khalidi also held successful fundraisers for Obama's campaign.

7) Che Guevara who advocated the "extermination" of the United States, and was involved in a foiled plot to bomb crowded department stores and New York City's Grand Central Terminal, had his portraits hung on the precinct captain's wall of Obama headquarters in Houston. The campaign formally only stated that it was "inappropriate."

8) During the presidential election campaign, Hamas advisor Ahmed Yousef was quoted as saying, "We like Mr. Obama. We hope he will win the election." Hamas is dedicated to the destruction of Israel and is on the United States' State Department list of leftist terrorist organizations.

9) The Communist Party USA actively supported Obama during the primary election and their leader Sam Webb recently said, "Just look at the new lay of the land...a friend of labor and its allies sits in the White House." He went on

to enthusiastically discuss Obama's agenda to nationalize the American financial system, the Federal Reserve Bank, and private industries such as energy and various other sectors. "All these...and many other things are within 'our' reach now...an opportunity of a lifetime," Webb exclaimed!

10) Obama's father wrote a thesis entitled "Problems With Our Socialism" that advocates 100 percent taxation of the rich, communal ownership of land and the forced confiscation of privately controlled land.

11) Obama's mother was a communist sympathizer from her youth. Obama has spoken of her beliefs: "The values she taught me continue to be my touchstone when it comes to how I go about the world of politics."

12) Obama's parents met in a Russian language class, generally unusual in the United States of the fifties, but a common activity for communists in that time period.

13) Obama's older brother, Abongo "Roy" Obama is a militant Marxist Muslim who made a pact with a hard-line Islamic group in Kenya to establish Sharia law there. Obama calls his brother "the person who made me proudest of all."

14) Obama's grandparents moved 2,000 miles so Obama's mother could attend a school where communism was openly advocated and whose

chairman testified to being a member of the Communist Party.

15) Obama's grandparents also attended a church known as "The Little Red Church" due to its promotion of communism.

16) Obama received the endorsement of the Chicago branch of the Democratic Socialists of America for an Illinois state senate seat in 1996.

17) Obama delivered the eulogy for Saul Mendelson, a lifelong communist activist.

18) Obama's physician, close friend and supporter Dr. Quentin Young, was a prominent member of the communist Bethune Club.

19) Obama's church, the Trinity United Church of Christ, is a leading proponent of Liberation Theology that is a religious overlay onto Marxism.

20) Obama admits that he regularly attended communist conferences at Cooper Union College.

21) Obama endorsed Bernie Sanders, who was the first self-described socialist to be elected to the United States Senate. The National Journal's 27th annual ratings listed only one Senator who had voted a more socialistic agenda than Sanders: Obama!

The media didn't touch any of the above questionable material because they are supporters of the collectivism agenda that Obama has been put in charge of implementing in America. So we have the "powers that be," the mainstream media, the entertainment community (Hollywood), the educational hierarchy, the intelligentsia and the useful idiots...are all onboard for the new utopian world. So is it any wonder that we old school conservatives will be left standing at the station as the train's caboose disappears into "Neverland."

Neverland, the movie: A parody, featuring Peter Pan as an older teen, with a gender identity dilemma, whereas the fairy Tinker Bell is a drugged out...and burnt out girl, the Lost Boys are pot heads, the Darling children are adopted by foreigners, Wendy Darling is a lesbian, Captain Hook is a gay, un-employed leather man and Tiger Lily is cast as a transvestite, will soon be coming to a neighborhood near you.

This "new communist world order" will allow you to retain your adolescence indefinably. You'll never have to outgrow your immaturities or take responsibility for your actions and/or poor choices. And...the government will take care of you from the cradle to the grave...or just eliminate you. The event will be opening at amusement parks worldwide, rather than on a magical, imaginary island.

Just think of it as "A Mind Game of Manipulative Illusions."

> "At what point shall we expect the approach of danger? By what means shall we fortify against it? Shall we expect some transatlantic military giant, to step the Ocean, and crush us at a blow? Never! All the armies of

Europe, Asia and Africa combined, with all the treasure of the earth (our own excepted) in their military chest; with a Bonaparte for a commander, could not by force, take a drink from the Ohio, or make a track on the Blue Ridge, in a trial of a thousand years. At what point, then, is the approach of danger to be expected? I answer, if it ever reaches us it must spring up amongst us. It cannot come from abroad. If destruction be our lot, we must ourselves be its author and finisher. As a nation of freemen, we must live through all time, or die by suicide."

~ Abraham Lincoln, January 27, 1838 ~

CHAPTER 29

While we've known from the very beginning that the mainstream media was not only cheerleading for him, but also shielding him on all fronts...from any personal information that might contradict, or betray the self-serving facade he has manufactured for America's gullible. So between the mainstream media and the intimidation factor of a visit from the FCC...suggesting that an audi*t might be in order if one continues down the wrong road, keeps the negatives (past and present) buried. We of course have the debunkers, but they are not immune from third-party pressure either. Even they have been known to dance around uncomfortable subjects when the wrong conclusion (True or False) could cast a negative shadow onto a high-ranking government official. The power of a tyrannical government can be very corrosive when it comes to controlling the masses and compromising their freedom.

The Department of Justice is currently pursuing a lawsuit against S&P in an apparent attempt to punish the company for downgrading America's debt rating back in August 2011. It's also a warning to Moody and Fitch not to follow S&P down that path of downgrading America's debt rating. Our nation's debt is in even greater economic peril today than it was two years ago, but this subtle warning to the rating agencies...from the DOJ, might just work in getting the economy back on track.

Obama and the Obama administration are sidestepping the House and Senate with Executive Orders (EO) that mimic legislation. They are blatantly ignoring our constitutional system of checks and balances as they attack our religious liberties, freedom of speech, and gun ownership rights by using EOs to forward their statist agenda. The establishment of a "shadow government" of unaccountable, un-vetted "czars" and numerous other subversions of our founding documents has been their vision from day one and has only grown more expansive and powerful with his second term.

The above is just a rehash of what we already know about the lack of transparency in this administration, but his re-election has unbridled him to move full speed ahead with his agenda. We hear nothing negative from our mainstream news channels, but we're receiving a lot of disturbing...and even unbelievable, information and from secondhand, third party sources. There's also a large...and growing, network of underground websites and bloggers. Because these stories sound so very important...and scary, one has to wonder why the media continues to ignore them...as if they "see no evil nor hear any evil." But then we are reminded of the media's bias toward the administration; that's the point where most of us, who want to know the truth, go to the debunkers... usually, Snopes and/or TruthOrFiction.

On Monday (January 21, 2013), renowned author and humanitarian Dr. Jim Garrow made a shocking claim about what we can expect to see in Obama's second term: "I have just been informed by a former senior military leader that Obama is using a new 'litmus test' to determine who among his military leaders will stay and who will be 'persuaded' to leave."

Get ready to explode folks. "The new litmus test of leadership in the military is whether they will fire on United States citizens or not...if commanded to do so. Those who will not are being removed."

Understand, this is not coming from Alex Jones or Jesse Ventura, or from anyone else the left often dismisses with great ease. Garrow is a well-respected activist and has spent much of his life rescuing infant girls from China, babies who would be killed under that country's one-child policy. He was also nominated for the Nobel Peace Prize for his work.

His bio on Amazon.com reads:

Dr. James Garrow is the author of The Pink Pagoda: One Man's Quest to End Gendercide in China. He has spent over $25 million over the past sixteen years rescuing an estimated 40,000 baby Chinese girls from near-certain death under China's one-child-per-couple policy by facilitating international adoptions. He is the founder and executive director of the Bethune Institute's Pink Pagoda schools, private English-immersion schools for Chinese children. Today he runs 168 schools with nearly 6,300 employees.

This comes on the heels of Sunday's report in the Washington Free Beacon (WFB) that the head of Central Command, Marine Corps General James Mattis is being dismissed by Obama and will leave his post in March.

The WFB article states:

"Word on the national security street is that General James Mattis is being given the bum's rush out of his job as commander of Central Command, and is being told to vacate his office several months earlier than planned."

Did General Mattis refuse to "fire on United States citizens?"

Virginia Beach Conservative Examiner.com: Published on Jan 23, 2013:

The Obama administration is openly escalating its campaign against private gun ownership, and shaking up the top ranks of the military command structure... but is it also preparing to make war on the American population? According to a person identified as a former senior military official, the answer to that shocking question is yes.

Garrow said that his source, a man regarded as "one of America's foremost military heroes," told him that President Obama is using a new litmus test for "determining who will stay and who must go" among top-ranked military leaders. That test is whether they will fire on United States citizens (if directed to do so) or not. Garrow also said that his source made the disclosure in order to "sound the alarm" over the administration's plans.

While Garrow has not yet revealed the identity of his source, it's important to note that Garrow himself is a man of considerable accomplishments.

He later joined Gary Franchi on WHDT World News to discuss this new "Litmus Test."

One would think that something of this magnitude would be all over the big news organizations, but it was disregarded because it wouldn't go over very well with the general public...and might even produce a cloud of suspicion and concern.

Having no other resources to verify or refute the allegation, I opted for the two big name debunkers, Snopes and TruthOrFiction. I entered the source's accusation: "Obama only wants military leaders who "will fire on United Sates citizens." Their answers (below) were less than reassuring.

Snopes said: Probably False. (I wasn't asking for your opinion, I already have an opinion.)

TruthOrFiction said: Unproven! (Excuse me, I already knew that much.)

Folks, it just doesn't get more blatant than this.

But getting back to the Virginia Beach Conservative Examiner's question: Is our government preparing to make war on the American population? I would also ask, "Is our government anticipating a push back from gun advocates if the new gun laws are extreme and constitute an attack on the Second Amendment?"

Homeland Security, under Obama, has already promulgated a booklet stating that the likely purveyors of terrorism would include gun owners, activists for limited government, and former military personnel. Silly in the extreme...absolutely, but someone in our government wrote the document.

In announcing his new gun control proposals, Obama said that he was not restricting Second Amendment rights, but allowing other constitutional rights to flourish.

He seems to understand the Constitution as a "set of suggestions."

I cannot endorse his performance in office, but he wins my respect for taking the steps he deemed necessary to ensure the safety of his family. (He just passed a bill that extended protection for him and his family, around the clock...for life, by the Secret Service.) So why would he want to prohibit me from providing a measure of protection for my family and myself?

The individual is not only best qualified to provide his own personal defense, he is the only one qualified to do so; and his right to do so is guaranteed by the Constitution.

The Founding Fathers, far from being ideologues, were not even politicians. They were an assortment of businessmen, writers, teachers and planters, in short... men who knew something of the world, which is to say, of "human nature." Their struggle to draft a set of rules acceptable to each other was based on the assumption that we human beings, in the mass, are no damned good...that we are biddable, easily confused, and that we may easily be motivated by a politician, which is to say, a huckster, mounting a soapbox and inflaming our passions.

The Founders also recognized that Government is quite literally a necessary evil, that there must be opposition, between its various branches, and between political parties, for these are the only ways to temper the individual's greed for power and the electorates' desires for peace by submission to coercion or blandishment.

The Constitution's drafters did not require a wizard to teach them that power corrupts; they had experienced it in the person of King George. The American secession was announced by reference to his abuses of power: "He has obstructed the administration of justice...He has made judges dependant on his will alone...He has combined with others to subject us to a jurisdiction foreign to our Constitution, and unacknowledged by our laws...He has erected a multitude of new offices, and sent hither swarms of officers to harass our people and to eat away their substance...imposed taxes upon us without our consent...He has fundamentally altered the structure of our government."

This is a chillingly familiar set of grievances; and the Founders foresaw its recrudescence. They realized that King George was not an individual case, but the inevitable outcome of unfettered power; that any person or group with the power to tax, to form laws, and to enforce them by arms will default to dictatorship, absent the constant unflagging scrutiny of the governed, and their severe untempered insistence upon compliance with law.

So, is the United States a "free country" today? Not hardly! Not compared to what it once was. Yet, very few Americans today challenge these Marxist institutions, and there are virtually no politicians calling for their repeal or even gradual phase out.

While the United States of America may still have more freedoms than most other countries, we have nonetheless lost many crucial liberties and have accepted the major socialist attacks on freedom and private property as normal parts of our way of life. The nation, whose founders included such individualists as Thomas Jefferson, George Mason, James Madison, John Adams and Patrick Henry, has gradually turned away from the principles of individual rights, limited constitutional government, private property and free markets. Instead, we have increasingly embraced the failed ideas and nostrums of socialism and fascism. We should hang our heads in shame for having allowed this to happen.

A new kind of fascism has taken over America: The merger of corporations and government whereby corporate power dominates. With the emergence of ever-larger multinational corporations, due to consolidation facilitated by the Federal Reserve's endless fiat money... the "corporatocracy" has been in a position to literally purchase the United States Congress.

A result of the corporate purchase of Congress is that many of the nation's laws have been re-configured to benefit "We The Corporations," rather than "We The People." Laws like NAFTA resulted in the outsourcing of the United States manufacturing base and the destruction of the "middle class." This is nothing less than the 1 percenters abusing the 99 percenters. Known as "crony capitalism," "mercantilism," "globalization," "the new world order," and/or "free trade"...this is not your grandfather's capitalism!

It is not too late to reverse these pernicious burdens and instead enact pro-freedom reforms to put our nation back on track again. But in many ways the Left has a head start over us on the pro-freedom Right. The enemies of "our" freedom do admittedly dominate the entertainment industry, television news media, and academia...but we have the tremendous strategic advantage that reality (including man's nature) is on our side; so, unlike the socialists and liberals (welfare-state fascists), we are not in the position of having to advocate a system which constantly tries to "make water run uphill"...or force human beings into a rigid utopian straitjacket based on the whims of some clique of central planning bureaucrats. We know that individual freedom for peaceful people within a constitutional republic works in practice; our country's history demonstrates that. The piecemeal abandonment of the principles and institutions that made America great has proved to be a dead-end road to failure.

Marxism, socialism and fascism have proved to be colossal failures all over the world. As Frederic Bastiat wrote in his classic "The Law"...just prior to his death, "let us now try liberty!"

I'm not suggesting that totalitarians are in charge, only that the multitudinous areas of diminished liberties, when combined into one big picture, gives a clear indication that Americans are at risk of no longer being wholly free, as Americans have traditionally understood that term. We may be on a slippery slope towards a semi-authoritarian hybrid state, where freedoms are reasonably widely enjoyed, but only at the sufferance of government officials, rather than as a natural right.

> "Necessity is the argument of every impingement of human freedom; it is the argument of tyrants and the creed of slaves."
>
> ~ William Pitt ~

Chapter 30

Throughout his life Woody Guthrie (of Dust Bowl Okies fame) associated with United States Communist groups, although he was seemingly never a paying member of any.

After landing in Southern California, Woody Guthrie was introduced to socialists and communists by newscaster Ed Robbin.

Guthrie later claimed that "the best thing I did in 1936 was to sign up with the Communist Party," but some still question whether or not he actually became a member of the party. He was noted as a fellow traveler... an outsider who agreed with the platform of the party while not subject to party discipline. Guthrie asked to write a column for the Communist newspaper, The Daily Worker. The column, titled "Woody Sez," appeared a total of 174 times from May 1939 to January 1940. Woody Sez was not explicitly political, but was about current events as observed by Guthrie. He wrote the columns in an exaggerated hillbilly dialect and usually included a small comic; they were published as a collection after Guthrie's death. Steve Earle said of Guthrie, "I don't think of Woody Guthrie as a political writer. He was just a writer who lived in very political times."

The Communist Party and its members have been with us for a very long time. Most of us can remember the 50s when America realized the Communist threat was knocking at our doors. Congress began investigating subversive groups (within Congress) and Americans began waking up to the relentless, incremental encroachment of our Republic. This awakening brought a renewed surge of traditional, conservative values as America regained its self-sustaining character and pride in America. But the malignancy did not go away...it only retreated to regroup and build on the progress it had made. In today's environment this socialist movement has every right to be confident with the outcome of their hundred-plus years of pushing America toward...and now, into the Socialist/Communist abyss.

Congress has always had...and continues to have, communists within its membership.

While most of the nation is still reeling from the tragedy at Sandy Hook Elementary School...and continues to mourn the innocent victims, others are already working to exploit the horrific event for political gain. After all, as President Obama's former Chief of Staff, Rahm Emanuel, once infamously said, "You never want a serious crisis to go to waste because a crisis provides an opportunity to do things that you thought you could not have done before."

This is a lesson that the president has learned...and remembered well.

The most recent article on the Communist Party USA website quotes Obama approvingly: "As a country, we have been through this too many times. Whether it is an elementary school in Newtown, a shopping mall in Oregon, a temple in Wisconsin, a movie theater in Aurora or a street corner in Chicago...these neighborhoods are our neighborhoods, and these children are our children. We are going to have to come together and take meaningful action to prevent more tragedies like this, regardless of the politics."

The article's author then writes: "Let us not forget that there are some who profit from the manufacturing and peddling of assault weapons, dealing in fear and offering constitutional and political cover for the unthinkable. We will continue to work to bring the necessary coalitions together that through common sense and a common stance...will work for a culture, government and country where such tragedies and crimes are indeed unthinkable and unheard of."

While neither the president nor the Communist Party USA used the precise term "gun control," there can be no doubt that they share the goal of placing further restrictions on the Constitutional right of American citizens to keep and bear arms. Obama has a long history of being anti-gun.

Using the mass murder of 20 small children to advance a political agenda aimed at restricting fundamental rights is simply ghoulish. President Obama, and his allies in the Communist Party USA, ought to be ashamed of themselves.

The Communist Manifesto, originally titled Manifesto of the Communist Party, is a short 1848 publication written by the political theorists Karl Marx and Friedrich Engels. It has since been recognized as one of the world's most influential political manuscripts. Commissioned by the Communist League, it laid out the League's purposes and program. It presents an analytical approach to the class struggle (historical and present) and the problems of capitalism, rather than a prediction of communism's potential future forms.

The book contains Marx and Engels' theories about the nature of society and politics, that in their own words, "The history of all hitherto existing society is the history of class struggles." It also briefly features their ideas for how the capitalist society of the time would eventually be replaced by socialism, and then eventually communism.

There is more to life than always increasing its speed; many people today are at the very least…running behind, and it seems that most are in danger of being run over by reality. They live in a virtual world of smoke and mirrors, games and electronics…unaware of our evolving world, but more importantly...uninformed and unconcerned about where America is being taken. Our "new norm" is just that to them…normal. They are oblivious to the decades-long transformation that has changed the face of America and the character of its once proud population.

No one is willing to say it out loud, but we are well into a socialistic framework and moving forward under the umbrella of "necessary benevolence." Unfortunately, history tells us...over and over again, that Socialism, over time...often capitulates to full-blown Communism. One could also suggest that America is already practicing Communism.

In his communist manifesto, Karl Marx describes the ten steps necessary to destroy a free enterprise system and replace it with a system of omnipotent government power, so as to affect a communist socialist state. Those ten steps are known as the Ten Planks of The Communist Manifesto. The following brief presents the original ten planks within the Communist Manifesto written by Karl Marx in 1848, along with the American adopted counterpart for each of the planks. By comparison it is clear that most Americans have, by myths or fraud and deception, under the color of law...by their own politicians in both the Republican and Democratic parties, been transformed into Communists.

We just have not reached the totalitarian phase yet; history tells us that the totalitarian or dictatorial period can only evolve "after the citizenry has been disarmed."

And if you think that is impossible you had better wake up, because Obama is already moving in that direction. The United Nations' Small Arms Treaty that Hillary Clinton was negotiating could take away our 2nd Amendment rights. And there are plenty of stupid people in congress and on the streets that will go right along with them.

Wake up America, this is why our founding fathers put the 2nd Amendment in our Constitution.

> "It does not require a majority to prevail, but rather an irate, tireless minority keen to set brush fires in people's minds."
>
> ~ Samuel Adams ~

Another thing to remember, Karl Marx in creating the Communist Manifesto designed these planks as a test to determine whether a society has become communist or not. If they are all in affect and in force, then the people are practicing communists.

Communism, by any other name (Marxism, Socialism, fairness doctrine, centralized planning...etc) is still communism and is very, very destructive to the individual and society!

The ultimate goal for Marxist socialists is the emancipation of labor from alienating work. Marxists argue that freeing the individual from the necessity of performing alienating work, in order to receive goods, would allow people to pursue their own interests and develop their own talents without being coerced into performing labor for others. For Marxists, the stage of economic development in which this is possible, sometimes called full communism, is contingent upon advances in the productive capabilities of society.

The 10 planks stated in the Communist Manifesto and some of their American counterparts are:

- 1) Abolition of private property and the application of all rents of land to public purposes.

Americans do these with actions such as the 14th Amendment of the United States Constitution (1868), and various zoning, school & property taxes. Also the Bureau of Land Management (Zoning laws are the first step to government property ownership).

- 2) A heavy progressive or graduated income tax.

Americans know this as misapplication of the 16th Amendment of the United States. Constitution, 1913, The Social Security Act of 1936; Joint House Resolution 192 of 1933; and various State "income" taxes. We call it "paying your fair share."

- 3) Abolition of all rights of inheritance.

Americans call it Federal & State estate Tax (1916); or reformed Probate Laws, and limited inheritance via arbitrary inheritance tax statutes.

- 4) Confiscation of the property of all emigrants and rebels.

Americans call it government seizures, tax liens, Public Law 99-570 (1986); Executive order 11490, sections 1205, 2002 which gives private land to the Department of Urban Development; the imprisonment of "terrorists" and those who speak out or write against the "government" (1997 Crime/ Terrorist Bill); or the IRS confiscation of property without due process. Asset forfeiture laws are used by (DEA, IRS, ATF etc).

- 5) Centralization of credit in the hands of the state, by means of a national bank with State capital and an exclusive monopoly.

  Americans call it the Federal Reserve, which is a privately owned credit/debt system, allowed by the Federal Reserve act of 1913. All local banks are members of the Fed system, and are regulated by the Federal Deposit Insurance Corporation (FDIC) another privately owned corporation. The Federal Reserve Banks issue "Fiat Paper Money" and practice economically destructive fractional reserve banking.

- 6) Centralization of the means of communications and transportation in the hands of the State.

  Americans call it the Federal Communications Commission (FCC) and Department of Transportation (DOT) mandated through the ICC act of 1887, the Commissions Act of 1934, The Interstate Commerce Commission established in 1938, The Federal Aviation Administration, Federal Communications Commission, and Executive orders 11490, 10999, as well as State mandated driver's licenses and Department of Transportation regulations.

- 7) Extension of factories and instruments of production owned by the state, the bringing into cultivation of wastelands, and the improvement of the soil generally in accordance with a common plan.

Americans call it corporate capacity, The Desert Entry Act and The Department of Agriculture. Thus they are written as "controlled or subsidized" rather than "owned." This is easily seen in these as well as the Department of Commerce and Labor, Department of Interior, the Environmental Protection Agency, Bureau of Land Management, Bureau of Reclamation, Bureau of Mines, National Park Service, and the IRS control of business through corporate regulations.

- 8) Equal liability of all to labor. Establishment of industrial armies, especially for agriculture.

Americans call it Minimum Wage and slave labor like dealing with our Most Favored Nation trade partner; i.e. Communist China. We see it in practice via the Social Security Administration and The Department of Labor. The National debt and inflation caused by the communal bank has caused the need for a "two income family." Women in the workplace since the 1920's, the 19th amendment of the United States Constitution, the Civil Rights Act of 1964, assorted Socialist Unions, affirmative action, the Federal Public Works Program and of course Executive order 11000.

- 9) Combination of agriculture with manufacturing industries, gradual abolition of the distinction between town and country, by a more equitable distribution of population over the country.

  Americans call it the Planning Reorganization act of 1949, zoning (Title 17 1910-1990) and Super Corporate Farms, as well as Executive orders 11647, 11731 (ten regions) and Public Law 89 - 136. These provide for forced relocations and forced sterilization programs, like in China.

- 10) Free education for all children in public schools. Abolition of children's factory labor in its present form. Combination of education with industrial production.

  Americans are being taxed to support what we call "public" schools, but are actually "government forced-tax-funded schools." Even private schools are government regulated. The purpose is to train the young to work for the communal debt system. We also call it the Department of Education, the NEA and "Outcome Based Education." These are used so that all children can be indoctrinated and inculcated with the government propaganda, like "majority rules," and "pay your fair share." Where are the words "fair share" in the Constitution, Bill of Rights or the Internal Revenue Code (Title 26)? No where is "fair share" even suggested! The philosophical concept of "fair

> share" comes from the Communist maxim: "From each according to their ability, to each according to their need." This concept is pure socialism! America was made the greatest society by its private initiative...work ethic! Teaching others and ourselves how to "fish" to be self-sufficient and produce plenty of extra commodities so that if desired, they could be shared with others who might be "needy." Americans have always voluntarily been the most generous and charitable society on the planet.

Does changing the words change the end result? By using different words, is it all of a sudden okay to ignore or violate the provisions or intent of the Constitution of the United States of America?

The people (politicians) who believe in the socialistic and communistic concepts, especially those who pass more and more laws implementing these slavery ideas, are traitors to their oath of office and to the Constitution of the United States of America...know your enemies.

But facetiously speaking, there is an upside to these historical cycles of "perceived" governmental benevolence; like old age...they have never lasted long.

The seductive notion of economic equality has appealed to many people throughout history. The pilgrims started out with the idea of equal sharing. The colony of Georgia began with very similar ideas. In New Harmony, Indiana (1825), Britain's Robert Owen...who coined the term "socialism"...set up colonies based on communal living and economic equality.

What these idealistic experiments all had in common was that they all failed.

They learned the hard way that people would not do as much for the common good as they would do for their own good. The pilgrims nearly starved learning that lesson. But they learned it. Land that had been common property was turned into private property, which produced a lot more food.

Similar experiments were tried on a larger scale in other countries around the world. In the biggest of these experiments, the Soviet Union under Stalin and Communist China under Mao...people literally starved to death by the millions.

In the Soviet Union, at least 6 million people starved to death in the 1930s, in a country with some of the most fertile land on the continent of Europe, a country that had once been a major exporter of food. In China, tens of millions of people starved to death under Mao.

Despite what the left seems to believe, private property rights do not exist simply for the sake of people who own property. Americans who do not own a single acre of land have abundant food available because land is still private property in the United States, even though the left is doing its best to restrict property rights in both rural America and the cities.

The other big feature of the egalitarian left is promotion of a huge inequality of power, while deploring economic inequality.

It is no coincidence that those who are going ballistic over the economic inequality between the top one or two percent and the rest of us, are promoting a far more dangerous concentration of political power in Washington; where far less than one percent of the population is increasingly telling the 300 million-plus Americans what they can and cannot do, on everything from their light bulbs and toilets to their medical care.

This movement in the direction of central planning, under the name "Forward" (Obama's re-election slogan), is in fact going back to a system that has failed in countries around the world...under both democratic and dictatorial governments and among peoples of virtually every race, color, creed, and nationality.

If someone wrote a novel about a man who was raised from childhood to resent the successful and despise the basic values of America, and who then went on to become President of the United States...that novel would be considered too unbelievable, even for a work of fiction. Yet that is exactly what has happened in real life.

None are more hopelessly enslaved, as those who falsely believe they are free...

> "Oh, what a tangled web we weave when first we practice to deceive."
>
> ~ Sir Walter Scott ~

Chapter 30: Part 2

It has been almost 50 years since the United States Supreme Court ruled that a Washington state law barring members of the Communist Party from voting or holding public-sector jobs was/is unconstitutional. Apparently, that's not enough time to remove the ruling from the state's legislative records.

Washington is one of a handful of states with similar laws still in existence despite their having been declared unconstitutional decades ago.

With few exceptions, most notably Georgia...where an anti-communist oath was administered to incoming Dunwoody City Council members as recently as last year. The laws are treated as part of a bygone era, not unlike state statutes prohibiting interracial marriage; the last of which was removed from Alabama's books in 2001 even though the Supreme Court ruled them unconstitutional in 1967.

Rep. Joe Fitzgibbon, D-Burien, first introduced a measure to repeal Washington state's anachronistic anti-subversives law last year, figuring, he says, that it would be an unceremonious end to a dead-letter statute originating from a dark period in our nation's history.

He was wrong. Though his bill passed out of the House Judiciary Committee, it did so on a party-line vote, with four Republicans opposed. With only so much political capital to expend on contentious legislation, House Democratic leaders declined to move it forward, and it never made it to the floor for a vote.

This year, Fitzgibbon lowered his sights and introducing House Bill 1062 with the "understanding" that it likely would not even get out of committee. By week's end, a key deadline for policy-related bills...the bill had not come up for a committee vote, thereby confirming his original understanding.

"There are some (Democratic lawmakers) that think this is a bad political issue for us, but I really don't," he said. "I don't think there is a lot of fear in our state these days about the prospects of a communist takeover."

That may well be, but even with many decades removed from the Red Scare, any suggestion of kowtowing to communists can still inflame passions.

Additionally, Washington, Georgia, Pennsylvania and California have laws requiring state workers to take an oath swearing they are not subversives or members of a group dedicated to overthrowing the government. At least five other states, Connecticut and Virginia among them...have laws prohibiting subversives from working in emergency management. Illinois has a statute barring communists from seeking elected office.

Thanks to a series of 1960s United States Supreme Court rulings that found them to be unconstitutional, those laws have long been basically unenforceable. The ruling that struck down Washington's statute on subversive activities, handed down in 1964, found that the definition of a subversive group was too vague.

Three years later, the Supreme Court ruled that Eugene Frank Robel, a worker at the Todd Shipyard in Seattle, had been wrongly fired from his job building warships over his membership in the Communist Party. "Robel put the final nail in the coffin" for laws limiting communists from public-sector jobs. If you cannot fire a communist working in national defense, what can you do?

While the Supreme Court struck down loyalty oaths that predicate public-sector employment on a lack of affiliation with a subversive group, it has upheld less-expansive pledges to defend the United States from its enemies and uphold the Constitution.

At least 13 states still have anti-subversives oaths laws on their books.

Periodically, a lawmaker seeking to stem the perceived tide of cultural decline will propose a new loyalty oath. Last month, a Republican state lawmaker in Arizona, Rep. Bob Thorpe, proposed legislation requiring high school students to swear an oath defending the Constitution before being allowed to graduate. That measure, House Bill 2467, is pending.

In general, though, such efforts are on the wane...a state of affairs not lost on the communists themselves.

"It is a good thing to get rid of these laws," says Libero Della Piana, vice chair of the Communist Party USA. "The reality is that people are more worried about foreclosures on their houses than subversives in their government."

I would say therein lies the problem. It is always about distortion, distraction and misdirection...all to create a smoke screen to prevent the voters from seeing the trees...for the forest. A large segment of today's general population does not have a clue about what's really going on in Washington.

The requirement, of some states...for a signed statement disavowing any communist or subversive affiliations is about as useless as a sign declaring a designated "Gun Free Zone." Of course they will sign a loyalty oath (truthfully or not)...but once inside, the pretender(s) can then promote his or her hidden agenda from within. Their true intent will disappear under the radar as it blends with the everyday flow of political corruption, until it is often too late to reverse.

Example: Since he began advancing his real agenda from 1600 Pennsylvania Avenue, numerous columnists/ writers have characterized Obama as "not caring about," "trampling upon" and/or "stomping on" the Constitution. I have agreed with most of their opinions and have a question I would like answered.

"Isn't failure to uphold the 'presidential oath of office' grounds for impeachment?" Just asking...

Probably, but we all know by now that oaths are not what they used to be, they are just hollow words today...a formality.

> "History is indeed little more than the register of the crimes, follies and misfortunes of mankind."
>
> From: "The Decline and Fall of the Roman Empire"
> ~ Edward Gibbon, English historian (1737-1794) ~

Chapter 31

One would think that with a little common sense and some knowledge of socialism and communism's history that America's population would be immune to such indoctrination. Well, we began losing the common sense element several decades ago, and our school systems (driven by governmental curriculums) have distorted and/or rewritten history to the point that most of the really ugly things have been smoothed over...and in some cases, it's as though they never happened. But how is it that over half of our populace does not see...nor understand, where this administration is taking us? I have to accept that a great number of people like the idea of the government (the tax-payers) taking care of them, but history tells us that eventually the government will run out of the other people's money...and by then, we will no longer recognize the America we once knew.

Conservatives have their Constitution. Progressives have their Narrative. The current battle for America is between these two concepts, and each side uses different rules to fight it. One set of rules is consistent with an unchanging objective, limited government and individual freedoms. The other side's rules are as fickle as their goals, which are never fully disclosed beyond the equivocal references to fairness and hyphenated forms of justice. They will have to remain vague and deny their true allegiances until a time when American voters will no longer squirm at the word "socialism."

And yet spotting them is not that hard. As a bird is known by his feathers, socialists are known by their Game. First tried and mastered in the USSR, the Game has since been popularized around the world, assuming various forms, names and colors...from red to brown to green. It is now taking hold in the United States under the blue web banners of Obama's campaign infomercials.

The laws of society and human nature are such that socialism can only be achieved through a certain sequence of steps and manipulations. For instance, the only way to attain material equality is to confiscate someone's property and give it to others. That necessitates a centralized mechanism of coercion, redistribution, and control. Such a system gives extraordinary corrupting powers to a small-centralized elite, while turning the rest of the citizenry into a compliant, obsequious herd.

All those who claim they can do it differently are doomed to retrace the same path. Once you unleash the ancient powers of collectivism, you have only two options, control the human herd or be trampled underfoot. Drawing blood is always an option, but there's also a "cleaner" way to control the crowds...by manipulating their minds with the cattle prods of collectivist morals and a fictional narrative that supplants the reality.

Let's call it The Mind Game of Manipulative Illusions.

The Game has existed since Cain and Abel, but it developed into an art form in the 20th century, with the rise of totalitarian regimes armed with state-controlled education, entertainment and the media. For a dictatorship to run efficiently, a sufficient number of people must give the regime a moral license to rule over them. The Mind Game of Manipulative Illusions secures and extends such a license.

Even the Soviet Communists, with all their tools of repression and fear, with all their power over everyone's life and death, were still pressed to play mind games to make the people feel good about the Party rule. Toward the end they went easy on the Game and relaxed their grip on the media, entertainment and education, accepting the policies of Glasnost. Once they lost the ability to control people's hearts and minds, they also lost their moral license and, with it, the country.

The Game can mutate and adjust to different cultures, but its basic rules always remain as follows:

Socialism is not just about taking away your money; it is also about making you praise the takers as your saviors. You are expected to feel good about being robbed of opportunities, talents and success. You must agree that "you did not build that." There must be a popular consensus that the crumbs you are getting back from the government are a sign of caring and largess...not a meager fraction of your actual earnings. Last but not least, you must sincerely believe that those in charge are trying to protect you from the thieves and your enemies... and those elements deserve to be destroyed.

Building up and maintaining such an illusion on a massive scale requires participation of the media, education and entertainment industries in a coordinated, long-term propaganda campaign. Once the illusion reaches a critical mass, those afflicted by it become immune to facts, numbers and/or rational arguments. Confronting them with logic will only cause more resentment, name-calling and sometimes…violence.

The little game of illusions that President Obama is running under the name of "tax cuts for the middle class" is part of the larger Game; it contains all of the above elements.

The plan is to pass yet another extension of Bush's tax cuts, to keep the status quo for most…while excluding families with a joint income of over $250,000. In plain talk, it is a tax hike. But calling things by their real names would be against the rules, and that is not how the Game is played. Listening to Obama now, one could never have guessed that these are the same Bush tax cuts that he had vigorously campaigned against in the past.

Simply put, Obama first discredits his predecessor's idea, and then steals it, bundles it with a job killing tax hike… and re-brands it as his own benevolent gift to the toiling masses.

Judging by the responses on Obama's official blog, WhiteHouse.gov and Twitter, many of his supporters believed they were actually going to get something out of all of this…but in reality, they are about to lose more than what they thought they had coming…due to the resulting cutbacks, layoffs, and price increases. The website "vaguely suggested" a possible $2,200 rebate to "families" if the Republicans would only "do the right thing" and work with Obama.

Join the herd and you will experience the collectivist sense of belonging, entitlement and empowerment by engaging in quixotic class struggle against the mythical windmills and all those mean-spirited capitalists who are conspiring to rob you of the rightful $2,200 disbursement you thought would be coming your way after Obama stuck it to the wealthy. Forget the phrase "policies that got us into this mess," the policies now are all about "doing the right thing."

You end up with a sincere belief that greedy corporations, Republicans, the Tea Party and the rest of the profligates opposing Obama's policies are the perfidious enemy who deserves to be punished and purged.

If you are wondering what kind of ignorant, misinformed and/or morally misguided fools would fall for this trick, look no further than Obama's most recent 56 percent job approval rating in the midst of a needlessly prolonged recession. The White House propagandist Stephanie Cutter knows her demographic and constructs simple phrases she believes they can understand. However, one question remains...if the Obama voters are the best and the brightest half of this nation, why does Ms. Cutter talk to them in the tone of a condescending kindergarten teacher?

The Game has a part for everyone, from top to bottom. As the top players obtain unprecedented powers, those at the bottom get high on the palliative illusion of safety and well-being. That illusion is as powerful as it is addictive, a mere exposure to the facts of life will cause the addict to writhe in agony. It is truly the Oxycontin for the masses. No presidential candidate can win on the promise of withdrawal; those who feel entitled to a pain-free existence will only vote for better and stronger illusions. The more the addiction spreads, the slimmer the chances of a realist ever occupying the White House again.

This can last as long as there are enough productive taxpayers to support the habit. Once they also get hooked, stop working, or the system runs out of resources, expect a fearsome, excruciating withdrawal of epic proportions. Until then, keep rational arguments to yourself unless you crave losing friends and alienating people. If you tell them that there is no such thing as a pain-free life, they will think you are some sadistic fascist who thrives on pain and takes pleasure in hurting people.

The problem with that attitude is that pain is nature's way to warn us of danger. If it burns, do not touch it. If it hurts, do not repeat it. People who are born without an ability to feel pain are incapable of learning safe behaviors and are doomed to live a short life of bumps, burns, broken bones and worse. A pain-free society would be even less viable.

The real choice, therefore, is between the occasional sharp pain of individual effort and the dull, permanent pain of collective misfortune, because re-distributive economies always end in misery, shortages, and corruption. Western Europe's gradual introduction to socialism is directly proportional to its gradual economic and moral decline, as evidenced by violent riots in response to inevitable austerity measures.

In the United States, the pain-free life will be even shorter if the country falls off a cliff.

When the painkillers become useless, The Game remedies it by directing the massive anger toward the opposition.

The perception of a relentless struggle with the opposition must be permanent and persuasive. Even in times of calm and prosperity the people must believe that the opposition is holding them hostage and only the firm, wise guidance of the People's Leader is saving them from imminent ruin. When the opponents are too few, too weak and too disoriented to put up a real fight, their power and influence must be exaggerated.

The Game has its logic: For socialism to work, there has to be unanimity and compliance. Dissent leads to system malfunctions, causing hardship for all those in the care of the state. That effectively makes the dissenter a traitor and a public enemy. The need to suppress opposition necessitates a totalitarian form of government. While we are not at that stage yet, the demonization of dissenters has already begun.

Until a time when the opposition can be eliminated completely, having opponents can still be useful; you can steal their ideas, take advantage of their desire to help the economy and blame them for any of your own failures. In the meantime, certain rules must be followed to control the public opinion and, through it, the opposition itself.

Maintain the perception of being constantly under attack. Do not examine the opponents' beliefs, nor answer their arguments. Discredit any media channels that offer them a platform. Enforce the following media template; the opposition is evil, treasonous, unfathomable and psychotic. They cannot be reasoned with. They are inspired by fascism and financed by a conspiracy of shady oligarchs. Defame their donors. Whatever the mischief you are planning to pull off, accuse them of doing it first; then proceed as planned, describing your actions as a necessary intervention. And above all, ridicule, ridicule, ridicule! Obama's standard comeback when challenged...

Imagine a scenario in which a theoretical group of left-wing radicals takes over America by playing the Game as described, then answer this question...how would their actions be different from what Obama, the Democrat Party and their allies are doing today?

The stated intentions and the feel-good, vague rhetoric are just words. If the results are the same, nothing else matters. We lose.

Socialist centrally planned economies invariably fail due to their inherent and integral failure to encourage, develop and nurture the essential potential of its people by a lack of incentive. Socialism is a failure because it suppresses the human spirit. Why else have so many thousands of people lost their lives in attempts to clandestinely escape their socialistic bondage and reach nations that embrace free market economies? In comparison, how many people have willingly left free market economies to move to socialist countries?

Due to its inability to foster, promote and develop the potential of people through incentives, centrally planned economies deprive the human spirit of ambition, aspiration, enterprise, determination and industry. What happens to the aspiration of a human being when there is essentially no reason to do anything? Nothing gets done.

Thus, lies the core flaw of collectivist economies: When you inform a laborer that it is essentially irrelevant whether they produce one wicket a day or a hundred, and it is also irrelevant whether those wickets are quality crafted or thrown together; that they will live in the same government owned apartment, shop at the same meager stores and be stuck in the same droning, monotonous job for the rest of their lives...their productivity falls steadily until almost nothing is produced. Multiply that effect by virtually every laborer in the nation, and you soon see why socialist economies are marked by long lines outside stores when the word gets out that they have soap, bread or eggs that day. Nobody is producing anything, thus nobody sells anything and therefore...there is nothing to buy.

At a time when the fault lines of capitalism are becoming exposed through the recent financial seismic shocks, it is a knee jerk reaction for the closet socialists to come out of the closet, dust off their tired rhetoric, and give it one more shot to convince the world to sing L'Internationale (Anthem of International Communism) in unison. The reason why each proponent of this deficient ideology, from Vladimir Lenin, to Mao Zedong, to John Lennon has failed is due to the barren wasteland that exists within the seductive allure of socialism to the poverty-stricken masses of the world. The fantasy of being able to "share the wealth of the state" is extremely tempting to those who toil in drudgery while the upper classes are whizzed by in their chauffeured limousines.

What they do not understand is that the state cannot create wealth, it can only administer it. Thus, the essence of socialism is one of universal impoverishment where even the hope that the lower classes can escape their poverty vaporizes along with the rest of the nation's productivity.

Socialism is the 20th century's greatest tragedy. Although its evangelists promised equality, prosperity and security, it has only produced misery, poverty and 100 percent of the time...it has all ended with tyranny.

Just as Madoff's Ponzi pyramid scheme initially showed staggering success, but then collapsed like the house of cards that it was, socialism demonstrates signs of success in its early stages. The essential problem is that all of the early gains, real or imagined, fade rapidly as the basic and inescapable deficiencies of the policies of a centrally controlled economy emerge.

I never thought that I would live to hear the Kremlin lecture Washington on the dangers of socialism (Vladimir Putin to Obama in 2012).

> "The democracy will cease to exist when you take away from those who are willing to work and give to those who would not."
>
> ~ Thomas Jefferson ~

Chapter 32

There is nothing new in the world today; the fools of humanity are destined to repeat...over and over again, the follies of the past. There's an old school saying that applies here: "We often return to where we've already been."

In our always changing world, "governmental change" is more often than not...nothing more than a new spin on past failures. The passage of time, coupled with the gullibility of the general public has always provided "many" politicians with unearned credibility.

Socialism and communism have been around, in various forms...since mankind first gathered together for survival. It always seems like a good idea in the beginning, but over time those utopian societies almost always mutated into some level of dictatorships...often including slavery, prison and even death. They have been dirty words in America for the last 60-plus years, but that's not to say that the promoters of these systems just gave-up and walked away. They understood that it would take time to bring Americans to accept the concept of this type of government and culture. They knew it could only be accomplished in a stealth-like manner, incrementally over a long period of time...from within. But even then, the marketing and promotional ideology plays an even bigger role in selling the product to the general public. It's now all about the "collective"...a level playing field for all. All for one...and one for all. "Collectivism," the euphemism for socialism sounds a lot more satisfactory to the average uneducated voters, but communism is still too strong a word to be tossing around.

I think most of us have viewed the word "collectivism" as a relatively newly coined word, but remember what the American Historical Association published in 1934 about giving careful consideration to what was being taught in our schools' social sciences classes...as far back as 1926. "The report concluded that the days of the 'individual' in the United States were coming to an end and that the future would be characterized, inevitably, by some form of 'collectivism' and an increase in the 'authority' of the State."

It is my guess that today's state-curriculum-schooled... and mainstream media educated voters, do not know or understand the differences and/or similarities between socialism, communism or fascism. I also doubt that they are familiar with how socialism can morph into communism or fascism. The Marxist socialists theory actually contends that socialism is just a transitional stage on the road to communism.

For many, many decades, the progressives have been propagating the false dichotomy that the choice confronting the world is only between communism and fascism. It should be obvious what the fraudulent issue of fascism versus communism accomplishes; it sets up, as opposites, two variants of the same political system and eliminates the possibility of considering capitalism...and by doing so, it switches the choice of ("Freedom or dictatorship?") into "Which kind of dictatorship?" Thus establishing dictatorship as an inevitable fact and offering only a choice of rulers. The choice, according to the proponents of the fraud...would be a dictatorship of the rich (fascism) or a dictatorship of the poor (communism).

It should be obvious and easily demonstrable that fascism and communism are not two opposites, but two rival gangs fighting over the same territory...and that both are variants of statism based on the collectivist principle that man is the "right-less" slave of the state. Both are socialistic in theory, in practice, and in the explicit statements of their leaders. Under both systems, the poor are enslaved and the rich are expropriated in favor of a ruling clique. Fascism is not the product of the political "right," but of the "left"...and the basic issue is not "rich versus poor," but man versus the state, and/or individual rights versus totalitarian government...which means, capitalism versus socialism.

The main characteristic of socialism and communism is the state's ownership of the means of production, and thereby, the abolition of private property. Under socialism, government officials acquire all the advantages of ownership, without any of the responsibilities, since they do not hold title to the property, but merely the right to use it...at least until the next purge.

Under fascism, citizens retain the responsibilities of owning property, without freedom to act and without any of the advantages of ownership.

In either case, the government officials hold the economic, political and legal power of life or death over the citizens.

Under both systems, sacrifices are invoked as a magic, omnipotent solution to any crisis, and "the public good" is the altar on which victims are immolated. But there are stylistic differences of emphasis. The socialist-communist axis keeps promising to achieve abundance, material comfort and security for its victims, in some indeterminate future. The fascist-Nazi axis scorns material comfort and security, and keeps extolling some undefined sort of spiritual duty, service and conquest. The socialist-communist axis offers its victims an alleged social ideal. The fascist-Nazi axis offers nothing but loose talk about some unspecified form of racial or national "greatness." The socialist-communist axis proclaims some grandiose economic plan, which keeps receding year by year. The fascist-Nazi axis merely extols leadership...leadership without purpose, program or direction, and power for power's sake.

A brave soul, John Mackey, CEO of Whole Foods, recently raised the specter of fascism when he was talking about the requirements of the top-down driven federal Obamacare system. Of course CNN quickly jumped in to defend Obama and his health care program while attacking Mackey, but he got the better of the exchange because the facts were on his side and Carol Costello came across as an ignoramus trying to make cheap political points.

"National Socialism, or fascism, was the ideology of Hitler's Nazi Party, a fact that scares most 'progressives' and even 'socialists' away from the use of the term. You realize when you say 'fascism' it brings up Nazi Germany and all sorts of ugly things," Costello challenged.

Mackey replied, "Apparently we can't use that word in America any longer, it's taboo; but while the term 'fascism' may have been a poor choice of words, it is technically true. He went on to note that traditionally, 'socialism' means that the government runs the means of production and in 'fascism' the means of production are still owned by private individuals but the government controls them. And what is happening is that our health care plan is moving...our health care system is moving away from free enterprise capitalism towards greater governmental control."

In the case of socialized medicine, it is a matter of the degree of control exercised by the federal government. Government direction can lead to outright ownership, which is probably where Obamacare is heading. All of these objectionable ideologies are on the left side of the political spectrum. Freedom and free enterprise are on the right side.

Fred Barnes wrote in The Wall Street Journal that Obama's inauguration speech proves that he is an "ideologically committed liberal" and not a "pragmatist or a centrist."

But Professor Paul Kengor is far more accurate when he describes Obama as a "hardcore leftist," a polite way of saying "Marxist."

The greatest threat to our economic prosperity and to the freedoms that we enjoy individually and collectively is not China or Russia or Iran. It is we. Numerous polls indicate that the majority of Americans profess to be in favor of smaller government and they strongly support the capitalist system. Yet, United States voters consistently endorse policies that grow government and inhibit free enterprise.

The typical American voter is ill informed and influenced by media and other biases while lacking effective comprehension of basic economic principles that are crucial to our nation's well being. Under these conditions, rather than frank debate and constructive action among politicians, it is rhetoric and marketing slogans that win elections. Factors such as a candidate's charisma, race and gender carry more weight than do competency and sound ideology.

The Orange County Register recently cited a study, co-authored by Yale University professor Gregory Huber, which identified "severe limitations in humans' ability to accurately and impartially judge the performance of politicians." Voters are influenced by rhetoric and marketing and by events such as hurricanes, shark attacks, even the outcomes of sporting events.

In his recent book "The Myth of the Rational Voter," economist Bryan Caplan expertly debunked a widely held notion among political scientists, known as the "miracle of aggregation." It presupposes that the collective errors of voters conveniently cancel out one another, thus neutralizing all biases among the uninformed electorate.

On the contrary, Mr. Caplan explains that the voting public is prone to systematic biases in a particular direction, most often in support of policies that grow government. More importantly, Mr. Caplan has identified the extent of the electorate's knowledge deficit and exposed its damaging effects on government policy decisions.

One of the primary causes of the voter knowledge gap is what economists term "rational ignorance." Given the extremely low probability that one vote will turn any election, it is irrational to expend the considerable time and effort necessary to become fully informed. Hence, voters act rationally and remain uninformed. Typical voters are educated passively by whatever information they become exposed to via the media, from talking with friends, etc. The result is that many voters cast a ballot largely based on emotion shaped by rhetoric and marketing slogans. The principle reasons for voting often relate to a sense of patriotic duty or to achieving personal emotional satisfaction.

In case you didn't already know, you are surrounded by a majority of ignorant/self-serving voters who will not have even noticed the subtle, incremental changes in America's foundation...well, not until it is too late and we have become the Socialist States of America.

The Heritage Foundation, a conservative think tank, and the Wall Street Journal have released their annual Index of Economic Freedom, which ranks 185 nations on the basis of rule of law, limited government, regulatory efficiency and open markets.

According to the survey, "the foundations of economic freedom are weakening around the world. Particularly concerning, is the rise of populist 'democratic' movements that use the coercive power of government to redistribute income and control economic activity."

As Winston Churchill once said, "Democracies are the worst form of government...except for all the others."

But freedom to choose leaders is no guarantee of wise leadership. As Heritage's study explains, there are no guarantees. Just as corrupt political systems keep poorer countries poor, democracies, too, can undermine wealth and prosperity.

In the post-Arab Spring Middle East, some democratically elected governments are adopting totalitarian practices reminiscent of revolutionary Iran or the Taliban. Economic freedom can not flourish under the arbitrary rule of authoritarians and despots, and it has declined significantly in Egypt, Tunisia, Algeria and Saudi Arabia, among other countries.

Over-reaching governments have debilitating economic effects. Economic favoritism and cronyism in advanced democracies also are economically stifling. The Heritage report catalogs a dozen ways government privileges for special interests hurt productivity and reduce efficiency. Resultant harm from "the pathology of privilege" also erodes political integrity by favoring the rich and powerful.

Whether government wealth redistribution is engineered by un-elected despots or by representatives elected in advanced democracies, the tendency can resemble the axiom that democracy should be more than two wolves and a sheep, voting on what to have for dinner.

Top-down income and wealth transfers compromise property rights and reduce incentives to work and invest, Heritage found. By contrast, promoting the rule of law and protection from arbitrary government regulation ensure fairness, which, "as documented in years of empirical data, promotes higher incomes and faster growth."

The United States increasingly is moving toward re-distributive economic solutions. It is ranked 10th-most free this year. But like Ireland, the United States has lost economic freedom, as judged by Heritage, five years in a row. Indeed, almost all "most-advanced countries" lost ground this year. Even top-ranked Hong Kong's score declined because of government spending increases and higher inflation.

Heritage blames the worldwide slowdown in economic liberalization on the lack of United States leadership, noting that trade flow declined with the stagnation of the United States' economy, and protectionism threatening consumers and businesses with higher costs and restricted supply.

Ill-conceived banking regulations such as the Dodd-Frank law generate uncertainty and anxiety. Investment freedom declines in the face of higher costs and new legal and tax liabilities such as those introduced by Obamacare.

United States policy-makers should take note, and would be well-advised to reverse government's detrimental trends, which not only resemble those of despots stifling prosperity elsewhere, but also affect other nations' well-being.

Our government continues its drive to take over more and more of our daily lives by always increasing the number of personal decisions it makes for us. Undoubtedly, individuals do make a lot of mistakes, and those mistakes can prove extremely damaging. Most of us can look back over our own lives and see the many mistakes we made, including some that were life altering.

Implicit in the wide range of efforts on the "Left" to allow government to take over more and more of our decisions for us, is the assumption that they are some type of superior class of people who are either wiser or nobler than the rest of us...our "betters" if you will.

Yes, we all make mistakes. But do governments not make bigger and more catastrophic mistakes?

Think about the First World War, nations on both sides ended up worse off than before, after an unprecedented carnage that killed substantial portions of the younger generations and left millions starving amid the rubble of war.

What about the Holocaust, and other governments that slaughtered even more millions of innocent men, women and children under Communist governments in the Soviet Union and China?

Even in the United States, government policies in the 1930s led to crops being plowed under, thousands of little pigs being slaughtered and buried, and milk being poured down sewers, at a time when many Americans were suffering from hunger and diseases caused by malnutrition.

The Great Depression of the 1930s, in which millions of people were plunged into poverty in even the most prosperous nations, was needlessly prolonged by government policies now recognized in retrospect as foolish and irresponsible.

One of the key differences between mistakes that we make in our own lives and mistakes made by governments is that bad consequences force us to correct and/or deal with our mistakes. But government officials cannot admit to making a mistake without jeopardizing their whole careers.

Can you imagine a president of the United States saying to the mothers of America, "I am sorry your sons were killed in a war I never should have gotten us into?"

What is even more unsettling about having our "betters" telling us how to live our lives, is that so many oppressive and even catastrophic government policies were cheered on by the intelligentsia.

Back in the 1930s, for example, totalitarianism was considered to be "the wave of the future" by much of the intelligentsia, not only in the totalitarian countries themselves but in democratic nations as well.

The Soviet Union was being praised to the skies by such literary luminaries as George Bernard Shaw in Britain and Edmund Wilson in America, while literally millions of people were being systematically starved to death by Stalin and masses of others were being shipped off to slave labor camps.

Even Hitler and Mussolini had their supporters or apologists among intellectuals in the Western democracies, including at one time Lincoln Steffens and W.E.B. Du Bois.

An even larger array of the intellectual elite in the 1930s opposed the efforts of Western democracies to respond to Hitler's massive military buildup with offsetting military defense buildups to deter Hitler or to defend themselves if deterrence failed.

"Disarmament" was the mantra of the day among the intelligentsia, often garnished with the suggestion that the Western democracies should "set an example" for other nations...as if Nazi Germany or imperial Japan was likely to follow their example.

Too many amongst today's intellectual elite see themselves as our shepherds and us as their sheep. Tragically, too many of us are apparently willing to be sheep, in exchange for being taken care of, being relieved of the burdens of adult responsibility and being supplied with "free" stuff paid for by others.

There are none so blind as those who will not see...(you cannot make someone pay attention to something that he or she does not desire to acknowledge).

> "Liberty is not collective (collectivism), it is personal. All liberty is individual liberty."
>
> ~ Calvin Coolidge ~

Chapter 32: Part 2

While Obamacare (enacted by Congress without even reading it) was framed as necessary and benevolent, it was in fact the classic con…"something for nothing." That "something" is now being slowly exposed as an ever-growing financial albatross with many, many questionable attributes. The "for nothing" (it was actually promoted as budget neutral) snake-oil-sales-pitch came with a very high price tag; not the least of which is more and more government control over our daily lives. And this was not just a by-product of the legislation; it was by design… about more and more control, and by extension…less freedom/liberties for the people.

Healthcare is one-sixth of our economy. If the government can control healthcare (Obamacare), they can control any…and everything.

Many people were probably bothered (as I was) by the idea that New York's Mayor Michael Bloomberg wanted to dictate how much sugary soda a person legally could purchase from restaurants, pushcart vendors and fast-food joints.

How dare Big Brother impose some bureaucrat's myopic vision of the dividing line between healthy and unhealthy!

It is a valid complaint, as far as it goes. It should be none of the government's business how much my belly hangs over my belt, or how far your derriere extends over the edges of the swivel chair at McDonalds.

Our obesity, should we choose to be obese, is our business. Where do they get off telling us to drink healthier or to eat more reasonably? After all, it is our money. Our choice. Our consequences. Well, not exactly.

Government, whose legitimate authority is supposed to be to protect peoples' rights, is instead becoming the fulfiller of wants and desires and provider of comfort and care. In particular, their health-care.

We, the public, who are so willing to hand over responsibility for our consequences to faceless bureaucracies, do not seem to connect the dots when the same bureaucracies insist that we quit running up the health care tab by consuming super-sized burgers, fries and 32-ounce Cokes.

An old adage applies here: "He who pays the piper calls the tune." After telling the government to pay the bills, why are we surprised the government imposes conditions on what it will pay for?

Consequently, the government increasingly calls the tune: Eat this, do not eat that, and drink only this much, not more.

Ironically, this Nanny State's effort to corral our appetites is, in a sense…a more fiscally responsible act than when we give Big Brother the responsibility to pay for our health care. At least the government recognizes the money pit isn't bottomless. There must be limits. And some bureaucrat, or politician, will be happy to set those limits.

This is the inevitable upshot when government plays nanny. Don't blame the bureaucrats and politicians. They are simply following our lead. We said, "Take care of us." They took our taxes and found that even those huge amounts of cash do not cover our even larger appetites for everything we insist the government provide.

To spend more responsibly, they will tell us what is acceptable behavior and what is not. If you were paying someone else's bills, wouldn't you insist on responsible behavior before cutting the check?

Unfortunately, we the public want our cheeseburgers and 32-ounce sugary drinks but do not want to pay for the consequences like cardiac care, diabetes treatment and joint replacements. Who is the irresponsible party here? The government? Well, not exactly.

The Sacramento Bee recently reported that government spending on health care in California now exceeds what is spent on the entire state general-fund budget. Medicare and Medicaid spending in California doubled over the past 15 years, even after adjusting for inflation.

We have come a long way. Many can remember a time when government spent next to nothing to provide such stuff.

The nonpartisan Congressional Budget Office estimates that nation-wide, spending on those programs will rise from 5 percent of the nation's gross domestic product today to 10 percent by 2037. That is one of every 10 dollars produced by the United States economy to pay for government-financed health care.

In 2011 the government spent six times as much on Medicare and Medicaid as on unemployment benefits. If food stamp spending has become a problem, and it has... the government spent 16 times as much on Medicare and Medicaid. If Social Security's finances are in trouble, and they are...government spent about 65 percent more on Medicare and Medicaid, according to the Bureau of Economic Analysis.

Even irresponsible spendthrifts, such as those at the controls of all these federal entitlements, know enough about balance sheets to recognize the government has to stop the fiscal bleeding. Consequently, we who cherish our personal freedoms increasingly are dictated to on matters as mundane as portion sizes for sugary drinks.

Couple this fiscal responsibility with the seemingly irrepressible urge to force people to do what the government deems worth doing, and we get laws like Obamacare, which tells us what health care services we may have... and like Bloomberg's drink limitations.

"Whichever way the wind blows"...it is almost universally true that politicians do not lead, they follow. They follow our lead. So, for the most part, we get the government we deserve.

[illegible]

CHAPTER 33

By this point in my writing, I was thinking that even though America has been attacked from every possible angle, she is still fighting...and that perhaps the worst was behind us. But there is no end to our enemies who are looking to transform America and everything it stands for. For the most part, our adversaries have come from within...but there are even darker international forces working to reduce America to a non-entity in a new one-world-order controlled by the super-wealthy, global elitists and high-ranking government officials from around the globe. Untold wealth is no longer enough for these ultra egos...they are now seeking the ultimate goal, complete control of the planet and everything within the kingdom...absolute control.

Is Bilderberg a secret conspiracy?

The Bilderberg Secretariat proclaims the conferences to be private in order "to encourage frank and open discussion." Frank and open discussion is a good thing in any forum but when those doing the discussing are some of the very most powerful financiers and media tycoons in the world it begs the question: If what they discuss is for the good of ordinary people why not publicize it? Isn't it a distorted use of the word "open" when no one can find out what they're taking about?

When such rich and powerful people meet up in secret, with military intelligence managing their security, with hardly a whisper escaping of what goes on inside, people should be suspicious. But the true power of Bilderberg comes from the fact that participants are in a bubble, sealed off from reality and the devastating implications of the black-science economic solutions on their conference table.

No...it's not a "conspiracy." The world's leading financiers and foreign policy strategists don't get together at Bilderberg to draw up their "secret plans for the future." It's much subtler than that. These meetings create an artificial "consensus" in an attempt to spellbind visiting politicians and other men of influence. Blair has fallen for this hook, line and sinker. It's about reinforcing...often to the very people who are on the edge of condemning Globalization, the illusion that Globalization is "good, popular and that it's inevitable."

Bilderberg is an extremely influential lobbying group. That's not to say that the organizers don't have a hidden agenda, they do, namely accumulation of wealth and power into their own hands while explaining to the participants that globalization is for the good of all. It is also a very good forum for "interviewing" potential future political figures such as Clinton (1991) and Blair (1993).

The ideology put forth at the Bilderberg conferences is that what's good for banking and big business is good for the mere mortals of the world. Silently banished are the critical voices, those that might point out that debt is spiraling out of control, that wealth is being sucked away from ordinary people and into the hands of the faceless corporate institutions, that millions are dying as a direct result of the global heavyweight Rockefeller/Rothschild economic strategies.

When looking at one of the (partially reliable) participant lists it should be remembered that quite a number of participants are invited in an attempt to get them on-board the globalization project. These are carefully selected people of influence, who have been openly critical of globalization. Examples are Jonathan Porritt (environmentalist at Bilderberg's 1999 meeting) and Will Hutton (British newspaper columnist at Bilderberg's 1997 meeting), but there have been many others. Most of this type of participants are happy to speak about the conference afterwards, and may even be refreshingly critical.

The Bilderberg organizers are accepted, by those "in the know," as the prophets of Capitalism. Will Hutton, deputy Editor of The Observer newspaper in London and left-leaning Economist, described private clubs of the elite as being masterminded by "The High Priests of Globalization." The ecclesiastical allusion is not accidental. The Bilderberg high priests are a force against good, out to wipe morality from the earth. For the organizers, Bilderberg Conferences are an annual ideological assault by the world's most power-hungry people. Not content with owning unimaginable amounts of money and property, they want to use that wealth to acquire even more power for themselves. Power is the most dangerous and addictive drug known to man. Will the craving be satisfied when a handful of men own and control everything on earth?

And just like the Nazi party in the 1930s, the global Capitalist Elite are rising in power by peaceful means. But there are some very uncomfortable and unexplained connections between Bilderberg and the Nazis through the Conference's founder, Prince Bernhard (pathological liar and Nazi background).

While it appeared peaceful on the surface, the Nazis used violence at the sharp end, the removal of dissidents by whatever means, the repossession of homes that men and women had worked a lifetime for, the needless deaths from starvation and geopolitical machinations... but terms relating to force are notable by their "current" absence from the annual meetings.

One can not help but wonder, once the Bilderberg organizers, Rothschild, Rockefeller, Kissinger and the rest of their cohorts have completed their scheme of enclosing all global goods and services into the hands of the elite, and taken total control of the media (of course they already control most of the mainstream media) to prevent the people from fully understanding the magnitude of their takeover...then what? What happens when the men who would be gods turn out to be the global devils?

If you are wondering who is responsible for so much of the capital-friendly and dissent-crushing law making, poverty and general misery in the world, this may be the place to look. This is the closest approximation to a transatlantic shadow government. And this is another hidden agenda at Bilderberg.

There may be other groups pulling the strings behind Bilderberg's Steering Group, possibly even high degree occult groups such as The Masons or Illuminati...but that is "conspiracy theory," Bilderberg is not.

There must certainly be some sociopathic minds behind Bilderberg since they go to so much trouble to promote policies that lead to exploitation, inequality and despair. These individuals seem oddly switched off from the suffering they are clearly causing. Surely only pernicious people would want to control the ideology of the world's mainstream press, and undermine natural political discourse. Public opinion and democratic institutions are a threat when you want to own the world.

The perverse objective of The Bilderberg Steering Group is to dress totalitarian ideology up to appear rational and push it out, un-attributable, for mass consumption under Chatham House rules. Meanwhile, outside the Bilder-bubble, "money-is-God" and globalization is the new religion. The greedy are given a pat on the back as they plunder the earth and do their best to destroy the human spirit.

The Bilderberg Group, is an annual, unofficial, invitation-only conference of approximately 120 to 140 guests from North America and Western Europe, most of whom are people of influence. About one-third are from government and politics, and two-thirds from finance, industry, labor, education and communications. Meetings are closed to the public.

The original conference was held at the Hotel de Bilderberg, near Arnhem in the Netherlands, between May 29 and 31, 1954. Interestingly, the 50s were a time of grave concern for America...as communism was working its way into America's consciousness. It has been an undercurrent ever since.

In his 1980 essay, The Bilderberg and the West, researcher Peter Thompson argued that the Bilderberg group was a meeting ground for top executives from the world's leading multinational corporations and top national political figures to consider jointly the immediate and long-term problems facing the West. According to Thompson, Bilderberg itself was not an executive agency, but that when Bilderberg participants reached a form of consensus about what was to be done, they had at their disposal...powerful transnational and national instruments for bringing about what they wanted to come to pass. That their consensus design is not always achieved, he concludes, is a reflection of the strength of competing resisting forces outside the capitalist ruling class and within it.

The Bilderberg group is not alone in its long-running effort to transform the current world order. There are other, ambiguous connecting organizations working toward the same goals with some big name members and/or attendees coordinating back and forth between the groups.

The Council on Foreign Relations (CFR) is an American nonprofit, nonpartisan membership organization, publisher, and think tank specializing in United States foreign policy and international affairs. Founded in 1921 and headquartered at 58 East 68th Street in New York City, with an additional office in Washington, D.C., the CFR is considered to be the nation's "most influential foreign-policy think tank."

Seven American presidents have addressed the Council, three while still in office...Bill Clinton, George W. Bush and Obama.

When Hamilton Fish Armstrong announced in 1970 that he would be leaving the helm of the Council on Foreign Affairs after 45 years, "David Rockefeller" became chairman.

The Trilateral Commission is a non-governmental, non-partisan discussion group founded by "David Rockefeller" in July 1973, to foster closer cooperation among the United States, Europe and Japan.

The dots are easily connected unless one doesn't want to see, but there's a larger group that just can't see it..."the enslavement conspiracy."

The Illuminati, Round Table, Council on Foreign Relations, Chatham House, the Trilateral Commission, the Bilderberg Group, Skull and Bones, the International Monetary Fund, and the United Nations, are all Brotherhood created and controlled, as are the media, military, CIA, Mossad, science, religion, and the Internet, with witting or unwitting support from the London School of Economics. At the apex of the Brotherhood stands the "Global Elite," identified throughout history as the Illuminati, and at the top of the Global Elite stand the "Prison Wardens." The goal of the Brotherhood...their "Great Work of Ages"...is world domination and a micro-chipped population.

"Telesis" is the purposeful use of natural and social forces; it is "planned progress." Telesis or planned progress, was a concept and neologism coined by the American sociologist Lester Frank Ward (often referred to as the "father of American sociology"), in the late 19th century to describe directed social advancement via education and the scientific method.

Power no longer resides in the church or the state, but in the manipulation of words, images and symbols... as in the power of reality engineering. In the past, the church and state held a monopoly on this power. Today, this power is with the media. The popular media was the first to show people other ways of life...outside the clenched provincialism and parochialism of their family and community. Cultural currents were able to cross-pollinate each other and the media was able to confer cosmopolitanism even on rural America. The media is the foundation of the emerging Global Village and the key to the alchemical Great Work of manifesting the Aeon.

Alchemy is an influential philosophical tradition whose early practitioners' claims of profound powers have been known from antiquity. The word aeon also eon, originally meant "life" and/or "being," though it also tends to mean "age," "forever" or "for eternity."

The influence of advertising and indoctrination... all promoted by the mainstream media, is how the government (over many, many decades) has finally dumbed the masses down enough to manipulate their minds and thereby control their lives.

In ritual, the contents of the mind are exteriorized into the environment. Objects that are symbolic of desires and abstract principles are manipulated physically, mimicking mental process. All of the props, tools, elements, and actions of ritual are means to activate, engage, and focus our attention and intent away from the truth, "their" reality-engineering power.

Media is also an exteriorization of the contents of the mind into the environment. Mass media is an environmental exteriorization of the contents of the collective minds. Any process that would unfold through ritual or meditative manipulation of word, image and symbol can be carried out on the mass scale, through the media, to the collective consciousness of humanity.

What words, images, values and traditions are holding us captive today? These controlling elements should be identified and isolated, we should then endeavor to sin against them in thoughts, words and deeds. Disrupt, disorientate, destabilize and destroy. We can create homo novis (new man) out of ourselves. The process will unfold at a level "below the individual and collective consciousness, where mind and matter are not yet differentiated."

I find the term "reality engineering" particularly interesting when used in connection with achieving the "alchemical Great Work of manifesting the Aeon" (the goal of the Illuminati) through the use of the mass media; and the creation of "homo novis," a term used by L. Ron Hubbard (Church of Scientology) in the original Dianetics. Dianetics is a set of ideas and practices regarding the metaphysical relationship between the mind and body.

The Illuminati conspiracy becomes even more bizarre when attention is focused on the backside of the United States' dollar bills. Since being designed in 1782 and printed on the back of the dollar bill since 1935, the Great Seal has had a mysterious image of the Egyptian pyramid with the Latin inscription Novus Ordo Seclorum (New Order of the Ages, but often mistranslated as "New World Order"), which is professed to be the ultimate goal of the Illuminati. Additionally, above the pyramid is a glowing, suspended capstone with the all-seeing eye of Horus, the Egyptian sun god. Interestingly, it is precisely the "Age of Horus" (When humanity will enter a time of self-realization, self-actualization and self-loving.), which the Illuminati are foreseeing as the beginning of the "end and the crowning of the Pyramid." Realizing that these facts about the symbolic image on our American dollar bill can be tied directly to the motto and plots of the Illuminati cult is a bizarre and somewhat disturbing reality.

And just as interesting is the fact that the inscription also appears on the coat of arms of the Yale School of Management, Yale University's business school. The Skull and Bones organization was founded in 1832...at Yale University.

In this Aeon of Horus there is no such thing as "sin." The very concept of something being sinful is a lie and an obstacle to self-fulfillment. Every person will be governed by his or her own self-will and self-interest. We will be allowed to truly be "lovers of our own selves"...and no one else will be able to say anything about it.

Many in the world believe that we are now entering the much-awaited Aeon of Horus or what others have called the Age of Aquarius. It is said to be a time of great spiritual awakening. A time of visitations from "ascended Masters" who will lead mankind in its evolution into a higher form of self. You can see this message being pushed in the music and broader entertainment industries, in politics, in education, in religion...in every worldly system.

They believe that with the coming of Lucifer, the Age of Horus will be at an end and Lucifer will commune with his chief human disciples of the Illuminati to begin energizing their "Great Work" to establish the "New Age"... his antichrist kingdom over the planet.

What is the main obstacle holding back all of mankind from these great advancements and supernatural revelations? Those who are still "stuck" in believing that their way to God is the only way, i.e. Christianity. The closer we move to this anticipated age, the more we will see concerted efforts to discredit Jesus Christ in every arena as well as a sharp increase in the disavowing of Christian principles...even by professing believers. The new agers call this our "awakening" as we transition out of the Age of Pisces into the Age of Aquarius; the Scriptures call it the great apostasy.

> Let no man deceive you by any means: for that day shall not come, except there come a falling away first, and that man of sin be revealed, the son of perdition; who opposeth and exalteth himself above all that is called God, or that is worshipped; so that he as God sitteth in the temple of God, shewing himself that he is God.
>
> 2 Thessalonians 2:3-4
> King James Version (KJV)

Chapter 34

The confiscation of wealth has begun, at least in Cyprus:

For a long time now, we have been watching and reading about the governments of many of the world's developed countries falling into bankruptcy...like dominos, and the social unrest and chaos that followed. The shell games that governments play with their citizens are well documented throughout ancient and modern history. But this problem is only getting worse.

At the highest level, what is the value of paper money? The paper money system (ever since it was de-linked from gold) is based on the faith and trust in the government behind it. The value of one's currency is only as strong as your ability to trust your government.

Since the financial crisis hit the world back in 2008, we have observed the lack of credibility and faith in governments. As the tide of excessive credit in the world receded, we could see who was swimming naked in the financial oceans. Governments, which aided the credit-fueled expansions by feeding its citizens the drug of easy credit, have all started showing signs of decay and declaring bankruptcy.

First to go are the smaller nations like Iceland, Greece, Ireland, Spain and now Cyprus. Soon the bankruptcy wave will spread to larger nations like Italy, France and Britain. Finally, we will see the largest nations fall prey to the wave of defaults. We have already seen the AAA credit rating of the United States, France, Britain and other large countries fall. That is the first step in the draconian measures that will get imposed on its citizens.

While I do not cast all governments as evil, I do cast their passion to rescue their citizens as misguided bungling. The governments are delusional in expecting that they can resolve all the ills that afflict us, and their attempts at rescues are nothing short of incompetence. There is no way to avoid the collapse of our current boom, brought about by reckless credit expansion. Yet the governments keep trying to avoid it, by ignoring it.

First they aid the credit expansion-induced overindulgence and when the game is up, they create hostile laws to make us pay for their overindulgences.

Let's talk about the unlimited printing of money that all governments have undertaken. Let's talk about the purchase of its own debt with its largesse of printed money. Let's talk about imposing a tax on savings in bank accounts. If we as citizens were to undertake any of these activities on our own, we would certainly be hauled off to jail.

This new imposition of a tax on personal savings in Cyprus is nothing short of robbery that the governments want to impose on its citizens. We have elected governments, which by definition are governments elected by the people, for the people. In this case, the government elected in Cyprus is by the people but not for the people.

Thank goodness that for now, the people have rejected this attempt, but this is a real wake up call regarding the extent governments will go to in their effort to grab our hard-earned money.

Unfortunately this kind of robbery is not unusual for governments. From the ancient days of the Roman, Spanish, Ottoman, British...and all other empires, governments have imposed draconian laws to loot the citizenry when they are done spending all the money they can get their hands on.

> "Hold on to the Constitution, for if the American Constitution should fail, there will be anarchy throughout the world."
>
> ~ Senator Daniel Webster, 1851 ~

The official oaths of office in the United States of America call for a solemn pledge to defend our Constitution against all enemies, both foreign and domestic. Yet our nation's system of checks and balances, as defined by the Constitution, are being systematically dismantled. Leftist intellectuals, radical activists, and elected government officials have forced us into a constitutional crisis of the first order.

Enemies of the United States of America...of both the foreign and domestic varieties would love nothing better than to destroy the very foundation of this nation...our Constitution!

Tyrannical leaders around the world and in all time periods since our founding have despised our Constitution because it represents everything despots hate: Government of the people, by the people, and for the people!

I am convinced that the greatest threat to our Constitution now comes from within our own borders, America's homegrown...domestic enemies. Never before has this document that was forged in the flames of the American Revolution come under such a withering attack from those who call themselves American citizens.

Even our own federal officials have systematically hacked away at the Constitution in recent years. Leftist members of the federal bureaucracy, regardless of which party was in political power...have proven to the American people time and again that they will stop at nothing to further their socialist agenda, including:

- ➢ The overt subversion of the Constitution.
- ➢ Continual sidestepping of one or more of the Branches granted power by the Constitution.
- ➢ Enactment of Executive Orders, mandates, regulations and/or other initiatives with little or no review or oversight.
- ➢ Overt deceit, distortion, and demagoguery to sway public opinion and bring discredit on the lawful procedures laid out in the Constitution.

The bottom line is this; the Constitution of the United States is being systematically assaulted in order to form a more socialized union!

Most Americans do not begin to realize how far we have already strayed from the principles our Founding Fathers laid down in the Constitution.

When Daniel Webster spoke of "anarchy throughout the world" more than 160 years ago, he could have been speaking of our own time! True anarchy is spreading worldwide, and even here in America.

By uncoupling government from the Constitution, we are starting even now to see the chaos and lawlessness that Webster predicted. It is easy to track how all this has happened.

Socialists in the media and academic world, liberals in Congress...the Hollywood elitists and radical demonstrators who seek their own agenda; these disparate groups have all worked to undermine the bedrock of American government.

The enemies of American exceptionalism know the Constitution is our nation's foundation and that its subversion will be the fastest way to change America into a society of "their" liking!

A one-sentence editorial that appeared in the Peoria Journal Star:

"A pen in the hand of this president is far more dangerous than a gun in the hands of 200 million law-abiding citizens."

Chapter 35

During his first term, Obama's spin was that he had no interest in gun control of any kind, but today he has an agenda...the one from the back burner that was just waiting for his re-election. Today, he's going on and on about gun control...telling us it is time to move on, we have waited long enough. Who the hell does he think he is? Is he more powerful than the Constitution? The 2nd amendment is in place to protect us from him! The 2nd amendment is in place to protect us from Dianne Feinstein! The 2nd amendment is in place to protect us from the whole damn bunch of these control freaks. That is why the 2nd amendment is there, and all the rest of the Constitution's amendments! Our elected officials are pushing to trash the Constitution and by extension...take away more and more of our Constitutional, guaranteed freedoms and liberties.

Is Obama positioning himself to carry out a hostile military takeover of the United States? There just seems to be a lot of thought provoking, Internet chatter around the subject these days. I have always believed it would be impossible for any one person to stage a military or hostile takeover of the United States. But we would not be the first country where the people paid dearly for their denial of the obvious. As in, "It couldn't happen here!"

During the past year, Obama has taken a number of actions that when added together clearly indicates that something is amiss; is it a developing plan for a military or hostile takeover of the United States? For the first time in my life, I not only believe it could happen, but that it could happen before the 2016 election.

To begin with, Obama has been tailoring the United States military to his personal agenda. He is filling the ranks with gays and lesbians who will now follow him to any extreme because he is their champion. He has all but shackled chaplains from preaching Christianity to the troops, who by the way, are not even allowed to have Bibles in some areas in the Middle East or any other semblance of Christianity. For the military coup de grace, he has been tailoring his top military leaders by asking them if they would be willing to shoot Americans (covered this issue earlier). Those who answered yes are placed in key positions while those who answered no are basically seeing the end of their military careers.

Additionally, the Department of Homeland Security has been stockpiling weapons and well over a billion rounds of ammunition...and "body bags." The federal government even has the NOAA (National Oceanic and Atmospheric Administration) stockpiling weapons and ammunition...and they are not going to be using them to predict the weather. This is unprecedented in American history and has no purpose or basis other than to be used against the American people. (As with my earlier question to the debunkers, Snopes and TruthOrFiction also danced around the subject matter in the preceding paragraph; they were unable to come up with anything on the subject...one way or the other.)

During the writing of this book, I have had friends "tactfully" ask me..."if this is really true...why hasn't Fox News addressed the situation?" (We, of course, know that the mainstream media is not going to acknowledge anything that would reflect negatively on their idol.) My answer was/is..."political correctness' muzzle." Glenn Beck, Pat Buchanan and other lesser known commentators, journalists and advocates for the truth...have paid high prices for speaking out against the administration.

The current massive push for gun control has only one purpose and that is to disarm the American people. There are more guns in private ownership than there are people in the United States. That would make a hostile takeover more difficult, costly and time consuming. However, the stockpiles of weapons and ammunition are for just that purpose, because Obama knows that there are a lot of Americans who will not give up their guns so easily. Attorney General Eric Holder has already warned gun owners to cower like smokers.

One of the problems with the guns in the hands of people is that the government doesn't know where they all are. That is why they are pushing for complete gun registration and background checks for everyone who owns a firearm, regardless of any grand-fathered clauses. Under Obamacare, they are even pushing doctors and medical staffers to gather information on their patients as to whether or not they own a gun.

Under the National Defense Authorization Act, the federal government has the legal right to indefinitely detain anyone they deem to be dangerous to the country. They do not have to produce any evidence, they do not have to obtain a warrant, and they do not have to give you the right to an attorney. All Obama or Eric Holder have to do is say you are a threat and that could be the last anyone sees of you for who knows how long.

Obama has also issued an executive order that gives him absolute power and control over all means of communication for any reason including an emergency. The executive order includes all television, radio, cable, Internet and cell phone communications.

Lastly, Obama is already placing drones in the skies over America. His chief puppet, Attorney General Eric Holder had ruled that not only are the drones legal, but that Obama also has the legal right to use them to shoot Americans on American soil. Holder was later forced to back away from his statement about the drones after Senator Rand Paul called him out...in front of Congress and the American people.

When you put this all together into one package, it is obvious that the stage is being set for Obama to use force in a hostile takeover of the United States. All he has to do is declare a state of emergency (most likely prompted by a forced economic collapse). This will allow him to control all forms of communication. Both military and DHS (Department of Homeland Security) trained personnel will then start rounding up everyone that has or still opposes Obama and detain them under the National Defense Authorization Act. Those who resist will face lethal force from the drones and/or the heavily armed military and DHS troops. Anyone resisting could be shot, since he claims to have the legal authority to do so.

If Obama feared a threat from another nation, he would not be slashing military spending, cutting our nuclear arsenal down to a third of what it was and he would not have the NOAA stockpiling weapons and ammunition. Everything Obama has being doing and putting in place is pointed inside the United States, not outside. We are the target(s), not Iran, Syria, China, North Korea or al-Qaeda.

If you do not believe this will happen prior to the 2016 election, then please explain to me the purpose of all these things that have been strategically placed at this time. I would suggest you do a little studying of history about nations like Germany, Russia, China and other socialist nations. They all thought it could never happen to them, but it did...and it all started with a tyrant just like Obama gaining power and outlawing guns!

Our government has been in the brainwashing business for decades, starting with MK Ultra...the CIA's mind control program sanctioned during the 1950s. The majority of parents send their children to government schools. What do they think their children are going to learn besides reading, writing, and arithmetic (even if they learn those subjects)? They're going to learn how, to learn...to love the State.

It reminds me of the film Dr. Strangelove, or "How I Learned to Stop Worrying and Love the Bomb" (1964).

In terms of government education, it is "How I Learned to Stop Worrying and Love the State."

In 1995, Eric Holder delivered the following message to the Women's National Democratic Club:

- "One thing that I think is clear with young people and with adults as well...is that we just have to be repetitive about this. It is not enough to simply have a catchy ad on a Monday and then only do it every Monday. We need to do this every day of the week and just really 'brainwash' people into thinking about guns in a vastly different way."

Brainwashing is designed to teach falsehoods, to get someone to throw away logic, experience, and observable facts and to adopt an irrational worldview. The facts are on the side of private gun ownership. There are two ways to change this:

1) Brainwash people in re-education centers (government schools) to get them to believe otherwise.

2) Use force when brainwashing does not work. It doesn't hurt to have a government-supporting media on your side to propagate the State-sponsored brainwashing.

Cults have become experts in brainwashing techniques. The goal "involves the systematic breakdown of a person's sense of self." The new self is found in the collective... the State-defined group. Think about Jonestown. Nearly 1,000 people willingly laid down their lives because they had been brainwashed by Jim Jones.

In nearly every government school across the nation students are fed a steady diet of group-thinking, anti-free market propaganda, and pro-government messages. Government education is said to be "free." When high school graduates go off to college, they are told that the government will make low-interest loans available to them, keep them subsidized on their parents' healthcare insurance policy until they are 26-years old, and possibly forgive their loans if they can not pay. Who made all this possible? The Government...the State!

The goal is to promote dependency so that it's hard to say no to the Cult of the State.

"Cults demand absolute, unquestioning devotion, loyalty and submission. A cult member's sense of self is systematically destroyed. Ultimately, feelings of worthlessness and 'evil' become associated with independence and critical thinking, and feelings of warmth and love become associated with unquestioning submission." This is exactly what our government wants... complete and unquestioning devotion to the State. The State becomes the substitute parent.

The philosophy of Georg F. W. Hegel (1770 - 1831), followed by Marxists, Fascists, Nazis, and the modern State in America expresses this view with chilling consistency:

- "The Universal is to be found in the State. The State is the Divine Idea, as it exists on earth. We must therefore worship the State as the manifestation of the Divine on earth. The State is the march of God through the world."

- After compiling these statements from Hegel's works, Karl Popper comments that Hegel's views mandate the "absolute moral authority of the state, which overrules all personal morality, all conscience."

A Breitbart contributor recently found video footage of Eric Holder's 1995 speech. The video was taken when Holder was the United States Attorney for the District of Columbia. He was speaking before the Women's National Democratic Club. This is the same speech where he openly admitted that the government had to "brainwash" people into not liking guns. That was the word he used. He also said over laughter from the audience that he wanted gun-owners to cower in the same way that smokers "cower outside of buildings." Here's what he said in context:

> "What we need to do is change the way in which people think about guns, especially young people, and make it something that is not cool, that it is not acceptable, it is not hip to carry a gun anymore, in the way in which we have changed our attitudes about cigarettes. You know, when I was growing up, people smoked all the time. Both my parents did. But over time, we changed the way that people thought about smoking, so now we have people who cower outside of buildings and kind of smoke in private and do not want to admit it. And that is what I think we need to do with guns."

Not that we did not already know what their agenda was, but here we have a clear testimony of the administration's goals as it pertains to guns. They want to brainwash people, and they want to make gun-owners ashamed of themselves for indulging in such a dirty habit like owning guns. And how do they do this?

First, they control the language by calling semi-automatic rifles "assault weapons." Then, the media sensationalizes events where the shooter uses an "assault weapon" to carry out his deed. Sometimes this requires changing the media script that describes the event in order to cast sole blame on the "assault weapon." (Some earlier reports said that Lanza left the AR-15 in the trunk of his car; others said that he used the AR-15 in the shooting; the media went with the latter because it was consistent with their agenda.) They fixate non-stop on the gun used and ask repeatedly, "Does anyone really need an 'assault weapon' to shoot a deer?"

Then, they do things like publish the names and addresses of people who legally own guns, comparing them not just to dirty smokers, but registered sex offenders. I do not think that makes them "cower" in shame, but it no doubt left those gun owners feeling a bit vulnerable as if their privacy had been violated.

Assuming they get their way, and they ban the "assault weapons," their next brainwashing campaign will be to get people afraid of handguns in the same way that people were scared of semi-automatic rifles. We will have a couple mass shootings involving handguns, and the media will do their job in sensationalizing the event and reporting non-stop about the handguns that were used. They will adjust the narrative and ask repeatedly, "Does anyone really need a handgun to shoot a deer?"

The campaign against the 2nd Amendment has been a complete psychological operation from the beginning, and the 1995 video of Holder proves it.

Alexander Tytler (1747 – 1813), a Scottish history professor at the University of Edinburgh, had this to say about the fall of the Athenian Republic some 2,000 years prior: "A democracy is always temporary in nature; it simply cannot exist as a permanent form of government. A democracy will continue to exist up until the time that voters discover that they can vote themselves generous gifts from the public treasury. From that moment on, the majority always votes for the candidates who promise the most benefits from the public treasury, with the result that every democracy will finally collapse over loose fiscal policy, which is always followed by a dictatorship."

Tytler believed that democratic forms of government such as those of Greece and Rome have a natural evolution from initial virtue toward eventual corruption and decline. In Greece, for example, Tytler postulated that "the patriotic spirit and love of ingenious freedom... became gradually corrupted as the nation advanced in power and splendor."

Tytler went on to generalize: "Patriotism always exists in the greatest degree in rude nations, and in an early period of society. Like all other affections and passions, it operates with the greatest force where it meets the greatest difficulties. But in a state of ease and safety, as if wanting its appropriate nourishment, it languishes and decays. It is a law of nature to which no experience has ever furnished an exception, that the rising grandeur and opulence of a nation must be balanced by the decline of its heroic virtues."

The average age of the world's greatest civilizations from the beginning of history has been about 200 years. During those 200 years, these nations always progressed through the famous "Fatal Sequence" quotation, sometimes known as the Tytler cycle.

Its earliest confirmed use is by Henning Webb Prentis, Jr., President of the Armstrong Cork Company. It was during a speech entitled "Industrial Management in a Republic," delivered in the grand ballroom of the Waldorf Astoria, in New York, during the 250th meeting of the National Conference Board on March 18, 1943.

"From bondage to spiritual faith,
From spiritual faith to great courage,
From courage to liberty,
From liberty to abundance,
From abundance to complacency,
From complacency to apathy,
From apathy to dependence,
From dependence back into bondage."

The Obituary follows:
Born 1776, Died 2012

The United States is currently somewhere between the "complacency and apathy" phase of Professor Tytler's definition of democracy, with almost fifty percent of the nation's population already having reached various levels of the "governmental dependency" phase.

Apathy is the greatest danger to our freedom.

Where does it all end? It does not end if we do not speak up!

> "When the government fears the people there is liberty; when the people fear the government there is tyranny."
>
> ~ Thomas Jefferson ~

CHAPTER 36

Lies, half-truths and the spinning of government created crises always frame the government's incremental, "distort and distract" methodology. Today our country is so torn apart and distracted by the ongoing, infighting over gun controls, gay and lesbian rights, abortions, Christianity, socialism, political correctness, immigration, self-serving charges of racism and any number of other social issues. Within each of these conflicts the levels of distortion varies of course...but certain factions are "in-your-face!" And for those, it is not enough that you don't have a strong opinion one way or the other, if you are not vigorously supporting their point of view...then you must be opposed.

The Associated Press recently announced that it would no longer describe illegal immigrants as "illegal immigrants," rather they are "undocumented immigrants." Shortly there after, The New York Times' star columnist.... Maureen Dowd, expressed her concerns that the Supreme Court seemed to have misplaced its progressive style book on another fashionable minority. She wrote, "I am worried about how the justices can properly debate same-sex marriage when some don't even seem to realize that most Americans use the word 'gay' now instead of homosexual."

She went on to say, "Scalia uses the word 'homosexual' the way George Wallace used the word 'Negro.' There's a tone to it. It is humiliating and hurtful. I don't think I am being overly sensitive, merely vigilant."

By comparing the word "homosexual" to "Negro" she gave their game away. Just as everything any conservative says about anything is racist, so now it will also be homophobic. It will not be enough to be clinically neutral (homosexual) on the subject.

Extremism seems to be the norm on today's college campuses. Actually, it's more likely that the extremists have taken control of the channels of power. The same thing happened on college campuses in the 1960s and early 1970s. The majority of students were in college to get their degrees so they could move on to develop their careers; they were not interested in protesting.

The radicals immediately beat down all dissenting opinions. Anyway, who cares? Football, fraternity life, a few tokes here and there, and sexual romps have more importance for the typical college student than protesting.

The radicals take advantage of student indifference, as do liberal politicians.

The latest radicalism is about abortion(s) at Johns Hopkins University.

The Student Government Association at Johns Hopkins University has denied official recognition to a group of pro-life students, and one SGA leader privately compared them to "white supremacists."

Voice for Life, a JHU student group that engages in pro-life activism, including counseling women outside of the front doors of abortion clinics, was twice denied official recognition last month. The SGA voted 10- to -8 to reject the group...cutting it off from student activities funding and building access for meetings, due to concerns that its activism constituted harassment.

I am not surprised at the attack and the absurd charge of white supremacy. Arguments for abortion are feeble. Pro-abortionists have to use extreme rhetoric to keep their lie alive, the fabrication about abortion being just the removal of a glob of tissue. Babies are not being aborted; it is only something akin to a vestigial organ like the appendix or a benign tumor.

But white supremacy? Can they be serious? These students might be smart, but their ignorance here is glaring. More abortions are performed on blacks than whites in terms of a percentage of the population.

<u>"He who controls the language shapes the debate."</u>

One should never doubt that while all this turmoil is raging, it is being cycled and recycled, 24 hours a day by the government-influenced media to keep the populace distracted and fighting amongst themselves. All the while, and under the radar...we are being relentlessly herded toward that utopian (socialist) new world order.

To explain how all this started and how long it has taken for the malignancy to morph into this all consuming, subliminal mind-control state, I am going to take a page from one of my earlier books (We the People, 2010).

Political Correctness started in a German think tank (The Frankfurt School) in 1923. The purpose was to find a solution to the biggest problem facing the implementers of communism in Russia. Why wasn't the wonderful idea of communism spreading?

The Frankfurt School's recommendations (amongst other things):

1) The creation of racism offences.

2) Continual change to create confusion.

3) The teaching of sex and homosexuality to children.

4) The undermining of schools and teachers' authority.

5) Huge immigration to destroy national identity.

6) The promotion of excesses.

7) Emptying the churches.

8) An unreliable legal system with bias against the victim of crime.

9) Dependency on the state or state benefits.

10) Control and/or dumbing down of the media.

11) Encouraging the breakdown of the family.

12) Ridicule and shout down opposition.

Sounds all too familiar, doesn't it?

The basic idea is to make the country wholly dependent on the State. By the dumbing down of education, the creation of huge state sector employment and large-scale immigration, the system effectively creates a captive audience to vote for them should the conservatives actually get back into power. But even if they did, there would be little that they could do to change things.

> "I can calculate the motion of the heavenly bodies, but not the madness of people."
>
> ~ Isaac Newton ~

CHAPTER 37

The Roman Empire was very, very much like us today; they lost their moral compass and their sense of values, in terms of who they were. And once all of those things converged, they were consumed by the proverbial black hole.

When I look at America today, it's not too hard to see many similarities. We've spread ourselves all over the place. We have incredible expenses (personally and as a nation)...and yet we refuse to implement modifications. Consequently, we push on with our out of control spending, growing the deficit, increasing subsidies and entitlement programs...even as our day of reckoning is looming ominously in the very near future. By not living within our means and making the necessary changes in our culture and government, we're not encouraging the essential adjustments needed in the population's attitude and expectations.

When it comes to wanting things, most people aren't really concerned about the national debt, they don't really think about the future; the only thing they really care about is, “Give me my check so I can eat next week.”

That is understandable, but we have not only allowed that mindset to grow, it has been promoted for many, many decades by our government and the marketing industry. If these unrealistic expectations are not addressed soon, we will face a fate similar to that of the Romans.

While this malignancy has been nurtured over a long period of time, overtly and subliminally...a couple of things stand out in my mind.

- In 1946, Dr. Benjamin Spock said we should not spank our children when they misbehave, because their little personalities would be warped and we might damage their self-esteem. We said...he is an expert and should know what he’s talking about... so we said OK.

- I think it (the disease) gained a lot of momentum when Madeleine Murray O’Hare complained that she did not want prayer in our schools, and we said OK. Then she said you better not read the Bible in school (1963). The Bible says thou shalt not kill; thou shalt not steal, and love your neighbor as yourself. And once again, we said OK. (She and two members of her family were later murdered [1995]; their dismembered bodies were not found for a number of years.)

Now we’re asking ourselves why our children have no conscience, why they do not know right from wrong, and why it doesn’t bother them to kill strangers, their classmates, and themselves. I think it has a great deal to do with "We reap what we sow."

Interesting how simple it is for people to trash God and then wonder why the world is going to hell in a hand basket. Funny how they believe what the newspapers and the mainstream media have to say, but question what the Bible says. And where did the idea come from that we should worship celebrities but we aren't allowed to worship God, as we understand Him? I know I am getting older, but there are a lot of us who are wondering...who are these celebrities anyway, and why should I give a crap about their lavish lifestyles and over inflated egos? I am more concerned about my country, how did the America we once knew fade away without a fight?

In the light of day, we can see America's destiny looming on the horizon. Like so many of the world's powerful nations, from time immortal, America is on the brink of collapse. And as with the others, the devastation is not being driven by external forces...but from forces within. A segment of our current administration seems hell-bent on pushing America into a financial abyss... even as our country is being torn apart by divisive rhetoric, demagoguery and class-warfare. As with the other nations, our financial dilemma has been driven... over a period of many decades, by the loss of traditional values: Christianity, personal character, accountability, responsibility, work ethic, common sense and respect for oneself and country. We have become a nation of takers... and we will all sink or swim if this ship of fools continues without a course correction.

The American republic has endured for well over two centuries, but over the past 50 years, the apparatus of American governance has undergone a radical transformation. In some basic respects...its scale, its preoccupations, even many of its purposes, the United States government today would scarcely be recognizable to Franklin D. Roosevelt, much less Abraham Lincoln or Thomas Jefferson.

What is monumentally new about the American state today is the vast empire of entitlement payments that it protects, manages and finances. Within living memory, the federal government has become an entitlements machine. As a day-to-day operation, it devotes more attention and resources to the public transfer of money, goods and services to individual citizens than to any other objective, spending more there...than all the other expenses combined.

The growth of entitlement payments over the past half-century has been breathtaking. In 1960, the United States government transfers, to individuals, totaled about $24 billion in current dollars, according to the Bureau of Economic Analysis. By 2010 that total was almost 100 times larger. Even after adjusting for inflation and population growth, entitlement transfers to individuals have grown 727 percent over the past half-century, rising at an average rate of about 4 percent a year.

In 2010 alone, government at all levels oversaw a transfer of over $2.2 trillion in money, goods and services. The burden of these entitlements came to slightly more than $7,200 for every person in America. Scaled against a notional family of four, the average entitlements burden for that year alone approached $29,000.

A half-century of unfettered expansion of entitlement outlays has completely inverted the priorities, structure and functions of the federal government, as they were understood by all previous generations. Until 1960 the accepted task of the federal government, in keeping with its constitutional charge, was governing. The overwhelming share of federal expenditures was allocated to some limited public services and infrastructure investments and to defending our Republic against enemies foreign and domestic. In 1960, entitlement payments accounted for well under a third of the federal government's total outlays...about the same fraction as in 1940, when the Great Depression was still shaping American life. But over subsequent decades, entitlements as a percentage of total federal spending soared. By 2010 they accounted for just about two-thirds of all federal spending, with all other responsibilities of the federal government making up barely one-third. In a very real sense, entitlements have turned American governance upside-down.

From the founding of our nation until quite recently, the United States and its citizens were regarded, at home and abroad, as exceptional in a number of deep and important respects. One of these was their fierce and principled independence, which formed not only the design of the political experiment that is the United States Constitution but also their approach to everyday affairs.

The proud self-reliance of Americans, that struck Alexis de Tocqueville in his visit to the United States in the early 1830s, extended to their personal finances. The American "individualism" about which he wrote ("Democracy in America") did not exclude social cooperation...the young nation was a hotbed of civic associations and voluntary organizations. But in an environment bursting with opportunity, American men and women viewed themselves as accountable for their own situation through their own achievements, a novel outlook at that time and markedly different from the prevailing attitudes of the Old World (or at least the continent).

The corollaries of this American ethos were, on the one hand, an affinity for personal enterprise and industry and, on the other, a horror of dependency and contempt for anything that smacked of a mendicant mentality. Although many Americans in earlier times were poor, even people in fairly desperate circumstances were known to refuse help or handouts as an affront to their dignity and independence. People who subsisted on public resources were known as "paupers," and for them..."necessities" were provided by the local communities and churches. Neither beneficiaries nor recipients held the condition of pauperism in high regard.

Overcoming America's historic cultural resistance to government entitlements has been a long and formidable endeavor. But as we know today, this resistance did not ultimately prove an insurmountable obstacle to establishing mass public entitlements and normalizing the entitlement lifestyle. The United States is now on the verge of a symbolic threshold; the point at which more than half of all American households receive and accept, some level of transfer benefits from the government.

The greater issue with big government is moral. Thomas Jefferson cautioned, "dependence begets subservience and venality...and suffocates the germ of virtue." Even Franklin Roosevelt warned that "continued dependence on government support induces a spiritual and moral disintegration that is fundamentally destructive to the national fiber. To dole out relief in this way is to administer a narcotic, a subtle destroyer of the human spirit."

Undoubtedly, many today would agree. But passive concurrence is not enough. We must first resolutely acknowledge the moral pre-eminence of free enterprise verses big government.

It is the moral arguments in favor of big government and opposed to capitalism, however misguided, that fosters popular support for government expansion. Government is deemed benevolent, while capitalists are characterized as greedy and exploitive. This is simply false of course. Free enterprise, rather than government, is the greater friend of small business, the middle class and, ultimately, of workers at all wage levels.

Real happiness is the product of "earned success," however modest, and governmental redistribution policies breed "learned helplessness," which is detrimental to the individual's well being...and otherwise.

But as Americans opt to reward themselves ever more lavishly with entitlement benefits, the question of how to pay for these government transfers inescapably comes to the forefront. The "taker mentality" has thus ineluctably gravitated toward taking from a pool of citizens who can offer no resistance to such schemes...the unborn descendants of today's entitlement-seeking population.

The prospect of careening along an unsustainable economic road is deeply disturbing. But another possibility is even more frightening...namely, that the present course may in fact be sustainable for far longer than most people today might imagine.

The United States is a very wealthy society. If it so chooses, it still has vast resources to squander. And internationally, because the dollar is still the world's reserve currency, there remains a great capacity for financial abuse of that privilege.

Such devices might well postpone the day of fiscal judgment, but not the day of reckoning for American character, which may be sacrificed long before the credibility of the United States economy. Some would argue that it is an asset already wasting away before our very eyes.

There was a time when our Christian values sustained us, but the government's plan for us does not include Christianity. Progressivism's influence has been overwhelmingly devastating in regard to America's core principles and traditions. Even our churches have been yielding to issues that decades ago would have been unthinkable. The situation today appears to be that you make adjustments...or you don't survive.

I recently read the proclamation by a Green Bay bishop that Christians who vote for someone supporting the gay or abortion agenda is putting their soul in jeopardy. His declaration came after some progressive/liberal churches published a list of hypothetical justifications for why Christians could turn a blind eye towards these outrageous offenses.

Let's scrutinize what passes as compassion for the unborn today. The most often referenced rationale for abortion, by the individual(s) and/or society, is the quality of life for the child. In other words, abortion is justifiable if some ambiguous standard called the "quality of life" is not met.

Pointing to uncomfortable situations such as when a child is likely to be born addicted to drugs often makes the case for abortion. Another so-called compassionate reason for abortion is when a young woman has had unhealthy relationships where she may not know who the father is or she is not ready to take on the crushing responsibility of raising a child.

What is painfully clear here is that abortion is overwhelmingly used to mitigate the sins of irresponsible individuals who have a "do it if it feels good" mentality. Misplaced compassion for the offenders ultimately holds no one personally responsible for his or her behavior.

Those same "benevolent" people would also propose that if there were a possibility that the child "could" be raised with some indeterminate disadvantage, it would be better to abort the pregnancy. I would challenge any of "those people" to find one person who was raised with the disadvantage of a too young mother, a single mother, abusive parents or any other disadvantage, that would rather have been aborted than be alive and living their life today.

The baby's parent(s) could solve all these problematic scenarios that are being used in defense of abortion as "the better choice," by unselfishly placing their child with loving parents through adoption.

A person's situation or narrative does not change the fact that the aborted baby was a living human being who deserved to be born and live. That is a fact and not a judgment call for anyone.

Since Roe v. Wade, we've given birth to a new materialistic culture of narcissism where reverence for life itself is gone. Life has become a commodity, and people use each other as cavalierly as they destroy innocent young life. As our reverence for life has diminished, so has our reverence for the institutions that surround and support it.

Scholars at the Brookings Institution observed in 1996 that Roe v. Wade contributed to the collapse of marriage and the dramatic increase in out-of-wedlock births. The idea that children were part of a sacred institution called marriage started disappearing.

In 1965, seven years before Roe v. Wade, less then 10 percent of American babies were born to unwed mothers...24 percent to unwed black women and 3.1 percent to unwed white women.

As of 2010, this was up to 41 percent of our babies born to unwed mothers...73 percent to black women and 29 percent to white women. Sixty percent of our out-of-wedlock births are to women in their 20s.

Soon, as our resources diminish to care for our growing aging population, we will start dealing with our elderly as we do our unborn.

But if everything is meaningless, who cares? The sense of honor, the sense of shame, disappears in this "culture of self."

Obama was proud to become the first sitting president to address Planned Parenthood the other day. But not proud enough to utter the word "abortion." The right to abortion is the sneakiest, most shamefaced of all American rights. It hides behind evasion, euphemism and cant.

So Obama sang a hymn of praise to Planned Parenthood at the organization's annual conference without mentioning what makes it so distinctive and controversial. He stated that its core principle is "that women should be allowed to make their own decisions about their own health." He excoriated opponents involved "in an orchestrated and historic effort to roll back basic rights when it comes to women's health."

Listening to him, you could be forgiven for thinking that the country is divided by a fierce dispute over whether women should be allowed to choose their own OB-GYNs or to get cancer screenings. In his speech, Obama used the word "cancer" seven times. About that he is happy to be forthright.

But imagine if he had been similarly frank about the core of Planned Parenthood's work: "In 2011, according to your annual report, your clinics or affiliates performed 330,000 abortions. That's a lot of abortions, over 10 years...that's more than 3 million. Thank you, Planned Parenthood. Think of all those women who wanted to terminate their pregnancies, and you were there for them. That's what you do. That's what you are about... and that's what this country is about."

Before that crowd, he might have gotten rousing applause, but talking in such honest terms would have been a gross faux pas. The unwritten rule when the left discusses abortion is that it shouldn't be called "abortion," but always "health" or, more specifically "reproductive health"...although abortion is the opposite of reproduction and, for one party involved, it's the opposite of health.

I can imagine these same types of Democrat apologists writing similar essays in the 1930s on how the Nazi Party was doing great things for infrastructure and social welfare programs in Germany. "Never mind that killing of the Jews thing," they would essentially argue. That's the underlying current of the Christian Democrat defense today..."never mind the killing of the unborn beings made in God's image thing." That's not to say that Democrats are Nazis, of course. It's to say that there is something extremely wrong with your priorities and moral compass when you try to find ways to excuse genocide. As a believer, I cannot imagine justifying that to God.

We have become a nation of promiscuous prudes. We have no morals and no boundaries; we are a society of "whatever."

Based on the Supreme Court's recent ruling on the Defense of Marriage Act, which defines marriage as a union between one man and one woman, regulations against other objectionable behaviors are now at risk. The justices ruled that when it comes to the benefits of marriage, a class of people cannot be discriminated against. The popularized expression of the ruling is that one should be able to marry whomever one loves. So, why stop at "homosexual marriage?" Proponents of polygamy are celebrating the recent Supreme Court ruling right alongside their pro-homosexual allies. Currently there are laws (varying by state) against incest and marrying your sibling, first cousin, offspring, or parent. We also have laws against marrying a minor and laws against polygamy. Although the justices stopped short of redefining marriage, legal challenges against laws on the books regulating marriage are going to flood the courts across our nation in the coming years. It would seem that the Progressives' version of Pandora's box (Greek Mythology) has been opened to release all human ills.

During these uncertain times I often reflect on the words of Timothy: "But the time will come when men will not put up with sound doctrine. Instead, to suit their own desires, they will gather around them a great number of teachers to say what their itching ears want to hear... they will turn aside from truth to myths."

> "Do not blame Caesar, blame the people of Rome who have so enthusiastically acclaimed and adored him and rejoiced in their loss of freedom and danced in his path and gave him triumphal processions. Blame the people who hail him when he speaks in the Forum of the 'new, wonderful, good society' which shall now be Rome's, interpreted to mean: More money, more ease, more security, more living fatly at the expense of the industrious."
>
> ~ Marcus Tullius Cicero ~

The Boston Marathon...Why?

Many in the media are asking how the Chechen Islamists who bombed the Boston Marathon got so radicalized while living in Massachusetts. One need only listen to those around them who have spoken out to glean the answer.

One person who knew the two men stated that they seemed strange and possibly violent, but knowing they were Muslim, did not want to appear insensitive or intolerant by speaking out. We know the real reason this individual did not want "to appear insensitive or intolerant" by airing his thoughts. He did not express those earlier concerns because it would not have been politically correct and he would have been called out as a racist.

Another stated that while, yes, he had heard one of them speak about how much he hated America and that our nation deserved to die; one must understand that being in Cambridge, everyone says those things and feels the same way. It was no different from what "everyone was saying."

In the aftermath, the politically correct media and commentators are all flabbergasted. Over and over, the media reported, "Dzhokhar was a normal American kid." They questioned, "What could be the terrorists' motivations?"

With the questions swirling of why two upwardly mobile young people in America could commit such acts, a good place to start would be the "educations" the two Tsarnaev brothers received from the celebrated Boston high school Cambridge Rindge and Latin School (CRLS).

The media has widely quoted retired CRLS teacher Larry Aaronson's shocked reminiscences about Dzhokhar. Aaronson told The Boston Globe, "This is a progressive town, the People's Republic, and how could this be in our midst?"

Well, he might start looking at his own classroom handiwork. Aaronson is an acolyte of the raving, America-hating, deceased "revisionist historian" Howard Zinn, who was a liberal elite darling. He claimed writer I.F. Stone opened his eyes to the racist, imperialistic horror that is America. After the Iron Curtain fell and certain Soviet documents became public, it was confirmed that he was a KGB covert influence agent.

Aaronson, who retired in 2007, used to brag to anyone who would listen that he had taught Zinn's textbook to CRLS students since the beginning of his career in 1981. He also proudly related that his students at CRLS had included actor Matt Damon and Damon's brother. He told how the Damon boys were taken with the anti-American history of Zinn.

In homage to Zinn upon his death in 2008, Larry started with this quote from the movie "Good Will Hunting." Quoting Matt Damon, "You wanna read a really good American history book? Read Howard Zinn's 'A People's History of the United States.' It will knock your socks off."

If you don't know Zinn's handiwork, here's a sample of his writing from "The Progressive" (a monthly magazine of politics, culture, and progressivism with a pronounced liberal perspective). Zinn's contempt for America and its citizens fairly drips from each and every word: "The deeply ingrained belief...no, not from birth but from the educational system and from our culture in general that the United States is an especially virtuous nation that makes us especially vulnerable to government deception. It starts early, in the first grade, when we are compelled to 'pledge allegiance' (before we even know what that means), forced to proclaim that we are a nation with 'liberty and justice' for all."

Then came the countless ceremonies, whether at the ballpark or elsewhere, where we are expected to stand and bow our heads during the singing of the "Star Spangled Banner," announcing that we are "the land of the free and the home of the brave." There is also the unofficial national anthem "God Bless America," and you are looked on with suspicion if you ask why God would single out America for his blessing ...a country with just 5 percent of the world's population.

Aaronson boasted that angry parents called him to say their children were talking about that bastard Christopher Columbus...his genocide, and how we have to question our history books and re-examine the evidence.

With that backdrop illuminated, let's return to the liberal media puzzling over "What could the Tsarnaev boys' motive possibly be?"

After the Marathon massacre, the media quoted the Zinn-acolyte, Aaronson, in their stories about the terrorist mass murderer. Aaronson was "utterly shocked by the news." The media reported that, "Aaronson taught social studies at Cambridge Rindge and Latin, where Dzhokhar was a student." The media reports continued, "Dzhokhar also lives just about three houses down from Aaronson's condo, so they would talk from time to time after Dzhokhar's graduation in 2011."

"I will say to you and to anyone who asks me," Aaronson told WBUR's David Boeri outside his home in Cambridge on Friday morning, "he had a heart of gold, he was a sweetheart, he was gracious, he was caring, he was compassionate."

ABC, CBS, USA Today, The New York Times, and CNN all carried versions of Aaronson's comments about "how normal" his neighbor and student Dzhokhar was. None of the media provided any other background on Aaronson and/or his brainwashing of students at CRLS with Zinn's history.

The media's reports studiously ignored the connections between Dzhokhar's anti-American lessons taught by a "social justice" weenie like Aaronson and the book by Howard Zinn, who took his cues from a KGB covert influence agent named Stone; who was later slyly celebrated in a Hollywood film known as Matt Damon's "Good Will Hunting."

As for the older brother Tamerlan's "education," it appears that he was a follower of a Lebanese-Australian extremist cleric whose messages of hatred for Western culture were prominent on Tamerlan's YouTube playlists, and he may well have been taught terrorist techniques during a recent trip abroad.

If you end up around the wrong people long enough and you are young enough and impressionable enough, then this kind of thing can happen. It would seem the brothers hung around people that did not like America and they somehow became inspired or influenced by their surroundings...and it's no wonder.

I'm not saying Aaronson was deliberately trying to indoctrinate or radicalize anyone, just that the young are more impressionable and the Tsarnaev brothers (due to their Muslim faith) were ripe for the subliminal message. He was certainly teaching from a biased point of view that surely had some level of support from CRLS.

This does not surprise me because throughout the writing of my books, I've often written about government sponsored curriculums designed to move America toward progressivism and eventually...a new world order. The transformation that Obama spoke of from the start of his tenure, began moving a very, very long time ago...a slow moving, indiscernible undercurrent. Incrementally and stealth like, the forces of collectivism have reached the point of no return and are now preparing to close the gates behind the hapless sheep.

Over 2,500 years ago, Sun Tzu wrote "The Art of War." In it, the Chinese strategist postulated: "One who knows the enemy and knows himself will not be endangered in a hundred engagements. One who knows neither the enemy nor himself will invariably be defeated."

Two millenniums later, Prussian military theorist Carl Philipp Gottfried von Clausewitz wrote a detailed exposition on the principles of warfare. His book, "On War"...was published after his death in 1831, posits, inter alia ("among other things"), that inadequate, incomplete, or incorrect intelligence will inevitably contribute to the "fog of war" and lead to "unexpected developments" that can obscure "the objective" in a conflict.

Unfortunately for us, our elected and appointed leaders in Washington appear to be completely unfamiliar with those two works. In the aftermath of last week's Boston Marathon terror attack, it is clear that those running our federal government...cocooned in federal buildings protected by high-tech security, metal detectors, bag searches, mail sensors, and armed guards and convoyed to and fro in motorcades of armored limousines, know neither our enemy nor what we need to do about it. It's not a new phenomenon...and it's only getting worse.

After thirty-plus years of attacks and more than 4,000 Americans dead, there is no excuse for such willful ignorance. Radical Islamists are still at war with us... and still killing Americans. Until our government accepts that fact, more and more Americans are likely to die at the hands of those waging jihad against us.

It is not that our government doesn't understand who we're at war with...they know exactly who the enemy is and why the extremists will never compromise their position; we are infidels (non-believers) and Mohammad dictates that "we" must be eliminated...from the planet. This administration is just unwilling to say...out loud, what we all know, "we're at war with Muslim extremists."

The Obama-Team's hollow rhetoric, dissembling and dubious record of effectiveness in fighting those who have declared war against us are especially troubling now that chemical weapons have been used in Syria. Obama has repeatedly described this as a red line...a game changer, but continues to sit on his hands. The aftermath of the White House's failure to articulate the true nature of the threat, identify who our adversaries really are and devise a strategy for dealing with them does not bode well for the American public here at home and/or America's interests overseas.

Liberals are always the first to complain when they "reap what they sow" and then have the nerve to ask "Why."

Footnote on Howard Zinn:

"A People's History of the United States" is a 1980 non-fiction book by American historian and political scientist Howard Zinn. In the book, Zinn seeks to present American history through the eyes of the common people rather than political and economic elites. A People's History has been assigned as reading in many high schools and colleges across the United States.

Quotes by Howard Zinn that actually make sense:

> "If those in charge of our society...politicians, corporate executives, and owners of press and television...can dominate our ideas, they will be secure in their power. They will not need soldiers patrolling the streets. We will control ourselves."

> "Nationalism is a set of beliefs taught to each generation in which the Motherland or the Fatherland is an object of veneration and becomes a burning cause for which one becomes willing to kill the children of other Motherlands or Fatherlands."

> "I'm worried that students will take their obedient place in society and look to become successful cogs in the wheel...let the wheel spin them around as it wants without taking a look at what they're doing. I'm concerned that students not become passive acceptors of the official doctrine that's handed down to them from the White House, the media, textbooks, teachers and preachers."

I would suggest that Zinn (who I first introduced in Chapter 6) had his own self-serving biases...and was aligned with the forces that are working to devalue America's exceptionalism.

While the media's sanitized line of thought, around the Boston bombing, sounds plausible...there are many unexplained oddities and un-addressed coincidences that were in play that day.

There is no doubt that the dynamics that day were varied and skewed; the only thing we know for sure is that the perpetrators were Muslim extremists.

We have been told again and again by experts and talking heads that Islam is a religion of peace and that the vast majority of Muslims just want to live in peace. Although this unqualified assertion may be true, it is entirely irrelevant. It is meaningless fluff, meant to make us feel better, and meant to somehow diminish the flaunting of these fanatics rampaging across the globe in the name of Islam. The fact is that the fanatics rule Islam at this time in history. It is the fanatics who march. It is the fanatics who wage shooting wars worldwide. It is the fanatics who systematically slaughter Christian or tribal groups throughout Africa and are gradually taking over the entire continent in an Islamic wave. It is the fanatics who bomb, behead, murder, or honor-kill. It is the fanatics who take over mosque after mosque. It is the fanatics who zealously promote the stoning and hanging of rape victims and homosexuals. It is the fanatics who teach their young to kill and to become suicide bombers.

Very few German people were true Nazis, but many enjoyed the return of German pride, and many more were too busy to care. Most just thought the Nazis were a bunch of fools. So, the majority just sat back and let it all happen. Then, before they knew it, they were owned, had lost control, and the end of their world had come. Many lost everything and ended up in concentration camps.

The hard, quantifiable fact is that the "peaceful majority"... the "silent majority," is cowed and extraneous. Communist Russia was comprised of Russians who just wanted to live in peace, yet the Russian Communists were responsible for the murder of about 20 million people. The peaceful majority was irrelevant. China's huge population was peaceful as well, but Chinese Communists managed to kill a staggering 70 million people. The average Japanese individual prior to World War II was not a warmongering sadist. Yet, Japan murdered and slaughtered its way across South East Asia in an orgy of killing that included the systematic murder of 12 million Chinese civilians; most killed by sword, shovel, and bayonet. And who can forget Rwanda, which collapsed into butchery. Could it not be said that the majority of Rwandans were peace loving?

History lessons are often incredibly simple and blunt, yet for all our powers of reason, we often miss the most basic and uncomplicated points: Peace-loving Muslims have been made irrelevant by their silence. Peace-loving Muslims will become our enemy if they don't speak up, because like the Germans, they will awaken one day and find that the fanatics own them, and the end of their world will have begun. Peace-loving Germans, Japanese, Chinese, Russians, Rwandans, Serbs, Afghans, Iraqis, Palestinians, Somalis, Nigerians, Algerians, and many others have died because the peaceful majority did not speak up until it was too late.

For the time being, the Islamic way may be peaceful in our country...until the fanatics move in.

In the United Kingdom, the Muslim communities refuse to integrate and there are dozens of "no-go" zones within major cities across the country where the police forces dare not intrude. Sharia law prevails there because the

Muslim communities in those areas refuse to acknowledge British law. But the United Kingdom is not an anomaly... the pervasive spread of radical Islam is worldwide.

As for us, who are watching it all unfold...we must pay attention to the only group that counts...the fanatics who threaten our way of life.

Just Saying...

I am sure I'm not the only one baffled by the gullibility of the average, everyday member of America's voting public. Every election comes with the responsibility to vote...but clueless voters are worse than absent voters. In our last big election we were voting on the future of America and our traditional American values...and over half of our voting population voted against America. I'm not suggesting they were knowingly being un-American, just questioning what they were thinking. How could they have been so blind to our current state of affairs? I couldn't help but be reminded of the old political adage that promoted an all-encompassing point...that voters are either uninformed or misinformed. One would think that line of thought would pretty much address the question of voter competence. Well, not exactly...I would add that, "We just don't know...what we don't know."

But a bigger concern, in my mind...is the "lemmings over the cliff" affect we're seeing in today's voting majority. In looking back into history I can see a historical pattern developing here, the naïve...and the pied piper phenomenon taking hold in America. With that insight, I would suggest that these mindless lemmings (and the rest of us) could become, at some point in time...Obama's conscripts.

Over the last several years, I have evolved and discarded several theories in an attempt to explain why it is that most people cannot see the truth...even when it smacks them in the face. Those of "us" who can see "the conspiracy" have participated in countless conversations among ourselves...addressing our frustration regarding the inability of most people to comprehend the extremely well documented arguments that "we" use to describe the process of our collective enslavement and exploitation. The most common explanation to be arrived at is that most people just "don't want to see" what is really going on.

Extremely evil men and women who make up the world's power-elite have cleverly cultivated a virtual pasture so grass-green that few people seldom, if ever, bother to look up from where they are grazing long enough to notice the brightly colored tags stapled to their ears. The same people who cannot see their enslavement to the pasture grass have a tendency to view "conspiracy theorists," those of us who can see past the farm and into the parlor of his feudal lordship's castle, as insane.

It's not that those who don't see that their freedom is vanishing under the leadership of the power-elite, "don't want to see it"...they simply can't see what's happening to them because their level of conscious awareness is blocking their view. All human endeavors are a filtration process.

There are over six billion people on the planet. Most of them live and die without having seriously contemplated anything other than what it takes to keep their lives together. Ninety percent of all humanity will live and die without having ever broken free of the first level of consciousness.

Ten percent of us will move past the first level of consciousness to explore the world of history, the relationship between man and government, and the meaning of self-government through constitutional and common law. We will discover the world of politics. We will vote, be active, and have an opinion.

Our opinions will be shaped by the physical world around us. We will have a tendency to accept that government officials, network media personalities and other "experts" are voices of authority. Ninety percent of the people in this group will live and die without having progressed beyond the second level of awareness.

The ten percent of us who moved forward to the third level of enlightenment found that the resources of the world, including the people...are controlled by extremely wealthy and powerful families (Rothschild, Rockefeller, Carnegie, J P Morgan, Ford Foundation and Vanderbilt) whose incorporated old world assets have, with modern extortion strategies, become the foundation upon which the world's economy is currently indebted. Ninety percent of the people in this group will now live and die without having experienced the fourth level of perception.

Ten percent of us will continue on and break through to the fourth level where we've discovered the Illuminati, the Freemasonry, the Bilderberg Group, the Skull and

Bones, and other secret societies. These societies use symbols and perform ceremonies that perpetuate the generational transfers of arcane knowledge that is used to keep the ordinary people in political, economic, and spiritual bondage to the oldest bloodlines on earth. Ninety percent of the people in this group will live and die without having moved to the next level.

Ten percent of us will pass on through the fourth and into the fifth level to learn that secret societies are so far advanced technologically that time travel and interstellar communications have no boundaries, and controlling the actions of people is what their members do as offhandedly as we tell our children when they must go to bed. Ninety percent of the people in this group will live and die without having moved out of the fifth level.

Ten percent of us will have evolved to the sixth level to where the dragons, lizards, and aliens that we thought were the fictional monsters of childhood literature, are real and are the controlling forces behind the secret societies (these monsters, dragons, lizards, and aliens represent the evil in mankind). Ninety percent of the people in this group will live and die without moving past the sixth level.

I do not know what is behind the seventh level of consciousness. I think it is where your soul is evolved to the point you can exist on earth and be the man Ghandi was, or the woman Peace Pilgrim was...people so enlightened that they brighten the world around them no matter what. The eighth level? Breaking through to the eighth stage probably reveals God and the pure energy that is the life force in all living things...that are probably...I think, one and the same.

If my math is correct there are only about 60,000 people on the planet who have broken through to the sixth level. The irony here is too incredible: Those who are stuck behind tiers one through five have little choice but to view the people who have pierced the levels beyond them, as insane. With each stage reached, exponentially shrinking numbers of increasingly enlightened people are deemed insane by exponentially increasing masses of decreasingly enlightened people.

Adding to the irony, the harder a "sixth or better leveler" tries to explain what he is able to see to those who can't, the more insane he appears to them.

Our Enemy, the State:

In the first two levels we find the great majority of people on the planet. They are tools of the state. Second levelers are the gullible voters whose ignorance justifies the actions of politicians who send first levelers off to die in foreign lands as cannon fodder. Their combined stations in life are to believe that the self-serving machinations of the power-elite are matters of national security worth dying for. And...the people who still accept the government's version of what happened at Sandy Hook, Boston, 9-11 and/or the Kennedy's (John, Robert and "possibly,"... even JFK, Jr.) assassinations...blissfully exist within this group also.

The third, fourth, fifth and sixth levelers are of increasing liability to the state because of their decreasing ability to be used as tools to consolidate power and wealth of the many into the hands of the power-elite. It is common for these people to sacrifice more of their relationships with friends and family, their professional careers, and personal freedom with each new level of consciousness they reach.

Albert Jay Nock (1870 - 1945), author of "Our Enemy, the State" (1935), explained what happens to those who enter the seventh and eighth realms: "What was the best that the state could find to do with an actual Socrates and an actual Jesus when it had them? Merely to poison one and crucify the other, for no reason other than they were too intolerably embarrassing (to the state) to be allowed to live any longer."

So now we know that it's not that our countrymen are so committed to their lives that "they don't want to see" the mechanisms of their enslavement and exploitation; they simply "cannot see"...just as surely as I cannot see what my next un-realized level of conscious awareness might provide.

Maybe this will help the handful of people in the upper levels to understand why the masses have little choice but to interpret "our" clarity as insanity, and perhaps it will help the people in the first two levels understand that living, breathing and thinking are just the beginning. But more importantly, it demonstrates that the meaningful quality of our life will always grow if we continue seeking the knowledge that ascending to the next level of consciousness provides...because with each and every step forward, there are fewer steps between God and ourselves.

America, the nation, is not just land and sea, it is the majority of the people comprising this area, and what we are seeing today does not even begin to resemble the America we (and our parents) knew. Do we just roll over? Of course not; we'll just fight with a renewed perspective. But there is something even more troubling than Obama in the new America today...it's the people who put him in the White House, whether actively...or passively.

> "Civilization, in fact, grows more and more mushy and frenzied; especially under democracy it tends to degenerate into a mere combat of crazes; the whole aim of practical politics is to keep the populace alarmed (and hence clamorous to be led to safety) by menacing it with an endless series of hobgoblins, most of them imaginary."
>
> ~ H. L. Mencken ~

The Bottom Line...

"Three hundred men, all of whom know one another, direct the economic destiny of Europe and choose their successors from among themselves," Walter Rathenau, 1909, founder of the mammoth German General Electric Corporation.

In the "Committee of 300," which has a 150-year history, we have some of the most brilliant intellects assembled to form a completely totalitarian, absolutely controlled "new society"...only it isn't new, having drawn most of its ideas from the Clubs of Cultus Diabolicus. It is striding rather well toward a One World Government, as described by the late, H. G. Wells in his book, "The Open Conspiracy: Blue Prints for a World Revolution."

While the Committee of 300 was modeled after the British East India Company's Council of 300...founded by the British aristocracy in 1727, it embraces a hand and glove alignment with the Illuminati elite in its major goals for world domination. Any leader(s) who dare to stand in their way will be removed...one way or another.

In the case of John F. Kennedy, the assassination was carried out with great attendant publicity and with the utmost brutality to serve as a warning to world leaders not to get out of line. Pope John Paul I was quietly murdered because he was getting close to the Committee of 300 through Freemasons in the Vatican hierarchy. His successor, Pope John Paul II, was publicly humiliated as a warning to cease and desist, which he did.

The Committee believes man's progress is tied to the earth's natural ability to support a given number of people...and therefore, it is necessary to limit the world's population. It goes without saying that the elites of the world will not allow themselves to be threatened by a useless population of commoners, and therefore...the masses must be thinned out. Well, it would seem to me that "the thinning out" is already well underway with 330,000 abortions last year, free contraception agents and/or morning after pills for women as young as 15. In 1980, the government's "Global 2000 Report" warned of overpopulation in the approaching decades that could seriously impact the quality of life for all.

The Committee of 300 looks to social convulsions on a global scale, followed by depressions, as a softening-up technique for bigger things to come.

The war on drugs, which the Bush administration was allegedly fighting, was for the legalization of all types and classes of drugs. Such drugs are not solely a social aberration, but a full-scale attempt to gain control of the minds of the people of the United States.

Their plan describes how they will use drugs to help stifle resistance to their New World Order scheme. Having been failed by Christianity, and with unemployment rife on every hand, those who have been without jobs for years, will turn away from the church and seek solace in drugs. Drug bars will take care of the unruly and the discontented. Would-be revolutionaries will be turned into harmless addicts with no will of their own. The drug overdose casualties and drug related killings would just be bonuses.

Today, through many powerful alliances, the Committee of 300 rules the world and is the driving force behind an agenda to create a "Totalitarian Global Government." Secret societies exist by deception. Each is a hierarchy with an inner circle at the top, which deceives those below with lies, such as claiming a noble agenda; thus, duping them into following a web of compartmentalized complicity.

The technique for keeping their illicit scheme secret is compartmentalization. Only the people in the inner circle, who are part of the capstone at the top of the pyramid, know the entire extent of the fraud. Illicit secret societies cannot withstand the light of day.

The Committee of 300 is the ultimate secret society made up of an untouchable ruling class and the world's wealthiest elite. Through their illicit banking cartel, they own the stock of the Federal Reserve, which is a private, for profit corporation that violates the United States Constitution and is at the root of the problem.

The list of associated organizations is long: Trilateral Commission, Bilderberg Group, Council on Foreign Relations (and "all its affiliated organizations"), United Nations, Illuminati order, Skull & Bones, International

Monetary Fund, World Bank, Bank of International Settlement, Club of Rome, Black Nobility, Chatham House, Round Table, Tavistock Institute for Human Studies (England's psychological warfare think tank), Associated Press, Reuters (Rothschild owned news monopoly used for brainwashing the masses), and many others, including the military establishment; all of which, whether they are dupes or adapts, work in favor of Great Britain's aristocracy and their one world government agenda.

But what are the goals of this secret elite group? We know the ultimate goal is world domination and total control, but how do they plan to achieve such a worldwide coup?

Their game plan has many tentacles that are far reaching and all encompassing, but even more importantly..."they" have been...and continue to be, patient.

One needs to understand that it is not just America that's going through this transformation...our decay is a mirror image of our global neighbors.

These individuals already have all the money anyone could ever dream of having, but money is not enough. They want global control of the people...enough said.

Below is a short list of "some" of their contrivances that we can relate to and/or see in real time...and the incremental advances they have made toward their goal of control.

- Take control of education in America with the intent and purpose of utterly and completely destroying it.

- The utter destruction of all national identity and national pride.

- The destruction of religion, but more importantly... the Christian religion.

- To export "religious liberation" ideas around the world so as to undermine all existing religions, and again...especially the Christian religion.

- To encourage the spread of religious cults such as the Moslem Brotherhood, Moslem fundamentalism and the Sikhs.

- Legalization of drugs and pornography.

- To introduce new cults and continue to boost those already functioning, which includes heavy rock and gangster music with its filthy, outlaw lyrics degrading women and advocating the killing of cops.

- Control of each and every person through means of mind control.

- Unemployables in the wake of industrial destruction will either become opium-heroin and or cocaine addicts, or become statistics in the elimination process we know today as "Global 2000."

- An end to all industrialization and the production of nuclear generated electric power in what they call "the post-industrial zero-growth society." Exempted are the computer and service industries. United States industries that remain will be exported to countries such as Mexico where abundant slave labor is available.

- To cause a total collapse of the world's economies and engender total political chaos.

- To weaken the moral fiber of the nation and to demoralize workers in the labor class by creating mass unemployment. As jobs dwindle due to the post industrial zero growth policies introduced by the Club of Rome, demoralized and discouraged workers will resort to alcohol and drugs. The youth of the land will be encouraged by means of rock music and drugs to rebel against the status quo, thus undermining and eventually destroying the family unit.

- To take control of all foreign and domestic policies of the United States.

- Penetrate and subvert all governments, and work from within them to destroy the sovereign integrity of nations represented by them.

- To give the fullest support to supranational institutions such as the United Nations, the International Monetary Fund, the Bank of International Settlements, the World Court and, as far as possible, make local institutions less effective by gradually phasing them out or bringing them under the mantle of the United Nations.

- To cause by means of limited wars in the advanced countries, and by means of starvation and diseases in Third World countries, the death of three billion people by the year 2000, people they call "surplus population."

- To keep people everywhere from deciding their own destinies by means of one created crisis after another and then "managing" such crises. This will confuse and demoralize the population to the extent that when faced with too many choices, apathy on a massive scale will result. In the case of the United States, an agency for crisis management is already in place. It is called the Federal Emergency Management Agency (FEMA). Of course we know how incompetent that agency is, it is a disaster itself...a governmental oxymoron.

- Organize a worldwide terrorist apparatus and negotiate with terrorists whenever terrorist activities take place. If you recall, it was Bettino Craxi who persuaded the Italian and United States governments to negotiate with the Red Brigades kidnapers of Prime Minister Moro and General Dozier. As an aside, General Dozier is under orders not to talk about what happened to him. Should he break that silence, he will no doubt be made "a horrible example of" in the manner in which Kissinger dealt with Aldo Moro, Ali Bhutto and General Zia-ul-Haq.

It is worth noting that the late Ayatollah Khomeini was a creation of British Military Intelligence Division 6, commonly known as M16, as exposed in 1985.

Given the extremes that M16 must have gone to...in creating a straw man like the Ayatollah Khomeini, it wouldn't be much of a stretch to suggest that a similar organization (perhaps the CIA) in America is responsible for creating our straw man...Obama.

As chilling as the above suggested possibility is, the reality of a "totalitarian like" government...can be a real "wake-up call."

Over the course of this administration, Americans have been slapped in the face with one example after another of government corruption seeping from the highest levels of the Obama-led Federal government.

During his first term, the Obama Justice Department sold more than 2,000 high-powered rifles to brutal Mexican drug cartels in an effort to "track" them, as a part of the now-infamous Operation Fast And Furious. The dangerous government initiative was revealed only when it was discovered that the Justice Department had the blood of American Border Patrol agents, and likely countless other murder victims south of the border, on its hands. Republicans vocally called for answers and for actions to be taken against those responsible for the fatally flawed program, but were largely drowned out and marginalized by the efforts of top administration officials controlling what aspects of the scandal made it into media reports.

Perhaps because of the easy avoidance of what should have clearly marked the beginning of the end of Holder's career in public service, the Attorney General was emboldened. Of course he was; Obama stood by him and ultimately covered everything up via executive privilege.

In early 2012, conservative organizations such as the American Center for Law and Justice accused the IRS of attempting to "intimidate and silence" multiple tea party groups that filed for tax-exempt status.

The accusation was flatly denied by the IRS at the time, with IRS Commissioner Douglas H. Shulman telling Congress last March: "There's absolutely no targeting... as you know, we pride ourselves on being a non-political, non-partisan organization."

Last Friday (5/10/2013), the IRS was forced to admit that it had in fact been targeting conservative organizations with the words "tea party" or "patriot" in their tax documents. The IRS apologized while blaming the controversy on low-level agents in its Cincinnati office. They also went on to assure "everyone" that their lapse of good judgment was not politically motivated. And of course, in the light of day...Obama was forced to step forward and condemn the IRS's "misguided actions"...and state emphatically, that such tactics will not be tolerated.

As reported on "Good Morning America," the IRS began targeting "The Tea Party or similar organizations" as early as March 2010. By June 2011, the unit had flagged over 100 Tea Party-related applications and the criteria used to scrutinize these organizations had grown considerably, flagging not just "Tea Party" or "Patriot" group names, but also groups that were working on issues like "government debt," "taxes" and even organizations making statements that "criticized how the country was being run."

The report, done by the Inspector General for the IRS, also shows that senior IRS officials in Washington were aware of what was going on as early as August 4, 2011.

According to the report, the IRS chief counsel held a meeting with the IRS's Rulings and Agreements unit "so that everyone would have the latest information on the issue."

"What we've long suspected to be the case is now confirmed to be true," said Niger Innis, chief strategist for TheTeaParty.net. "The Obama administration has used the IRS as a political weapon."

Now, Holder's Justice Department stands accused of extra-judicially spying on reporters working for The Associated Press by monitoring incoming and outgoing calls on AP office phones, phones used by AP reporters in the House of Representatives press pool, and, most egregiously, work and private phones of individual reporters.

The Justice department's actions make a few things very clear. It believes that Federal agents can spy on Americans without warrants...because it is actively involved in doing so. The agency feels inclined to deliver reprisal to organizations that "wrong" its Federal allies. It is unconcerned with the consequences of spying, bullying and abrogating the Constitution because part of its reason for doing so...is to control the very media that could potentially elicit public outrage.

While the Justice Department has been involved in its own dirty deeds, our Internal Revenue Service has been hard at work controlling the public message in its own way...by requesting additional information from any group that applied for tax-exempt status and was obviously conservative in its political leanings. Now, it has been revealed that the IRS's reason for doing so was not only to make it difficult for those organizations to proliferate, but also to collect intimate details about certain groups' financial dealings...which, in some cases, were strategically leaked to the press.

But never fear, the Justice Department announced yesterday that it would conduct a thorough investigation of the IRS's misdeeds.

And no less disturbing is the on-going, stonewalling travesty of the Benghazi nightmare. Those men were left to die for reasons still unanswered...because the factual answer(s) would probably reflect negatively on some in the administration's hierarchy.

The common threads in all of this administration's secrecy and lying are a general rejection of a government's moral obligation to tell the truth, a disturbingly brazen willingness to evade and avoid the restrictions imposed by the Constitution...which were deliberately built around our government, and a glib, unspoken attitude...that the government can do as it pleases so long as it can politically get away with it.

As Obama's ability to continue blaming circumstances, lack of knowledge and/or the Republicans for these governmental intrusions, becomes less and less convincing...his credibility becomes more and more suspect.

A "straw man" can only stand as long as he is propped up; once his capability to promote "the agenda" is compromised...and his "sponsors" start to retreat, he becomes a liability.

Global corporations, for the last 100-plus years, have been consolidating their power and influence through on-going mergers around the world. Their persuasive power and control has, long ago...reached a level where limits or boundaries no longer apply. With unlimited funds, worldwide armies of lobbyists and a complicit and/or compliant media...global governments no longer represent their populace; their loyalty lies with the powers that be. And to compound the charade, these puppet-governments...through their media, with its endless pro-government campaigns, slanted advertising and just general propaganda ads...are not only able to convince the mindless to vote for "the right person," but that they elected the best man for the position, and that he would actually be representing them...and their best interest.

In a reality-based world, government officials (at every level) would wear their sponsors' name(s) on their lapel... kinda like NASCAR drivers.

A short list of the names I recognized from the list of current members of the Committee of 300:

Michael Bloomberg, Zbigniew Brzezinski, Warren Buffet, George H.W. Bush, David Cameron, Bill Clinton, Benjamin Rothschild, David René Rothschild, Evelyn Rothschild, Jacob Rothschild, Leopold Rothschild, Elizabeth II, Queen of the United Kingdom, Bill Gates, Timothy Geithner, Mikhail Gorbachev, Al Gore, Alan Greenspan, John Kerry, Henry Kissinger, Paul Krugman, Joe Lieberman, Mack McLarty, Rupert Murdoch, Nicky Oppenheimer, Colin Powell, Susan Rice, David Jr. Rockefeller, David Sr. Rockefeller, Nicholas Rockefeller, David Rubenstein, Robert Rubin, Nicolas Sarkozy, Klaus Schwab, Sidney

Shapiro, Olympia Snowe, George Soros, Arlen Specter, Dominique Strauss-Kahn, Paul Volcker, John Walsh and William Prince of Wales.

I find it somewhat ironic that within such a powerful group of the global elitist, that two of its members once resided in my hometown, in rural Arkansas.

Our world is undergoing immense changes. Never before have the conditions of life changed so swiftly and enormously as they have changed for mankind in the last fifty-plus years. We have been carried along...with no means of measuring the increasing swiftness in the succession of events. We are only now beginning to realize the force and strength of this storm of change that has come upon us. These changes have not come upon our world from without. No meteorite from outer space has struck our planet; there have been no overwhelming outbreaks of volcanic violence or strange epidemic diseases; the sun has not flared up to excessive heat or suddenly shrunken to plunge us into Arctic winter. These changes were brought on by mankind; quite a small number of people, heedless of the ultimate consequence of what they were doing, one man here and a group there, have made discoveries and produced and adopted inventions that have changed all the conditions, of our social lives...as we once knew them.

Though none of us are yet clear as to the precise way in which this great changeover is to be effected, there is a worldwide feeling now that changeover or a vast upheaval is before us. Increasing multitudes participate in this uneasy sense of an insecure transition. In the course of one lifetime, mankind has passed from a state of affairs that seems to us now...to have been slow, dull, ill-provided, and limited, but at least picturesque and tranquil-minded, to a new phase of excitement, provocation, menace, urgency, and actual or potential distresses. More and more, our lives are intertwined with one another...a worldwide morass, and we cannot get away from that fact. We have become nothing more than non-descript, political pawns in a "winner-takes-all"... global chess game.

About the Author: Richard McKenzie Neal

One should never equate education and/or intelligence to wisdom...

Richard was born in Hope, Arkansas (Bill Clinton's boyhood home), in 1941 and his father was gone prior to Richard turning two years old. He never knew the man, but attended his funeral as a sixteen-year-old.

Before boarding a Greyhound bus for California, at seventeen, Richard knew two stepfathers and a number of others who were just passing through. During those teen years, before succumbing to the beckoning allure of the outside world, Richard worked at an assortment of low-paying jobs. Summers were spent in the fields... picking cotton and/or watermelons and baling hay. He also worked as a plumber's helper and a carhop at the local drive-in burger stand.

After dropping out of school, eloping and landing in California, he soon realized how far out of his element he had ventured. And without the guidance of his "Constant Companion," Richard would have spent a lifetime floundering in a sea of ignorance and ineptness...and his books would not exist.

Richard's first book (Fridays With Landon) was driven by his son's life-altering heroin addiction. He had hoped not to author a sequel, but left the book open-ended due to historical concerns, which did in fact...resurface. For 25 years the family has endured the emotional highs and lows associated with the chaotic, frustrating and more often than not...heartbreaking task of rescuing one of their own, from the always ebbing and flowing tide of addiction.

The unintended sequel (The Path to Addiction...) was triggered by a mind-numbing relapse after 30 months of sobriety. The second book was then written to bring closure...one-way or the other. The author advanced several possible scenarios for the ending of that book, but only one of those possibilities was favorable.

His third book (The Long Road Home...) is a philosophical journey that we'll all experience as our time here begins to dwindle.

The fourth book (We the People) was driven by what he saw as the dismantling of America and the circumventing of its Constitution. Additionally, the ominous cloud of socialism and a New World Order looming over Washington motivated him to speak up, in spite of political correctness' muzzle.

The fifth book (The Compromising of America) was written to confirm and document the realities of those fears and concerns chronicled in the preceding book. While those fears and concerns were driven by the current administration, his nightmare now is the possibility of that same administration being returned to office, for another four years, in 2012. He has grave apprehension regarding America's future should the unthinkable happen.

The sixth book (America...Hanging By A Thread) was intended to complete the trilogy...but America is in even more peril today.

The current book (The New World Order) continues to document and record the events as things become more transparent.

All seven books were written after retiring from a rewarding, thirty-six years in the oil industry.

Our success should be measured by what we gave up (what it cost us) to obtain it...and not by what we accomplished and/or accumulated.

> "I have no respect for the passion of equality, which seems to me...merely idealizing envy."
>
> ~ Oliver Wendell Holmes Jr. ~

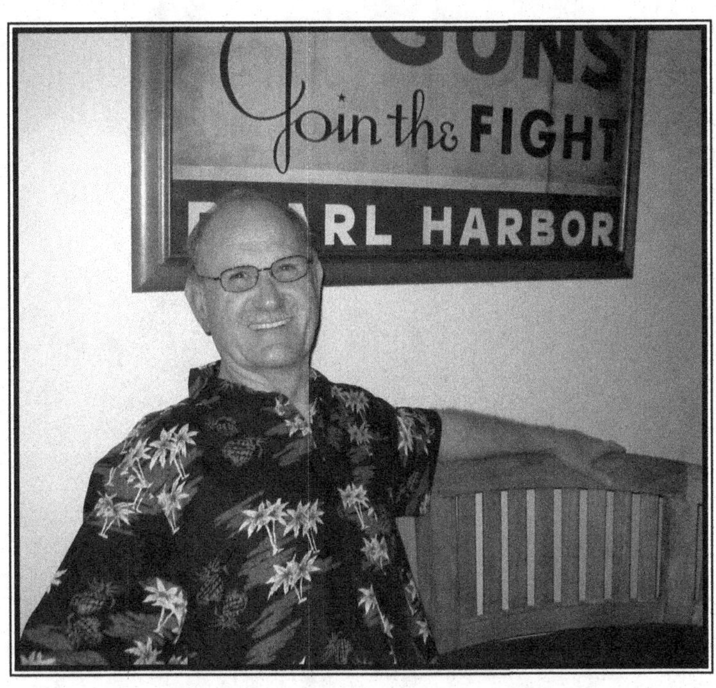

Contributors:

Gayla Crall

Victoria Davis

Landon Neal

Debra Stone